AAHE'S SERIES ON SERVICE-LEARNING IN THE DISCIPLINES

Writing the Community

Concepts and Models for Service-Learning in **Composition**

Linda Adler-Kassner, Robert Crooks, and Ann Watters, volume editors

Edward Zlotkowski, series editor

STERLING, VIRGINIA
Originally published by AAHE

Published in cooperation with the National Council of Teachers of English

Acknowledgments

This monograph was published in cooperation with:

National Council of Teachers of English
1111 W. Kenyon Road
Urbana, IL 61801-1096
toll free 1-800/369-6283
www.ncte.org

Writing the Community: Concepts and Models for Service-Learning in Composition
(AAHE's Series on Service-Learning in the Disciplines)
Linda Adler-Kassner, Robert Crroks, and Ann Watters, *volume editors*
Edward Zlotkowski, *series editor*

Opinions expressed in this publication are those of the contributors and do not necessarily represent those of the American Association for Higher Education or the National Council of Teachers of English or their members.

About This Publication
 Printed in the United States of America. For information about additional copies of this publication or other AAHE or Stylus publications, contact:

Stylus Publishing, LLC.
22883 Quicksilver Drive
Sterling, VA 20166-2102
Tel.: 1-800-232-0223 / Fax: 703-661-1547
www.Styluspub.com

ISBN 1-56377-006-7
ISBN (18 vol. set) 1-56377-005-9

Contents

Foreword

by Edward Zlotkowski

The following volume, *Writing the Community: Concepts and Models for Service-Learning in Composition,* represents the first in a series of monographs on service-learning and the individual academic disciplines. Ever since the early 1990s, educators interested in reconnecting higher education not only with neighboring communities but also with the American tradition of education for service have recognized the critical importance of winning faculty support for this work. Faculty, however, tend to define themselves and their responsibilities largely in terms of the academic disciplines/interdisciplinary areas in which they have been trained. Hence, the logic of the present series.

The idea for this series first surfaced approximately three years ago at a meeting convened by Campus Compact to explore the feasibility of developing a national network of service-learning educators. At that meeting, it quickly became clear that some of those assembled saw the primary value of such a network in its ability to provide concrete resources to faculty working in or wishing to explore service-learning. Out of that meeting there quickly developed, under the auspices of Campus Compact, a new national group of educators called the Invisible College, and it was within the Invisible College that the monograph project was first conceived. Indeed, a review of both the editors and contributors responsible for many of the volumes in this series would reveal significant representation by faculty associated with the Invisible College.

If Campus Compact helped supply the initial financial backing and impulse for the Invisible College and for this series, it was the American Association for Higher Education (AAHE) that made completion of the project feasible. Thanks to its reputation for innovative work, AAHE was not only able to obtain the funding needed to support the project up through actual publication, it was also able to assist in attracting many of the teacher-scholars who participated as writers and editors.

Three individuals in particular deserve to be singled out for their contributions. Sandra Enos, Campus Compact project director for Integrating Service and Academic Study, has been shepherd to the Invisible College project. John Wallace, professor of philosophy at the University of Minnesota, has been the driving force behind the creation of the Invisible College. Without his vision and faith in the possibility of such an undertaking, assembling the human resources needed for this series would have been very difficult. Third, AAHE's endorsement — and all that followed in its wake — was due largely to AAHE vice president Lou Albert. Lou's enthusiasm for the monograph project as well as his determination to see it adequately supported have been critical to its success. It is to Sandra, John, and Lou that the monograph series as a whole must be dedicated.

Other individuals to whom the series owes a special note of thanks include Matt Bliss, who, as my graduate assistant, helped set up many of the communications mechanisms that got the project going, and Jeannette MacInnes, coordinator of student programs at the Bentley Service-Learning Project, who has served in an information clearinghouse role and more.

The Rationale Behind the Series

A few words should be said at this point about the makeup of both the general series and the individual volumes. Although Composition may seem a natural choice of disciplines with which to begin, being both a staple of undergraduate education *and* sufficiently broad to accommodate multiple pedagogical goals and strategies, "natural fit" has not, in fact, been a determinant factor in deciding which disciplines/interdisciplinary areas the series should include. Far more important have been considerations related to the overall range of disciplines represented. Since experience has shown that there is probably no disciplinary area — from Architecture to Zoology — where service-learning cannot be fruitfully employed to strengthen students' ability to become active learners as well as responsible citizens, a primary goal in putting the series together has been to demonstrate that fact. Thus, some rather natural choices for inclusion — disciplines such as Anthropology, Geography, and Religious Studies — have been passed over in favor of other, sometimes less obvious selections from the business disciplines and natural sciences as well as several important interdisciplinary areas. Should this first series of volumes prove useful and well received, we can then consider filling in the many gaps we have left this first time around.

If concern for variety has helped shape the series as a whole, a concern for legitimacy has been central to the design of the individual volumes. To this end, each volume has been both written by and aimed primarily at academics working in a particular disciplinary/interdisciplinary area. Many individual volumes have, in fact, been produced with the encouragement and active support of relevant discipline-specific national societies. For this volume on Composition, in fact, we owe thanks to the National Council of Teachers of English (NCTE).

Furthermore, each volume has been designed to include its own appropriate theoretical, pedagogical, and bibliographical material. Especially with regard to theoretical and bibliographical material, this design has resulted in considerable variation both in quantity and in level of discourse. Thus, for example, a volume such as Accounting contains more introductory and less bibliographical material than does Composition — simply because there is less familiarity with and less written on service-learning in Accounting. However, no volume is meant to provide an extended introduction to service-learning *as a generic concept*. For material of this nature, the reader is referred to such texts as Kendall's *Combining Service and Learning: A Resource Book for Community and Public Service* (NSIEE, 1990) and Jacoby's *Service-Learning in Higher Education* (Jossey-Bass, 1996).

I would like to conclude this preface with a note of special thanks to the three coeditors of this Composition monograph, Linda Adler-Kassner, Robert Crooks, and Ann Watters. Not only have they demonstrated great skill and resourcefulness in putting it together, they have also maintained throughout the entire process a remarkable level of patience and professionalism. In all they have done, they have set a high standard for the volumes that follow.

December 1996

Introduction to This Volume

Service-Learning and Composition at the Crossroads

by Linda Adler-Kassner, Robert Crooks, and Ann Watters

The past five years have seen a microrevolution in college-level Composition through service-learning. We call it a "revolution" because in the growing number of schools where service-learning has been implemented, either on a course-by-course or programmatic basis, both faculty and student participants report radical transformations of their experiences and understanding of education and its relation to communities outside the campus. We also have to call it a "micro" revolution, though, because despite the growth and success of service-learning in the Composition discipline, a great many composition instructors know little if anything about it. Representation of service-learning at annual meetings of the Conference on College Composition and Communication, for instance, has grown from a single panel in 1991 to a handful; one of us proposed a special MLA session on service-learning two years ago and received a polite rejection on the grounds that while the proposal sounded interesting, none of the members of the evaluating committee had heard of service-learning or understood what its relevance to the MLA might be.

The need to increase the visibility of service-learning on and across campuses has not been lost on its proponents, but neither has it always been a priority. Like many young academic movements, service-learning (in Composition and elsewhere) has been considerably preoccupied with logistical and administrative issues. Forming relationships and developing projects with off-campus organizations, getting students back and forth between the campus and project sites, coordinating academic and nonacademic schedules, designing and evaluating new kinds of assignments, integrating service projects with academic ones — all these are demanding tasks that have consumed much of the time and energy of what Tom Deans in this volume aptly calls the "early adopters" of service-learning (see p. 29).

Not only carrying out these tasks but also documenting and reporting the results have been crucial to development of service-learning programs, to attracting new faculty participants with reports of success, and to avoiding repetition of unsuccessful projects and strategies. At this point, a new phase in the expansion of service-learning, especially in the area of Composition, seems due for several reasons. Basic logistical and administrative procedures have been developed and refined through trial and error to the point that they are largely institutionalized in many colleges and universities. New faculty participants can sometimes find considerable start-up support, and new community and institutional participants can find both assistance and well-developed models to aid them in setting up service-learning programs. Also, to consolidate the early gains of the service-learning movement in these logistical and administrative areas and thus facilitate further growth, there is an increasing need to secure the place of service-learning in the academy. As Deans rightly observes, service-learning is more often identified as a cross-disciplinary program whose main focus is pedagogy and service, rather than as a method of teaching multiple skills, including those included in more traditional classes, and conventionally understood now as legitimate areas of scholarly research. Ensuring that service-learning makes the transition from the first conception to the second is an uphill struggle against departmental, disciplinary, and other institutional interests (see p. 30). Finally, as Nora Bacon points out in her essay, administrative and logistical problems themselves have unearthed what turned out to be larger theoretical problems that now need attention for sake of the long-term health and success of service-learning.

In putting together the collection of essays for this volume, we have been especially attentive to these various junctures, and have sought to present both accounts of past successes and problems and also larger assessments and visions of the future of service-learning and Composition. In the remainder of this introduction, we highlight some of the benefits and problems of service-learning and composition highlighted by the essays in this volume, and then outline further areas of work to be done.

Benefits of the Service-Learning/Composition Combination

Motivation

Both faculty and students widely attest to the increased motivation produced by the alliance of Composition with service-learning. Though the evidence is largely anecdotal, it points to a source in the sense that service-learning makes communication — the heart of composition — matter, in all its manifestations. Whether teaching, learning, planning and executing assignments, exploring the writing process, or even grading papers, students and instructors feel a greater sense of purpose and meaning in the belief that their work will have tangible results in the lives of others. In the most successful cases, such as the one related in this volume by Nora Bacon, participants in service projects make the crucial transition from students to writers. This transition allows a less-obvious role shift for instructors, as well: from carrot-and-stick-wielding lesson drivers to facilitators for student-directed and collaborative writing projects. Closely related to this sense of the importance of service-related communication is a greater sense of responsibility and accountability.

In an ordinary composition class, if the work that is produced is less than it ought to be — regardless of how the fault is distributed — the failure is first a private matter between student and instructor. Either or both may make the matter public in various degrees by assigning a poor grade, issuing informal or formal reports and complaints, and so forth, but neither is required to nor has much incentive to do so. In a service-learning course, concealing failure is much more difficult. As Bacon observes, every writing project (and the assertion could be extended to every service project) has a bottom line, a specific desired effect that is either obtained or not. Furthermore, service-learning is likely to provoke greater-than-usual interest from faculty and administrative colleagues in the successes and failures of courses. In part this results from the newness of service-learning, but even more because everyone in the college community, whether or not they participate directly in service-learning, seems to recognize that the stakes are high in the new kinds of connections that are being forged between the academy and the community.

Making Connections

E.M. Forster's often-quoted phrase "only connect . . ." has been the central theme of many discussions of service-learning and Composition. However clichéd that may seem, the forces that favor disconnection seem very strong in this era, while those favoring connection are limited. Points of security — like those found in a building where different electric or mechanical keys are required to attain points of access — are ubiquitous. We point this out not to suggest that such measures are signs of paranoia unrelated to any real threats but to highlight the long-term danger of an all-too-common response to social problems: fortifying divisions rather than trying to construct connections. Service-learning is a crucial focal point of efforts in the latter direction.

Reinventing the College Community

When we fortify the divisions between parts of a community — and in doing so abet and accelerate the uneven development that will increasingly reify those divisions — the effects are felt on all sides. In a campus context, external barriers tend to get reproduced internally, as faculty, students, and staff maintain a distance and thus further organize themselves around perceived similarities and against perceived differences. Thus, the historical movement toward fragmentation has additional consequences, especially for students. Attending college means for many a transition to being a fuller participant in a larger social world, and the college experience is important in shaping that participation. Whatever tends to restrict the range of student contact to the campus tends to define lasting limitations on an individual's sense of community.

Service-learning helps to bridge such divisions by bringing people together with positive common causes and collective tasks that foster communication and social bonds. Every response to service-learning experiences we have encountered emphasizes the value and pleasure of making these new connections. They are particularly important in composition classes for a couple of reasons. Composition is one of the first courses taken for most students, and thus provides a crucial opportunity to set a tone and pattern for the whole college experience. More importantly, the emphasis on communication encourages students to articulate these experiences — discursive connections being crucial in producing and reproducing material ones.

While the service experience may seem the most immediately satisfying aspect of a course to students, the academic side of the project, which often entails building discursive bases to support further collegiate and lifelong service-learning experiences, is probably of more lasting value. Certain is that other segments of the college community get transformed, as well. At Stanford, a number of faculty colloquia on service-learning have brought together teachers and scholars from diverse disciplines; during one summer, faculty from four different disciplines — History, Political Science, Communication, and Composition — worked together at a week-long retreat sponsored by Campus Compact to develop a coherent approach to integrating service-learning in the disciplines. At Bentley College, service-learning has been from the start an intensely cross-disciplinary program in several ways. Instructors who wanted to teach service-learning courses struggled with implementation, found themselves frequently attending workshops and meetings and having informal conversations across departments. These interactions converged nicely with a learning-communities program that sprang up about the same time, resulting in several service-learning course clusters — composition paired with sociology, government, philosophy, and computer information system courses, for instance. These clusters not only allow instructors to share the administrative burden of managing service-learning but also provide a much richer sense of what actually goes on in courses outside our own departments than most of us have ever had an opportunity to know.

The College and the Local Community

The most immediate effect of service-learning is to rearticulate the college or university as part of rather than opposed to the local community. This is a crucial and difficult rearticulation. Sometimes a large portion of the college population — especially the student portion — have no past relation to the surrounding community, and often come from different class, ethnic, or national backgrounds, as well. Conversely, on large commuter campuses such as Minnesota's, students have connections to the parts of the urban or suburban communities from which they commute, but not to other parts of the community, and certainly not to the monolithic campus. Students' futures tend to be different, as well, as job options are sharply differentiated based on possession of a college degree. Given such differences, there is little incentive for substantive communication between academy and community; and the lack of it gives rise on the one hand to the fear and security measures on campus, and on the other to resentment toward a college community that seems to have no investment in community interests and instead contributes traffic and parking problems and kinds of commercial development of little value or even detrimental to the community. Service-learning not only creates interactions that tend to offset the effects of these divisive forces; it actively draws up differences to support shared or mutually compatible goals. As the Community Literacy Project in Pittsburgh exemplifies, service-learning at its best assumes "the goal of intercultural collaboration . . . asks people to take rhetorical action together, across differences, to change their relationship from that of commentators on diversity to collaborators" (Peck, Flower, and Higgins 1995: 214). Composition courses, with their focus on rhetoric and communication, offer an excellent vehicle for such collaboration. Furthermore, the writing done for such courses, whether it takes the form of writing in the community or more-traditional academic writing relating to service projects, creates a record that can be shared with the community collaborators to solidify relationships and encourage collaborative reflection that forms a basis for future work.

The College and Society

The kind of written record produced in service-learning courses, with its concomitant reflection and analysis, can help to move the school and the surrounding community toward greater consciousness of their connected places in larger social systems. The work of colleagues such as Bruce Herzberg, Paul Heilker, and Eli Goldblatt focuses — albeit through different means and assumptions — on enabling students to make this transition from the personal and intersubjective toward analyses of larger political, ideological, and institutional forces and processes that shape the social conditions governing personal experience and interaction.[1] There is much work to be done in this area, but past results suggest convincingly that service-learning in the context of Composition can increase students' conception of the social far more effectively than either textbooks or experience alone. Through such writing, whether in the form of a newsletter for a nonprofit institution or an analytic essay for class, students begin to rewrite the social.

The effects are likely to be much less immediately evident than the personal effects of service, but ultimately more important to the extent that such writing addresses the causes of social problems and not just the symptoms.

Expertise, Teaching, and Evaluation

Like any other undertaking, service-learning is neither automatically successful nor inevitably beneficial. The essays in this volume are valuable for the future of service-learning and Composition not only because they offer models for success but also for the explicit and implicit delineation of problems.

The great majority of those who teach composition are trained in English, a disciplinary designation that covers a lot of ground but is most often centered in literary studies. As many composition programs and courses have moved toward some version of "writing in the disciplines," the model of disciplinary expertise that our higher education is based on has posed serious difficulties. How do we teach or evaluate writing about other people's areas of expertise? One common answer — that we are concerned with transferable rhetorical skills rather than "content" — runs contrary to the very notion of "writing in/across the disciplines." Constructive responses to E.D. Hirsch's *Cultural Literacy* (1988), which argues that we are engaged in inculcating students into a common culture, add political reasons also for questioning whether teaching and evaluating writing can or even should be dissociated from content. The move to service-learning exacerbates these dilemmas. As Nora Bacon points out, sending students out into the community means that assigning an "academic exercise" is no longer an option (see pp. 41-42). The experts in the area of community-based writing are particular people directly involved in the course, people whose authority instructors don't want to challenge — any more than they want to risk their own authority. Bacon further points out that "success" in community-based work is not an abstract or complex concept but rather a "bottom line": Writing is supposed to produce certain outcomes (see p. 44). This means that many of the evasions we resort to in evaluation or discussion ("The argument is well made, though I'm not convinced by it. . . .") are bound to sound like the equivocations that they are. Besides, one of the central motivations for service-learning is that there are pressing community issues that students should get involved in. Surely, then, the content — not just what is talked about, but what is said — ought to matter.

But do we also, as Paul Heilker suggests here, need to think about how it is said? Heilker argues that a responsible composition course should work to help students learn "writing as social action" (see p. 72), to use the discourses they will actually need and that will have efficacy in the world outside the academy. This version of service-learning thus offers students real rhetorical situations in which to work: real tasks, real audiences, real purposes for writing. Students at Minnesota's General College, for instance, are admitted because they are considered "underprepared" for admission to degree-granting colleges. For them, connections with real audiences who are often part of their home communities have been invaluable.[2] But we also need to help both students and practitioners of service-learning understand that we have some responsibility to help students get through college, as well as operate outside it; and that our standards of evaluation usually reflect those of academic discourse. Heilker's essay asks, however, what is this discourse for, and why should we support its perpetuation by teaching it? Some might cynically argue, for example, that it only alienates students from their communities. Furthermore, Heilker suggests that academic discourse carries a particular ideological stance, and that pressing ideological analysis on students may be counterproductive as well as dubious from an ethical standpoint. But this position elides another question in its different stand against teaching a particular mode of ideological analysis: Are we as instructors not engaging in service-learning both because we want to change our communities in specific ways and because we find it an effective "content" through which to teach students skills associated with academic writing? Is it enough to get students engaged and involved without promoting specific attitudes, interpretations, and outcomes — whether those are related to the community, the academy, or both?

All Connections Are Not Equal

Making connections across various social boundaries, as demonstrated by the programs at Michigan State University and Arizona State University described in this volume, is one of the great values in service-learning. However, the simple fact of creating physical proximity does not automatically undo ideological divisions; it may in fact reinforce and strengthen them. The dangers lie on both sides of the service-learning conjunction. Rosemary Arca's essay (beginning on p. 133) demonstrates the problems inherent in assuming that ideas about what community service is are the same for students across the socioeconomic spectrum. But by asking her community college students to reconsider what they think service is and where it takes place in their lives, she argues that even those who say they cannot afford community service — because of personal, time, or financial constraints — realize that they do perform such service in their everyday lives. Arca believes that arriving at this conclusion can move students toward developing even deeper connections between their lives and the academic enterprise, connections that can be critical in helping them make relevance of the project of education.

Some practitioners object to the term "service," because they feel that it locates service-learning in a tradition of philanthropy in which "superior classes" magnanimously render service to their "inferiors." This argument, for example, is advanced by president Eduardo Padron, of Miami-Dade Community College, whom Lillian Bridwell-Bowles discusses in her essay in this volume. Whether or not anyone involved actually frames the interaction in these terms, it is clear that service-learning interactions have the potential to reinforce both of these perceptions. Even when their service experiences are positive, Bruce Herzberg notes how difficult it was for his students to transcend their own deeply ingrained belief in individualism and meritocracy (see p. 63). Nor are further interactions in and of themselves likely to change this. Herzberg goes on to note that student interactions with disenfranchised and marginalized people often do little to increase their understanding of systemic injustice, since those subject to it may have also imbibed the lessons about individualism and equal opportunity (see p. 63).

But there is an additional factor at work here. The larger issue is that students always arrive at and set out on their service-learning project from some ideological perspective.[3] This doesn't simply mean that they have some prejudices or biases that can be easily corrected when "reality" disproves their misconceptions. Rather, it means that all their experiences, whether in school or out in the community, are filtered through a whole system of ideas that shape the experiences themselves in ways that have little to do with conscious good intentions or resistance — these are described, for example, in the essay by Wade Dorman and Susann Fox Dorman (beginning on p. 119).

The same is true for faculty members. In fact, one considerable part of the presumptions students take with them into the community is an academic ideology that faculty instructors may be least able to help them analyze critically as ideology, because of our own investment in it. But we would be naive to ignore academic ideologies, or to assume that their effects are always productive. Eli Goldblatt, for instance, asserts that "to teach literacy within the confines of the college [is] to accept an impoverished account of literacy that claims text alone can provide the reader enough reality to read the world" (1994: 77). Advocates of theoretical approaches in English and other disciplines are sensitive to the problem of ideology when they insist that our choice is not whether to "be theoretical" or not, but rather which theories we will practice and how. Indeed, an ideology is an unacknowledged theory of experience. Conscious theorizing does not liberate us from ideology but rather encourages critical reflection that may make us less subject to particular ideologies.

The problem of ideology is made even more difficult by the phenomenon that Samuel Weber, adapting a concept from Freud, calls "isolation" (1987: 29-30). Through isolation, an individual can hold contradictory ideas or attitudes, provided the ideas never come to consciousness simultaneously. In his essay here, for instance, Herzberg describes an instance of isolation common in service-learning: a sharp disjunction between a student's attitude toward the individual she worked with and her attitude toward a social group that this individual represented. He also notes that even when his students are able to understand systemic discrimination and disenfranchisement when they read about it, they have difficulty connecting the concepts to the homeless people they work with. In the first case, the student's attitude toward the homeless individual (an affective response) has nothing to do with her attitudes toward homeless people as a group (theory of homelessness, however incoherent and unconscious it may be). In the second case, such inadequate theories of homelessness have been replaced by what we think are more adequate theories, but the latter remain equally isolated from everyday experience as individuals. We can gain further insight by seeing that both problems identified here are versions of the larger problem of the relation between "theory" and "practice." Both the ideologies that participants in service-learning arrive with and those they may assimilate through reading and discussion are theories of social reality, but we lack adequate models for the actual or possible relations between such theories and the experience of social reality. The model most often cited in discussions of experiential learning is Kolb's learning cycle (see figure on p. 10).

The model seems a reasonable starting point, and is flexible in that there is no specific starting point for the learning cycle; we can use it to track learning for those who start with experience or practice. However, it seems limited in that the movement of learning is presumed to be essentially linear, though cyclical — development is mapped as a one-directional path with a set itinerary. More importantly, perhaps, it fails to account clearly for ideological conditioning of experience that is always already in place, and which arguably shapes the experience itself.

The Work Ahead: Communication Theory and Communities

Rhetoric offers a great deal to theorizing service-learning and Composition, or the theory/practice connection more generally, because it has always viewed communication as a kind of technology, a form of action aimed at producing effects. As opposed to what? According to Richard Lanham, as opposed to "philosophy," which views communication rather as a means of revealing existing truths. As a theory of communication as action, rhetoric tends to bridge the gap between theory and practice. That gap, in fact, can

Kolb's learning cycle

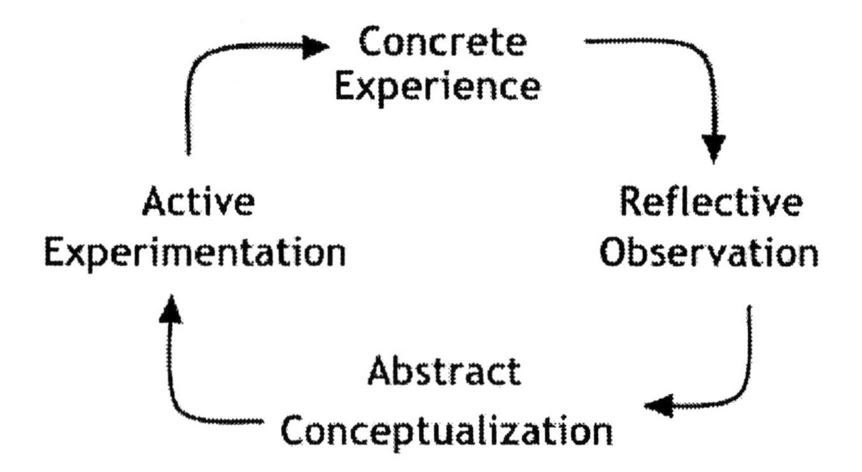

be seen as an effect of the ascendancy of philosophy over rhetoric in the modern academy (1993: 154-194). But more than traditional rhetoric is needed if we are to avoid seeing experience as simply an effect of rhetorical action. Instead, we need something like a "rhetoric of practice" that understands the effects of practice to be reciprocal with those of verbal rhetoric. A part of such a double rhetoric would need to be a consideration of politics and ideology that goes beyond the entrenched championing of seemingly rigidly opposed positions such as "community" and "academy." Actions in the community or the academy are never independent of context, which means that they are always assimilated to larger political movements and ideologies — like the tenure debate in academia, or the struggle for funding among nonprofit agencies — whether we are aware of that or not. On the other hand, that does not mean that actions are only about ideology. What we do need, though, is a better understanding of how ideologies connect and affect interactions and understanding among students, instructors, academic and nonacademic institutions, and community members, each of whom may bring different ideologies and politics to the table.

Redefining the Academic Institution

These are small glimpses of large vistas of theoretical work that needs to be done, but getting it done will partly depend on addressing at least three institutional issues that pose obstacles to the growth of service-learning in Composition.

Course/Term Structures

The academy operates in a special temporality that is one of the factors that tends to separate it from the rest of the community. Dividing up our time into class time-blocks and quarter or semester terms is a tradition little moved by the scattered experiments in more flexible scheduling.

Like any other way of segmenting time, ours has both advantages and disadvantages. From the perspective of service-learning, however, class and term blocks can be a huge and even crippling obstacle, especially in community-based writing projects. As a number of service-learning practitioners have noted, such projects often make much larger and more complex demands on student writers than do ordinary writing classes. To some extent, this burden can be mitigated by the careful selection and design of projects, but in many cases what is possible within the limits of one class in one term simply does not serve the best interests of students or the organizations they work with. In the near run, we will no doubt continue to wiggle along as best we can in the familiar straitjackets, but if service-learning continues to grow, eventually we will have to design "courses" in a much more flexible way than we now do, and this transformation will affect the entire curriculum, not just service-learning.

Discipline/Department Structures

If class and term schedules impose sometimes debilitating temporal constraints on service-learning, disciplinary and departmental structures create others of a more spatial nature. The community organizations we work with in service-learning are concerned with their own goals, not with disciplinary ones, and the kinds of projects they want students to undertake often reflect this. One way to address this problem, for example, is to implement service-learning in interdisciplinary two- or three-course clusters. Departmental barriers arise here in a different form, however, when we are forced to react to late staffing or course scheduling changes with other departments.

Further, while both Composition and service-learning seem relatively undertheorized, the reason is not simply their relative newness as recognized academic programs; it has more to do with the nature of the programs and how they fit into university structures. In the case of Composition, one would expect it to be a locus of theory, given that so much of the theoretical work of the past 30 years has focused in some way on discourse and communication. But as we all know, composition programs have historically been treated as poor relations to literary studies, staffed largely by poorly paid adjuncts with heavy teaching loads and little time or incentive for scholarly work. The fact that composition specialists have moved away from training students in literary studies and toward general academic discourse or writing in/across the disciplines has greatly increased the value of their courses, in our view, but has not helped the stature of composition programs. As Tom Deans points out, cross-disciplinary programs are vulnerable both to withering away from neglect and to losing focus and purpose in the effort to garner broad institutional support.

The problem is not simply that such programs fall through the cracks of existing departmental structures and the corresponding lines of funding, but that traditional disciplines and departments may well resist cross-disciplinary programs as competitors for turf and resources. One result is that the effort faculty members put into the development of such programs goes largely unrewarded, whether in salary or tenure and promotion considerations (see Zlotkowski 1996: 26). So far, the responses to these challenges, both in Composition and in service-learning in general, have been largely tactical. Fearing that entrenched disciplinary and departmental forces are too great to be overcome through direct competition for resources, cross-disciplinary programs try to allay fears and win support without drastically compromising ideological or theoretical principles. On another front, practitioners of service-learning and Composition are producing the kind of scholarly work that supports claims to legitimacy within the bounds of academic traditions. The essays contained in this volume demonstrate how strong and valuable such work can be, but we also think that service-learning proponents will eventually have to look for ways to reshape departmental structures to meet the needs of those both in and outside the academy who view the world in terms of issues and problems that cannot be neatly divided or fit into problems of Sociology, Composition, History, Engineering, and so forth.

Evaluation Procedures

As we have already noted, several of the essays in this volume raise problems of evaluation that occur in service-learning composition courses. Nora Bacon sums up an ideal outcome in saying that in the best cases, those in such courses learn to function "not as *students* but as *writers*" (see p. 42). In such cases, students may not care about the grades, and it may even seem petty to assign them. But where students do care intensely about grades, service-learning exposes the most glaring flaws of traditional evaluation procedures. Much service-learning work ought to be judged at least in part by those in the community, who are at least as much involved as is the instructor. In addition, most service-learning projects are collaborative projects, and the community settings aggravate the problems of evaluating any individual performance in a collaborative project. Even worse, the individual grading system reinforces in a most profound way a belief in "individualism and meritocracy" that many of us would join Herzberg in seeing as a major obstacle to the understanding service-learning seeks to provide. Minor adjustments to traditional evaluation procedures will not address these problems; the sort of adjustments that would involves a more radical transformation of higher education than we can now imagine.

Conceptualization of Purpose

Neal Stephenson's cyberpunk novel *Snow Crash* (Bantam, 1992) posits that there are two distinct kinds of language that human society has been and can be organized around:

- symbolic language (the kind we are all used to), which enables flexible, creative, and critical thinking; and
- binary language (the kind used to program computers), which provides a set of instructions for carrying out various tasks and procedures.

The debate over "education" versus "vocational training" in higher education has often presented the two goals as starkly contrasting alternatives approximating Stephenson's two languages. The philosophical and ideological roots of this debate are too long and complex to rehearse here and are not particularly relevant to the fact that this has become a highly unproductive infight among academics who would be better served by concentrating on improving the academy's relations with the nonacademic world. Service-learning promises to help us do that — by connecting education with real projects in the community, to real goals in the classroom, and to a real connection between "theory" — that is, ways that we think about working in the world — and "practice." While service-learning's concern with immediate social problems and effects and experiential learning may seem remote from academic theory, there's really no disjunction at all. For us, theory is not an end in itself, but rather a means for producing profound social changes by reconfiguring the discursive systems through which we construct the meaning of the experiential world. Indeed, we have never seen the "theory revolution" that began roughly in the late 1960s as the introduction of theory into the humanities; we have seen it rather as a shift of theoretical orientations away from disciplinary objects seen in isolation (the "verbal icon" and so forth) toward an attempt to discover interrelationships among and between knowledge groups previously conceptualized as isolated from one another.

Furthermore, our insistence on the need to teach "theory" in every aspect of the curriculum arises from a firm rejection of oppositions between "academic theory" and "practical applications": The most important turns in the current phase of theoretical work have been toward bringing conceptual abstractions together with the experiential — history, contingency, politics, culture, and the like. Theory now is not an armchair exercise — if it ever was — but a movement toward systematic cross-disciplinary approaches to analyzing and transforming the experiential world.

The composition/service-learning/theory conjunction seems a particularly rich site for advancing "observation-based theory building," to borrow a phrase from Linda Flower (as quoted in Peck, Flower, and Higgins 1995: 219), for several reasons:

• Both service-learning and Composition, but especially the former, are relatively undertheorized; further work is both an intellectual need, to understand what we are engaged in (here, where the effects of service-learning are most immediate, and often on particularly vulnerable members of the community), and a strategic need, to secure institutional places.

• Both service-learning and Composition have been crucial contact points for academic and nonacademic communities — service-learning obviously, but Composition also because communication and writing skills have been an area of such great concern and an easy point to observe the "results" of education.

• The combination of service-learning and Composition, both in practice and in theory, has helped to raise questions about each, as well as about larger disciplinary, institutional, and social issues.

As several of the essays in this volume demonstrate, important theoretical issues are already arising in the attempt to define the proper place of service-learning in the academy. As a form of experiential learning, service-learning is prone to being identified with the "vocational training" side of the opposition, as well as with "do-goodism" and social activism. Discussions about what service-learning is and how it can serve the goals of the academy and the community have been productive internally as well as externally, prodding practitioners toward valuable clarification of the significance, purpose, and implementations of service-learning and composition. Our colleague Edward Zlotkowski wrote recently that

> *With the curtailment of support for a federally sponsored national service movement, service-learning proponents must more than ever face two fundamental decisions:*
>
> - *Do they represent a movement of socially and morally concerned activists operating from an academic base or a movement of socially, morally, and pedagogically concerned academicians?*
> - *What ultimately takes priority in their discussions and writings: the suitability of moral and civic concepts such as "charity," "citizenship," and "justice," or the pedagogical rationales that allow engineers and dancers as well as sociologists and political scientists to see service-learning as directly relevant to their work? (1996: 26)*

We add to this a third one: How do we position ourselves and our students as practitioners of service-learning, and what is the relationship of that learning to the academic endeavor? Are we participating in what Benjamin DeMott criticizes as "the new civility," a belief that "the Republic is suffering from rampant intemperateness on the one hand . . . and distaste for associated living on the other" (1996: 11), or do we want to perpetuate what he calls, drawing from Richard Hogarth, a democratic tradition that "obligate[s] citizens to resist 'the constant pressure to undervalue others, especially those who do not inhabit our own publicly articulate world'" (19)?

These are, of course, significant decisions. If it is not enough to clarify conceptualizations of service-learning, there is the additional pressure of Zlotkowski's argument, that service-learning is not likely to survive, much less grow, unless it is recognized as a genuine academic endeavor. We do not believe that we can make these decisions in terms of the existing education/training distinction, however, because the label of "vocationalism" is as damaging as "social activism" to academic credibility. Service-learning cannot continue to be what it has so valuably been, an effort perceived as one focused only on work in the community. Instead, we need to ensure that added to ongoing discussions about the relationship between service-learning courses and the community, and the nature of service-learning, is one about aspects of teaching and learning that are rewarded in the academy, including the process of promotion and tenure — like a focus on traditional academic content, and close work with students on difficult issues of theory and practice. The prospect of such fundamental changes in the academy shows what Tom Deans means when he writes: "Writing and community service, as articulated within WAC and CSL circles, both aspire to be 'modes of learning' . . . and processes of discovery rather than trendy add-ons and quick-fixes. Both are 'instrumental' rather than 'additive'" (see p. 29).

The initial establishment of service-learning is now an accomplished fact, in no small part because it has found a natural ally in composition. But the successes push us toward a critical juncture, where the academy must be transformed to accommodate the possibilities of service-learning and composition, or these programs must modify their own visions to fit into traditional academic roles. The essays in this volume are offered as reflections on where service-learning and composition have been, and as maps to suggest where they should go.

Notes

1. This case is convincingly made in Herzberg's essay in this volume, originally published in the October 1994 *College Composition and Communication.* Eli Goldblatt's (1994) essay does not concern a composition course but is recommended to readers for the relevant issues it raises and the perspective, which is related to but in some respects very different from those of Herzberg and of Heilker.

2. This is discussed more extensively in Adler-Kassner 1995.

3. We use "politics" in this introduction to mean conscious positions on social and political issues, and "ideology" to mean unconscious assumptions and categories that underpin a view of the world, including those that might be less conscious.

References

Adler-Kassner, L. (December 1995). "Digging a Groundwork for Writing: Underprepared Students and Community Service Courses." *College Composition and Communication* 46(4): 552-555.

DeMott, B. (November 9, 1996). "Seduced by Civility." *The Nation.*

Goldblatt, E. (1994). "Van Rides in the Dark: Literacy as Involvement in a College Literacy Practicum." *The Journal for Peace and Justice Studies* 6(1): 77-94.

Herzberg, B. (December 1995). "Response [to Linda Adler-Kassner]." *College Composition and Communication* 46(4): 555-556.

Hirsch, E.D. (1988). *Cultural Literacy: What Every American Needs to Know.* 2nd ed. New York: Vintage.

Lanham, R. (1993). *The Electronic Word*. Chicago: University of Chicago Press.

Peck, W.C., L. Flower, and L. Higgins. (May 1995). "Community Literacy." *College Composition and Communication* 46(2): 199-222.

Weber, S. (1987). "The Limits of Professionalism." In *Institution and Interpretation*, pp. 18-32. Minneapolis: University of Minnesota.

Zlotkowski, E. (January/February 1996). "Linking Service-Learning and the Academy: A New Voice at the Table?" *Change* 28(1): 21-27.

Service-Learning: Help for Higher Education in a New Millennium?

by Lillian Bridwell-Bowles

Sometimes, givers benefit as much as receivers. In the case of the service-learning movement, American higher education may stand to gain as much as those who are being served in programs such as the ones described in this collection.

We are facing an identity crisis in who we are and what our goals are, precipitated, among other things, by the spiraling costs of maintaining our educational institutions. Our constituencies — students, taxpayers, employers — are demanding greater accountability, more outcomes for their investments. At my own institution, our own regents, whose role is to advocate for the University, have challenged the academy's most sacred cow — tenure — in their attempts to reduce the faculty so that they can control personnel costs. As one Minnesota legislator said when she described the size of the financial request the administration has made to the legislature for 1997, "I don't know what planet they are coming from." We faculty need to "get out more," in the words of another state policymaker.

In addition to raising the question about the relevance of a tenured faculty, demands for "real-world" connections also imply that faculty members in many of our colleges and universities are largely removed from the workaday world of business and industry in a postindustrial society. We are characterized as "privileged" or "ivory tower," with lifelong job security, as a class apart, separated from late-1990s problems of joblessness, downsizing, and poverty. Some faculty members exacerbate the problem by responding in esoteric ways to these attacks, championing complex concepts such as academic freedom, the integrity of independent research, and free speech. These topics don't lend themselves to sound bite rhetoric, and academics aren't generally inclined to learn the art of the sound bite. It's not our job; we have thought that it was our job to see things in more complex terms.

While many faculty members are clinging to tenure, students who complete an undergraduate degree find it increasingly difficult to find the kinds of long-term careers that the baby boomer generation enjoyed before downsizing. Students, parents, and legislators ask what kind of marketable, "value-added" skills and abilities can be guaranteed by increasingly expensive baccalaureate degrees. These kinds of political and economic pressures have forced nearly every institution in the country to reevaluate its mission. The cry for school reform was a little late arriving in the halls of academe, but there is no question that we are now under great pressure to be more directly accountable to our communities.

Service-learning programs are one of the more attractive of the new generation of initiatives that schools are adding to meet the needs of students and society in the 21st century. Popular guides to colleges and universities, aimed at entering college students and their parents, tout service-learning programs as pluses in "Value-Added Math 101." The *U.S. News & World Report 1997 Annual Guide to the Nation's Best Colleges* contains a story on "the new honors programs," featuring an upbeat picture of Robyn Painter, an honors student at one of my alma maters, the University of Georgia. She appears to be enjoying a service-learning project, hammering a nail for Habitat for Humanity. For Painter and other students like her, service-learning provides the opportunity for intimacy, the chance to "get to know and work with faculty members" (Fischer 1996). These kinds of close relationships with faculty members are advertised as a competitive advantage when large universities attempt to recruit students like Painter.

But if the future described in an essay on controlling academic costs in the same guide comes to pass, close contact with faculty members may be a thing of the past in the classroom. Mel Elfin (1996) argues for the efficiencies of computers compared with faculty, saying that faculty need to do other things, beyond the classroom, perhaps even instead of teaching in the classroom. He takes on "academic technophobes" who worry about technology as a substitute for faculty and asserts that

> *the computer is destined to eclipse the professor-centered classroom. It will free faculty from routine and repetitive chores in the classroom, enabling them to devote more time to doing what they should do best — closely monitoring and mentoring students. Such one-on-one relationships are becoming increasingly important as colleges place more emphasis on so-called experiential-learning programs that take place outside the classroom. Realizing the educational value of learning by doing and growing by doing, many schools now offer college credits for participation in off-campus internships, independent study and research projects, volunteer service and undergraduate teaching assistantships and for enlisting in local community development activities. (93)*

In too many classrooms at large universities, faculty members are teaching sections with hundreds of students, who complain that they never see a faculty member up close. More faculty members would be needed to work with students one-on-one or to mentor them in off-campus programs. "Value-Added Math 101" may need a remedial prerequisite.

Nevertheless, experiential learning is a good idea. Elfin applauds plans at Connecticut's Trinity College to involve its nearly 1,750 students in community service in the deteriorating Frog Hollow area surrounding its

Hartford campus. The president of Furman University, in South Carolina, agrees: "We have found that undergraduates who are involved in real-world experiences like internships take more responsibility for their own education and develop greater self-confidence and sharper communication skills" (Elfin 1996: 93). And, of course, Elfin's article cites the benefit most often advertised to students and their bill-paying parents: Students develop contacts in real-world programs that can help them get jobs. Elsewhere in the issue, college placement advisors speak of their efforts to coordinate internships and service programs to provide students with a competitive advantage. Of course, the contributors to this collection also argue for even more benefits such as better learning when the contexts for new ideas are "authentic" and when direct involvement in something important increases motivation.

But in the same issue of *U.S. News & World Report*, the president of the Miami-Dade Community Colleges describes his reasons for eliminating service-learning projects there: "We were trapped in a do-gooder mentality but had nothing to show for it" (Schrof 1996: 123). Many of the contributors to this volume have wrestled with the "missionary mentality" that students and faculty sometimes bring to service-learning. At Miami-Dade, president Eduardo Padron replaced the community service project with a neighborhood scholarship program that is "truer to the colleges' educational mission at a fraction of the price" (123) and put the institution back in the black. This example raises one of the many difficult questions higher education faces: how to choose an appropriate set of goals among many worthy ones. Miami-Dade has a long history of experimenting with computer-assisted instruction, but apparently Elfin's technological substitute teachers have not yet worked well enough to allow such a major commitment to service-learning.

One of the factors that may distinguish institutions from one another in the future will be their ability to afford "special" programs, such as service-learning, which provide students with direct contact with faculty, more appropriate environments for learning, and, some would argue, a competitive advantage. Proponents of service-learning in this volume make a case not only for the merits of this enterprise but also for its value compared with other worthwhile endeavors. They also argue that we really can get "two for one" or "more with less," especially when they demonstrate that students learn skills such as writing more rapidly because they are highly motivated in environments where effective communication matters to them personally. But it's a tough sell to many beleaguered faculty members. We need the kind of data provided here if we are to recruit large numbers into this movement.

The bibliography at the end of the collection alludes to many essays that fit into what the editors have described as a first wave of descriptions of service-learning courses. With any new initiative in higher education, we typically find essays that contain individual testimonials from those who have tried the innovation, found it exciting, and hope to attract others. My casual search on the World Wide Web (WWW) revealed 464 sites filled with powerful testimonials. One student at the University of Michigan puts it this way: "Simply invite someone to see the world as it really is through community service combined with critical reflection and people will change themselves. The experience of truth in community is too powerful to ignore" (University of Michigan, Office of Community Service Learning, Project Community homepage, http://www.umich.edu/~ocsl). The editors of this collection assert that the "early adopters" have resolved most of the early logistical problems so that faculty members at institutions across the country can now share their successes.

I see an analogy here with the wave of testimonials for computers in composition classrooms. Computers were going to revolutionize the way students learned to write and, according to some, relieve writing teachers of the tedium of correcting and responding to student papers. The early adopters, and I was one of these, spent a great deal of time consulting with colleagues about how to solve the logistical problems in computer-assisted writing labs. In a more mature phase, we now know that computers have dramatically altered our methods of producing writing and of communicating, but they have not magically replaced teachers. If anything, they have made the need for smaller student-faculty ratios more dramatic, not to mention the costs for maintenance of software and hardware and technical assistance for increasingly more sophisticated networks.

Those of us who argued for computers for more basic reasons — they simply would be everywhere and we had to prepare students for this new world — see an analogy here for service-learning. Service-learning courses may not be justified because they help us to economize, using the world as our new classrooms and the Internet as our library. We have to provide instruction in the contexts that will prepare our students for the brave new world that they are entering — not just so that they can survive, but because they might make it better. And if colleges and universities do not make stronger connections to the world, many of them will simply not survive, or at least not as we have known them.

In the second stage for any educational innovation, however, we also have to ask difficult questions about *why* we're doing something, *and*, especially these days, why we are doing something instead of something *else*, given the critical shortage of dollars. Given the pressures on higher education, as the editors of this book have pointed out, it is time for a more critical analysis of the purpose of service-learning programs and courses inside the academy. What is their history and how have they evolved? What are their objectives? What are the pitfalls associated with service-learning? Why is Composition Studies an appropriate site for these courses — or at least a typical one? The essays in this collection go a long way toward answering all these questions.

Many schools have had long-standing community service projects. A major impetus for such projects, especially at the secondary level, came when the Clinton administration connected community service to the school reform movement. Jim Kohlmoos, senior advisor for the Office of Elementary and Secondary Education, describes service-learning as "an ongoing effort to break down the barriers and build bridges — to create a lasting connection between the constantly changing needs of the community and the educational effort to address them." Such programs can put public institutions "back in touch with the people they are set up to serve," according to Kohlmoos (1994: 2). Michigan State, for example, has a strong partnership with secondary schools in its service-learning programs. The University of Minnesota's National Service-Learning Cooperative Clearinghouse on the WWW (http://www.nicsl.coled.umn.edu) offers information about 14 partner organizations and universities that are sponsoring service-learning programs nationwide. While the promise of a year or more of national community service for all students has not yet materialized, grass-roots efforts are increasing daily in the nation's secondary schools.

At the college level, the institutions represented by the contributors to this collection have had long-standing requirements for community service or experiential learning and often a formal program office to administer the requirement. Other schools merely endorse individual faculty members' efforts to offer courses with a service requirement, sometimes publishing opportunities in fliers or on WWW pages. Arizona State's established program is representative of many of the outstanding programs described in this collection and provides a good overview for those new to the field.

ASU's official documents define service-learning as "an academic experience where you learn and develop by participating in dynamic community service projects that are integrated into your academic curriculum" (Brack 1996). A student spends between six and eight hours working with children at one of the Service Learning Project Sites, and receives six or seven academic credits for the class. Students often read, write about, and emulate workplace writing, collected in such books as *Writing in the Workplace* (Southern Illinois University Press, 1993). They also collaborate with other students via electronic communication. For example, a student might post a query ("Where's some good material on quadratic equations for junior high kids?") on a computer listserv and seek help from other tutors. In progress reports and final reports, the rhetorical task is to explain the benefits of the project to a supervisor, a typical kind of reporting task across business and industry. Like most others, ASU's program calls for active reflection in the form of journals the students keep for themselves or for partners or instructors who engage in an informal dialogue.

Arizona State University's flier advertises a number of benefits to students: academic credit, real-world applications for classroom concepts, real-world work experience for resumes, and a personal investment in the community outside the university. Students are also supposed to develop skills in solving problems, making decisions, communicating, thinking critically, planning, and participating in collaborative groups. Further, according to their materials, the experience can improve academic writing skills, increase content knowledge, and provide for career exploration. The recipients, mostly children, benefit through improved reading skills, help with homework, one-on-one attention, an introduction to computers, and multicultural awareness. Many of these arguments seem valid simply at face value, though some quantitative data to back up these claims no doubt does help to persuade funding sources that the investments of increased time and money are worth the effort.

The ASU program represents the most common model — a course combined with service — but there are other models. An entirely different kind of service-learning opportunity is available in lieu of traditional "study abroad" programs. The WWW homepage for the International Partnership for Service-Learning (http://www.studyabroad.com/psl) advertises the chance to study cultures and serve in 11 countries, e.g., tutoring children on Native American reservations in South Dakota, serving food to destitute children in one of Mother Teresa's homes in Calcutta. The costs are comparable to tuition rates at low- to moderately priced private colleges (e.g., $3,800 for a January term or $7,700 for a semester in Calcutta, including airfare). These prices again raise the question about who gets to do this kind of service and benefit from these outstanding opportunities.

Linda Adler-Kassner and Terence Collins in the General College of the University of Minnesota had different aims as they employed urban high school students who were deemed "at risk of not fulfilling their educational experience" in a service project they conducted in conjunction with Penumbra Theatre, Minnesota's only professional black theater company. Students worked in internships at the theater in a range of positions — from writing newsletter copy, to stuffing envelopes, to ushering, to working with the theater's dramaturg. They enrolled in college courses designed to help them develop connections between these experiences and college work. The program also helped connect them with people who might reinforce their desires for a college education and develop realistic goals. This kind of program might be described as a "pipeline" project, involving students in service-learning projects with role models who serve as inspirations or show them how to obtain a higher education.

But when they began their project in 1990, Adler-Kassner and Collins found that models like the one they used — working with at-risk students to facilitate their transition to college — were lacking. Instead, in a monograph entitled *Writing in Service-Learning Courses*, they noted two paradigms that characterized service-learning projects at the time: (1) a focus on a "'service ethic' or citizenship responsibility" and (2) the "career ladder" approach, in which students use an internship to apply academic coursework and gain experience that can help them land a job. In their review of the writing assignments students produced in a range of projects, they encountered a persona adopted by the student that they describe as the "educated [student], descending into the world of the 'served,' 'slumming,' 'not the other' . . . the person who enters the world of the 'other' and gets to define that other, or for work-experience career ladder projects, as a now-experienced functionary in a corporate culture" (1994: 3). For their own purposes, they wanted to "take service-learning projects in directions that do not merely serve the process of replication of elite, 'otherizing' structures, which do not simply (or only) serve as training sites for would-be functionaries, and which do indeed build the critical competence and self/communal esteem for our students."

Coming as they do from a program that takes risks with students who are themselves often members of communities typical of those served by service-learning courses, it comes as no surprise that Adler-Kassner and Collins should have a political agenda for service-learning that was and still is more inclusive than simply a "service ethic" or "career development." Whether students come from disadvantaged communities or from communities of privilege, one of the goals of this program and others like it is to help students develop a more sophisticated analysis of society and their roles as educated citizens within it. Many of the essays in this collection demonstrate the enormous shift that has taken place in service-learning since Adler-Kassner and Collins wrote that essay, as leaders now work with students from a variety of backgrounds to develop connections among learning, work, and society.

That Composition Studies and writing across the curriculum programs should be popular venues for service-learning is no accident. Quite often, our profession supplies the leaders on campus who are committed to pedagogical reform. The cross-disciplinarity of our work, as Tom Deans points out in his essay, is another reason. Those of us in Composition Studies have come to understand that literacy within the walls of academe is as foul a fish as Ken Macrorie's "Engfish," a type of writing found only in the rarefied atmospheres of English classrooms, one that smells when it is taken out of that environment. For decades we have issued calls for "authentic" writing and "real-world" assignments (described well in Paul Heilker's essay), and in recent years, our theorizing about literacy has explicated a social constructivist view of language that makes it impossible to justify "pretend" writing. Nora Bacon tells us that "Stanford launched its Community Service Writing program just after composition theory took its 'social turn'" (see p. 39). For Rosemary Arca's basic students, writing about the connections between their worlds and the academy gives them what Paulo Freire has described as "the means for authentic thought." Chris Anson's essay gives us some practical suggestions for journal assignments that can provide students with more critical tools for this "authentic thought."

As we look away from the myths of the isolated writer in an ivory tower, we discover, over and over again, the rhetorical power of writing in particular social contexts. The need to connect with our communities and the need to communicate cut across every field in a modern college or university. And they may also be a cure for the alienation and despair that many of us see among students on our campuses. As contributors Wade Dorman and Susann Fox Dorman put it, "Students who see no relevant connection between learning and life don't try to store the learning for life, but only through the final exam" (see p. 119). Gay Brack and Leanna Hall describe the service-learning as a successful cure for the "empty assignment syndrome" (see p. 143).

"Praxis" as an issue suggests theory to academics as often as it suggests service. And, as Bruce Herzberg worries, if we don't connect service-learning to systematic analyses of social ills from multidisciplinary perspectives ("social imagination" is a term he borrows from Kurt Spellmeyer), our programs become places where we are doing missionary work with emotionally charged opportunities for personal writing about individual conversions (grist for the "easy A"). Others might argue that personal, individual growth might motivate students to learn more about the systemic causes for societal ills, but no one defends a condescending version of voluntarism as an important goal for critical pedagogy at the college level.

As old disciplines die out and evolve into new fields to solve human problems in a new millennium, we see interdisciplinary hybrids of every sort. David Cooper and Laura Julier describe a partnership of service-learning, American Studies, and Composition in their American Thought and Language courses, which encourages students to engage in a critical dialogue with American ethical traditions and democratic institutions in preparation for their own service experiences. Writing, cultural critique, and the knowledge gained from firsthand experience and "experiential immersion" (see p. 82) are essential steps in solving complex social problems. Those of us who remember Linda Flower's early problem-solving strategies for individual writers see signs of our profession's evolution in her tangible, community-based, and collaborative version of "problem-solving." At Michigan State, Patti Stock reports that adolescents enrolled in its "Write for Your Life" project taught the literacy experts that merely studying social problems was not enough. In fact, uncovering negative statistics on social problems such as AIDS, teen pregnancy, child abuse, and homelessness was making the students despondent. Literacy scholars had thought that information would be empowering, but they quickly learned from the young students that analysis without action was inadequate. In many ways, this is the fundamental lesson that our colleges and universities can learn from service-learning projects. Analysis combined with action is the cornerstone of this new movement.

Academics, students, and various public constituencies are confused about the purpose of higher education in America as we near the end of this millennium. As we look closely at service-learning in this volume, many advantages seem clear. It offers us a new way of thinking about the function of higher education. For more than 2,500 years we have evolved institutions designed literally to isolate students from the "real world." I was reminded of this on a walking tour of Oxford, as tourists peeked at privileged students through cracks in medieval walls. The luxury to read and to think and to write apart from the world has had its clear advantages for certain kinds of societies. So what is the appropriate combination of academic learning and experience in our society? Is service-learning so important to higher education that it should be encouraged at the expense of something else? Does service-learning deliver multiple outcomes so that we can get two (or more) outcomes for the price of one? Should all students have this opportunity? The editors of this book and the authors of its individual articles have given us much to consider as we wrestle with these questions. If they are correct, higher education can benefit from learning how to serve.

References

Adler-Kassner, L., and T. Collins (1994). *Writing in Service-Learning Courses*. Technical Report No. 9. Minneapolis: Center for Interdisciplinary Studies of Writing, University of Minnesota.

Brack, G. (1996). "Classes and Internships in Community Service." Tempe, AZ: Service Learning Project, Division of Undergraduate Services, Arizona State University.

Elfin, M. (September 16, 1996). "The High Cost of Higher Education." *U.S. News & World Report*.

Fischer, D. (September 16, 1996). "The New Honors Programs." *U.S. News & World Report*.

Kohlmoos, J. (1994). "Thoughts on Community Service Learning." Keynote address to the New England Conference on Community Service Learning, December 7, 1994. [Greenwood Press, Inc. website, http://www.greenwood.com/eeeeart.htm]

Schrof, J. (September 16, 1996). "Crunch Time for Community Colleges." *U.S. News & World Report.*

Writing Across the Curriculum and Community Service Learning: Correspondences, Cautions, and Futures

by Tom Deans

Last year I gathered every other week for a lunch meeting with faculty from across the disciplines at my university who were planning and implementing, most for the first time, service-learning courses. We were a small group from Art, Consumer Studies, Education, English/Writing Program, Philosophy, Public Health, and Nursing, each of whom had received a small grant from the provost's office to introduce community service learning practices to our courses.[1] The criteria for the grants required that (1) the courses integrate students' community service experience into course content; (2) the faculty develop the service component cooperatively with community agencies; (3) the students' service meet community needs; and (4) the course require systematic reporting, reflection, and assessment by students about their community service. Within these broad guidelines, we "service-learning fellows" initiated new ways of bringing community service into our teaching and our students' learning, and the ways we did so varied enormously, from having freshmen undertake writing projects for community agencies as part of a composition course to having graduate students in public health do comprehensive evaluations of community agencies for their major projects. We were, to use a phrase Barbara Walvoord borrows from sociology in describing the development of writing across the curriculum in American colleges, "early adopters."

Through the experience of this faculty group and the service-learning component of my own introductory college writing course, the correspondences between community service learning (CSL) and writing across the curriculum (WAC) became more and more apparent to me. The following connections surfaced:

• Writing and community service, as articulated within WAC and CSL circles, both aspire to be "modes of learning" (Emig 1977) and processes of discovery rather than trendy add-ons and quick-fixes. Both are "instrumental" rather than "additive" (Thaiss 1988: 94).

• WAC and CSL require a significant departure from traditional teaching and learning in college courses (i.e., fewer traditional tests; less lecturing; not just consumption of texts and knowledge, but production of them; more active, collaborative, and student-centered learning; emphasis on process as well as product; different assessment measures; etc.). One consequence of this departure is the need for more time and effort in the planning and teaching of such courses; another is that WAC and CSL can reenergize teaching.

• While WAC and CSL are cross-disciplinary, there is no standard WAC or CSL model or practice to be "imposed" on a discipline or course from without. Each discipline and instructor needs to discover what will work within a particular context to enhance disciplinary learning, and have the authority and flexibility to adapt WAC and CSL to his or her own means and goals.

• Both can prompt faculty to adopt new perspectives on the values and conventions of their home disciplines. This fresh and different perspective may prompt faculty to reevaluate how discourse and service work in their own particular disciplinary contexts — and this may have implications for their scholarship and teaching.

• WAC and CSL, while generally highly valued by a small core group of faculty and viewed as worthwhile by university administration (and, notably, by students, parents, and the larger culture), are perceived as low-prestige activities by much of the faculty. Both fall on the losing side of the prevailing value binaries of the modern research university: generalist knowledge/specialist knowledge; teaching/scholarship; "soft" service/"hard" research. As a consequence, WAC and CSL must meet with not only attitudes not always friendly — or more often, simply indifferent — to their propagation but also promotion and tenure systems that devalue them. (Why spend the many hours redesigning one's course to have students do more writing or service-learning when one can devote that time to writing an article, which will reap more professional rewards?)

• Within the disciplines, both WAC and CSL can fall prey to the perception that they take time away from "content" and lower intellectual standards.

• CSL, like WAC, is emergent in both secondary and higher education and could be another valuable site of school-university collaboration.

Behind these similarities, and both WAC and CSL, lie deeper questions for educators, such as: What kind of literacy do we value in school? What is the meaning and purpose of liberal education in a democratic society? What ways will graduates of our institutions use language, and how shall we teach them? (Russell 1991: 307). To further interrogate my initial observations of correspondences between the two movements — and those abiding questions — I turn to the history of WAC and what it might mean for the future of CSL.

History: Against the Grain

As David Russell (1991) chronicles in his insightful *Writing in the Disciplines*

1870-1990: A Curricular History, student writing has always played some role, even if often misunderstood or marginalized, in American higher education. So, too, with service. Although I am aware of no similar account of the history of service or experiential learning, I don't presume that community service learning burst full-born from the head of Zeus onto campus. As my colleagues and I recognized when we discussed our courses, and service-learning more generally, service to the community has been central to the mission of our institution from its founding as a land-grant university (as many other universities have histories, whether religious, public, philanthropic, or otherwise, that value service); so, too, countless efforts of students, faculty, and staff, both in and out of the classroom, demonstrate an ongoing commitment to serving the needs of the university and wider communities.

However, the history of writing in the disciplines should give service-learning advocates pause. Russell's history documents again and again how the modern university resists change, especially the cross-disciplinary sort championed by WAC and CSL adherents. Despite the enthusiasm and vision of a committed few, efforts at increasing and reforming student writing across the disciplines have been repeatedly resisted and thwarted, even when well-intentioned, well-designed, and well-funded.[2]

> *[Cross-curricular writing] programs failed not because they lacked substance but because they could not overcome institutional inertia, which the differentiated structure of mass education creates. Cross-curricular writing instruction goes against the grain of the modern university, with its research orientation, specialized elective curriculum and insular departmental structure — all of which makes it extremely difficult to change faculty attitudes toward writing instruction. (1991: 268)*

Russell also widens this claim to include all interdepartmental programs, a rubric under which service-learning would fall, and the reason why most community service programs at colleges and universities remain distinct from the disciplines, and instead are claimed by administrative structures in Student Affairs, where they remain largely disconnected from the academic curriculum.

> *There is no specific constituency for interdepartmental programs within the structure of the American university . . . because the academic community is fragmented, and there is thus no permanent defense against the slow erosion of programs under the pressure of well-defined departmental interests. (298)*

Such programs often end up in an "institutional no-man's land."

Yet there is something new and different about the current CSL movement, just as there was something new and different about WAC when it emerged about 25 years ago. Russell discerns the critical feature distinguishing the emergent WAC movement from its predecessors as the attempt to "reform pedagogy more than curriculum."

> *In most of its theory and much of its practice, writing to learn overshadows learning to write. This is one reason WAC has eclipsed all of its predecessors. It asks for a fundamental commitment to a radically different way of teaching, a way that requires personal sacrifices, given the structure of American education, and offers personal rather than institutional rewards. . . . A group of faculty who are personally committed to WAC can ride out any administrative changes (and perhaps increase their number), for the reforms are personal rather than institutional, and their success depends on conversion not curriculum. But on an institutional basis, WAC exists in a structure that fundamentally resists it. (295)*

Russell also notes, importantly, that as WAC evolved, it built on the personal commitment of a few, but also learned to use the fragmented structure of the university to its benefit.

> *[T]he current WAC movement has elements in it that do not ignore or attempt to supplant institutional divisions; rather they work through the disciplines to transform not only student writing but also the ways disciplines conceive of writing and its teaching. The WAC movement (and, with it, elements of the academic disciplines themselves) are attempting to develop new traditions of inquiry that examine the structure of academia's divisions and the ways that students and faculty may learn to travel among them, not transcend them. (299)*

This shift is evident in the preference of many for the title "writing in the disciplines" over "writing across the curriculum."

Service-learning seems to be following a similar trajectory, slowly and incrementally building on the personal commitment of early adopters interested in exploring new forms of pedagogy, while steering clear of reform that would threaten disciplinary formations or insist on radical critique. This approach of "service-learning in the disciplines" rather than a pan-curricular reform effort is a strategic (even if not consciously plotted) and, I think, wise one. Yet it is not without costs. Daniel Mahala (1991) laments similar developments in WAC, arguing that

> *the deeper questions that WAC implies have too often been quickly muted in the interests of insulating the tenuous consensus on which WAC is built from the clash of powerful professional and ideological interests in the university. Instead of addressing the most contentious issues, WAC programs*

have often maintained political invisibility, tailoring theory to institutional divisions and the demands from teachers for "methods that work," rather than really interrogating prevailing attitudes about knowledge, language, and learning. (773)

CSL needs to be aware of and to strategically navigate the competing draws, evident throughout the history of WAC, of acclimation to institutional structures and commitment to a progressive vision of teaching and learning.

The Future: Follow WAC's Path?

In the history of WAC there is also hope. Today, WAC is in a relatively healthy state, with a footing in at least 427 American and Canadian colleges and universities, equaling 38 percent of those who responded to a 1987 survey (McLeod 1988: 103). Among those programs, there is dizzying variety and innovation. According to Susan McLeod (1989), "A reform movement which began little more than a decade ago (a microsecond in institutional terms) seems well on its way to becoming part of the established order" (242). There is already a strong base of WAC scholarship (see Ackerman 1993; Bazerman and Russell 1994; Bizzell and Herzberg 1986; Herrington and Moran 1992), with continuing inquiry and dissemination of theory and practice through graduate programs, book-length studies, textbooks, academic journal articles (not only Composition journals), conferences, and networks (personal, professional, electronic). This turn toward more systematic research has helped WAC gain footing in institutions where research is highly valued. This commitment to research is, certainly, an area that community service learning advocates need to address.[3] There is little research available in service-learning (and even less about service-learning and composition), and what is out there is almost entirely from (and read by) those in departments of education, another constituency too often devalued by other academic disciplines.

Of course, one cannot simply demand research and expect it to promptly surface. WAC started through recruiting faculty to attend voluntary workshops, emphasizing intrinsic rewards such as more-gratifying teaching rather than extrinsic institutional rewards, seeking foundation and university funding, and slowly building on the enthusiasm and word-of-mouth success of the "early adopters." As WAC faculty and administrators gained more-secure places in the academy (aided by the ascent of Rhetoric and Composition as a discipline), early research in support of WAC, such as Janet Emig's and James Britton's, was recognized, and new research on all aspects of WAC burgeoned (and continues to). CSL should note the grass-roots approach of the emergent WAC days (and read the literature on those workshops, noting especially that the programs that tended to be more successful crafted their approach to particular institutional contexts and garnered faculty as well as administrative support).[4] Only by motivating faculty and by helping faculty recognize the value of process writing for their home disciplines did WAC take root. Although I can't claim any firsthand knowledge of early faculty WAC workshops, I imagine that some of them must have been like the bimonthly lunches I attended with the first group of service-learning fellows at my university: voluntary, collegial, discussion-based, a mix of the practical and theoretical.

With her recent *College English* article, "The Future of WAC," Barbara Walvoord (1996) becomes the latest of the WAC prognosticators. (For earlier predictions about WAC, see Herrington and Moran 1992, Afterword; McLeod 1989; Thaiss 1988.) She suggests that WAC adopt a "social movement organization" ethos and engage several "micro" and "macro" challenges. According to Walvoord, the first macro challenge for WAC, if it is to grow and thrive, is to work with other movements and organizations that share WAC's reform agenda. She mentions such organizations as the American Association for Higher Education (a notable supporter of CSL), university-based higher education research centers, funding agencies, and governing bodies. Walvoord predicts that "the most likely scenario over the coming decade is for a multitude of educational reform programs to coexist in a shifting kaleidoscope, with some programs disappearing as they can no longer draw funds or faculty, and new programs arising" (69). She also mentions that "another possible collaborative role for WAC is what the movement literature calls dissemination of tactics or personnel, or becoming a network though which other movements form" (70). Already, WAC programs at some universities have allied with such cross-curricular initiatives as critical thinking or computer literacy. Certainly CSL could share in, and contribute to, WAC's kaleidoscopic and collaborative vision. This notion echoes Christopher Thaiss's suggestion that "one way to measure the success of your WAC workshops is to see, over the years, how many other cross-curricular initiatives sprout up" (1988: 99).

CSL could be well served by capitalizing on WAC's institutional success (the benefits would run in the other direction, too, of course). After all, WAC and CSL advocates would likely share not only a similar educational reform agenda but a combination of administrative savvy and scholarly capability needed to launch cross-curricular initiatives. Also, most CSL academic projects have writing at their center, whether the projects be text-based, or reflection on service-learning projects be through journal, expressive, or analytical writing. It did not surprise me that the first faculty CSL fellows at my university included the director of the writing program, and the second included a WAC participant from another department.

Toward a Nascent Service-Learning in the Disciplines

Reflecting on the future of WAC, Russell (1991) concludes that "disciplines must find or create places where student writing matters to the disciplinary community" (302). He adds, "Finding ways to harness the efforts of the disciplines — where the faculty's primary loyalty and interests lie — will perhaps achieve more in the long run than structurally separate programs, no matter how well intentioned and well-financed" (304). Therein lies both the challenge and opportunity for service-learning, as well.

That challenge is a tall order, and one that must be addressed locally, within particular institutional contexts and community needs. While some universities and secondary schools have active and exemplary service-learning programs up and running (and interest seems to be increasing), service-learning is perhaps still too young to be considered a national "movement." I have suggested one paradigm that CSL should at least pay attention to, if not imitate. As always, lockstep imitation will lead to narrow vision and limited success. WAC, a collection of diverse people, practices, theories, and events more than any singular thing, has created a forum for dialogue about teaching and learning and demonstrated a capacity to grow, despite setbacks and institutional resistance, because of its resourcefulness, timeliness, and its dynamic practitioners and theorists. From the efforts of early adopters, to workshops, to growing faculty and administrative support, to collaboration between university and secondary teachers, to research, to prominent roles in such organizations as CCCC and the National Writing Project, WAC has demonstrated the long and winding road that even very good ideas and practices need to travel if they are to take root.

Making predictions is precarious business, and I shy away from the role of CSL fortune-teller. CSL may atrophy in the face of institutional inertia; or reveal itself as a public relations fad in response to shrinking funds and growing public cynicism about education; or remain the pet project of a few enthusiasts. But I hope not, and it need not. Community service, like writing, is an invaluable mode of learning; and CSL advocates, by carefully reading the history of WAC and strategically working within our institutions, can help others discover its value for the academic disciplines.

Notes

1. A new group of faculty receives grants each year. The 1994-95 final report of the first committee, describing the courses and evaluating the program, has been published by the University of Massachusetts Chancellor's Office. For a copy, contact David Schimmel, Hills South, University of Massachusetts, Amherst, MA 01003.

2. See Russell, especially pp. 261-270, on initiatives at Colgate and Berkeley.

3. See Giles et al. (1991) for some general research questions and issues. Also see Kraft and Swadener (1994) for an overview of available research, a service-learning bibliography, and descriptions of several CSL courses at Colorado colleges and universities. For other references, see the annotated bibliography in this volume.

4. See Fulwiler 1981 and 1984; Fulwiler and Young 1990; Herrington 1981; McLeod 1988.

References

Ackerman, J. (1993). "The Promise of Writing to Learn." *Written Communication* 10:334-370.

Bazerman, C., and D. Russell. (1994). *Landmark Essays on Writing Across the Curriculum.* Davis, CA: Hermagoras Press.

Bizzell, P., and B. Herzberg. (1986). "Writing Across the Curriculum: A Review Essay." In *The Territory of Language,* edited by D. McQuade, pp. 340-354. Carbondale, IL: Southern Illinois University Press.

Emig, J. (1977). "Writing as a Mode of Learning." *College Composition and Communication* 28:122-128.

Fulwiler, T. (1981). "Showing Not Telling in a WAC Workshop." *College English* 43:55- 63.

——. (1984). "How Well Does Writing Across the Curriculum Work?" *College English* 46:113-125.

——, and A. Young. (1990). *Programs That Work: Models and Methods for Writing Across the Curriculum.* Portsmouth, NH: Boynton.

Giles, D., E.P. Honnet, and S. Migliore. (1991). *Research Agenda for Service and Learning in the 1990s.* Raleigh, NC: National Society for Internships and Experiential Education.

Herrington, A. (1981). "Writing to Learn: Writing Across the Disciplines." *College English* 43:379-387.

——, and C. Moran. (1992). *Writing, Teaching and Learning in the Disciplines.* New York: MLA.

Kraft, R., and M. Swadener, eds. (1994). *Building Community: Service Learning in the Academic Disciplines.* Denver: Colorado Campus Compact.

Mahala, D. (1991). "Writing Utopias: Writing Across the Curriculum and the Promise of Reform." *College English* 53:773-789.

McLeod, S., ed. (1988). *Strengthening Programs for Writing Across the Curriculum.* San Francisco: Jossey-Bass.

——. (1989). "Writing Across the Curriculum: The Second Stage and Beyond." *College Composition and Communication* 40:337-343.

Russell, D. (1991). *Writing in the Disciplines 1870-1990: A Curricular History.* Carbondale, IL: Southern Illinios University Press.

Thaiss, C. (1988). "The Future of WAC." In McLeod 1988.

Walvoord, B. (1996). "The Future of WAC." *College English* 58:58-79.

Community Service Writing: Problems, Challenges, Questions

by Nora Bacon

I have a section in my file cabinet labeled "CSW Success Stories." In it are stored testimonies gathered over seven years — teachers' reports, students' reflective essays, program evaluation forms — demonstrating the accomplishments of the Community Service Writing (CSW) program at Stanford and one of its daughters, the Community Service Writing program at San Francisco State University.

For my present purposes, I am going to limit myself to retelling just one of those stories, assuming that in the context of this book, it will be enough to show which model of service-learning I have in mind and why I advocate its inclusion in composition courses. Then I'd like to shift gears: I will tell a couple of "CSW failure stories" to illustrate the problems we confront when students write for community organizations. Although the failure stories can't offer much in the way of inspiration, they highlight the theoretical complexity of community service writing and they show how fundamentally it challenges some long-standing assumptions about writing and learning to write.

Stanford launched its Community Service Writing program just after composition theory took its "social turn," shifting its focus from the cognitive processes of individual writers to the relationship between texts and their social context (for overviews of the relevant literature, see Dyson and Freedman 1991; Nystrand et al. 1993). But the program was not developed only in response to composition theory. It grew in response to observed needs — community organizations needed help with writing tasks, the staff of Stanford's Haas Center for Public Service saw that students needed opportunities for service experience linked to their academic courses, and instructors in the English Department believed they needed meaningful writing tasks with audiences beyond the classroom. It was as the program expanded and we began to shape courses to accommodate community-based writing that we learned how it blended — or collided — with the theories of writing that informed our teaching practices.

The stories below are intended to show, first, how community service writing advances the conventional goals of writing instruction, and, more important, what difficulties we have faced in the effort to integrate community-based writing tasks into courses at Stanford and San Francisco State. Several problems that first presented themselves as administrative challenges have persisted, finally emerging as theoretical and empirical questions.

Esperanza

Stanford's Community Service Writing program was piloted in the fall of 1989, when I required it in one section of English 1 and my colleague Richard Holeton offered it as an option in another section. I had a wonderful class that semester, one of those groups that "gels" from the start and remains engaged and committed for the duration. None of us knew what to expect of the community-based writing assignment, but we embarked on it with a positive spirit: I was eager to see my students work collaboratively and learn to shape their prose for a "real-world" audience, and they appreciated the opportunity to practice their academic skills in the service of public, socially useful work.

The most impressive team of student writers was the five-person group writing for the South Bay Sanctuary Covenant (SBSC), a church-sponsored organization that shelters and aids Central Americans fleeing political persecution. They were asked to create an issue of *Esperanza*, the SBSC's newsletter, and to write research papers on related topics.

Inspired by the South Bay Sanctuary Covenant's work and the dedication of the people they met there, these students threw themselves into their writing task with remarkable energy. Alone or as a group, they interviewed several refugees and two church workers who had just returned from El Salvador, went to their congressman's town hall meeting to question him about legislation relevant to political asylum, and combed through the SBSC's library. One weekend they drove to San Francisco to see *Romero* and the next they drove to Berkeley where they could gain access to government documents unavailable at Stanford just after the Loma Prieta earthquake. Finally, they wrote articles for a six-page newsletter (twice as ambitious as anything the SBSC had printed before), edited one another's work, borrowed a computer equipped with PageMaker, and worked until the small hours of the night to get the newsletter camera-ready before their deadline.

These students were understandably proud of what they had achieved. In an evaluation of the assignment, one wrote, "The project fostered a 'can-do' attitude. When our group saw the inside of an organization like the Sanctuary Covenant, we realized the impact that a single individual can make." The project also fostered a transformation in their attitude toward U.S. foreign policy. At the beginning of the term, the students professed themselves neutral on the issue of U.S. intervention in Central America and ignorant about political asylum; by the end, they were opposed to intervention, highly critical of the ARENA party, and prepared to argue for specific legislation to extend political asylum to Salvadoran refugees.

The students' newly developed positions appeared in *Esperanza* and were elaborated more fully in their research papers. Although I was willing to scale back the course's research paper requirement for these students in recognition of the many hours spent on the community-based writing, they declined my offer. They explained that their contacts at the SBSC had introduced them not only to some pressing issues they wished to explore but to a network of community organizations where a vast, essential body of current information was available. One student took an incomplete in another course so she could complete the research on a 20-page paper about the repatriation of Salvadorans from refugee camps in Honduras, drawing from an array of English- and Spanish-language articles, pamphlets, government documents, interviews, and letters. Another, whose paper earned a solid A when he brought it to my office for a conference, refused to hand it in before he had the chance to discuss his views with a representative of the FMLN who was scheduled to visit the campus the following week.

The staff members at the South Bay Sanctuary Covenant were as impressed by this group of writers as I was. They printed bylines on all of the newsletter's articles and added a sidebar on the back page thanking the students for "donating their time to community service." Some time later, after working with two other teams of freshman writers, they changed the publication schedule of their newsletter to coincide with the academic quarters.

After each of the Community Service Writing program's first three years, I gathered together program evaluations from students, teachers, and community-agency staff to compile an overview of "sources of satisfaction" and problems. Among the satisfactions most frequently identified were these:

- The writing was meaningful because it had a "real" audience and purpose.
- The assignment exposed students to new people and environments.
- The project gave students valuable information about or insight into social issues.
- Students took pride in their final products.
- The assignment lends itself to collaboration.
- The assignment gave students a leg up in work on a research paper.
- The writing made a genuine contribution to the community organization.
- Students working with community service agencies were highly motivated and thoroughly engaged in their writing.

The *Esperanza* team was the first group of students I knew to fulfill the promise of community service writing. In the years since 1989, CSW courses have provided similar experiences for hundreds of students at campuses across the country.

Real Audiences and the Problem of Authenticity

I suppose the *Esperanza* team remains my favorite success story for sentimental reasons; the students were in my first CSW class, and their political awakening as they learned about U.S. intervention in Central America mirrored my own experience as an undergraduate learning about the war in Vietnam.

But it's also my favorite because of the student who refused to give me his research paper and because the group as a whole was so little concerned about getting me a copy of their newsletter. For these students, a central goal of community service writing had been achieved: They were not writing just to satisfy their teacher or to earn a grade. They had come to care deeply about what they had to say; they wanted, in the newsletter, to spread the word to a wider audience and, in their research papers, to work out a coherent and well-argued defense of their views. They were functioning not as *students* but as *writers*.

Other students do not make this role shift. Some students, in fact, turn their papers in to their teachers but fail to submit them to community agencies for distribution to the "real" audience. This problem occurs when a program is young, and it can be solved with administrative measures: Written guidelines for students can emphasize their obligation to follow through on commitments to community organizations, or a teacher can require sign-off from community agencies before awarding grades (Bacon 1990; Crawford 1993).

But why does it happen? What does it mean? Because the classroom is such a contrived and atypical rhetorical environment — where the reader often has more knowledge about the topic than the writer, where she reads not to learn but to evaluate so that the writer may learn, where the purpose of communication is easily subordinated to the purpose of demonstrating mastery of a skill or satisfying a requirement — we tend to see the classroom as artificial, while we perceive an off-campus readership as real. We design CSW assignments in an effort to create *authentic* acts of communication. Apparently students who submit their papers to their teachers and not to their community-based editors experience the classroom context as more authentic.

Margaret Mansfield (1993) describes a graduate course in Writing for the Public in which, she says, her students quickly discovered the paradox in her effort to establish an authentic context for their writing:

> *On the one hand, they were supposedly placed in a real world committee situation, and were writing memos to each other, to me, and sometimes to people outside the classroom to obtain or convey real, needed information.*

On the other hand, they were also writing memos to be graded by me, Moffett's "same old person, the English teacher." (72)

Community service writing assignments pull students out of the classroom more dramatically than Mansfield's assignment did, but the paradox still obtains. The distinction between the artificial classroom and the real world is overly simplistic; really, students are being asked to write for *both* a teacher and a community audience, and perhaps it is not surprising that the teacher — with whom they have more contact, and whose power may be more salient in their lives — sometimes comes first.

In nonacademic settings, writers often have to anticipate the needs of multiple audiences — a supervisor or editor, perhaps, in addition to some (possibly heterogeneous) set of readers for whom a document is ultimately intended. "It seemed the situation I had set up in the classroom was not so 'inauthentic' after all," Mansfield observes; "perhaps it was the 'single audience' assumption underlying most students' perceptions of the academic writing situation . . . that was really inauthentic" (73).

Experience with community-based writing, then, gives us a new perspective from which to view academic writing. It denaturalizes academic writing, for us and for our students, introducing self-consciousness about the business of writing for a teacher. While the teacher is in some respects a unique sort of audience, whose interests and power impose a unique set of constraints, she is quite real, and the classroom is a real rhetorical context. Given the opportunity to reflect on academic writing in the light of an alternative rhetorical situation, students may interrogate the classroom as a context for writing: Why is writing valued in undergraduate classes? In what ways and to what extent do teacher expectations determine the content and form of school writing? Why is the essay the preferred genre in so many disciplines? What values are implied by the privileging of essays? What, in other words, is the relationship between the form and function of writing in composition classes, and how does this compare with the form and function of writing in other classes, or in particular nonacademic settings?

These questions have relevance to the dispute over whether composition courses should be designed to initiate students to the "academic discourse community" (Bartholomae 1985; Bizzell 1982; Elbow 1991; Harris et al. 1990). Many of us have reservations about drawing students into an institution that mixes the most honorable of our culture's values with the most elitist. While we recognize our responsibility to prepare students to succeed as academic writers, we insist on a *critical* process of initiation. A course that sets academic writing side by side with nonacademic writing invites comparative analysis; it doesn't guarantee critical distance from academic writing, but it offers the possibility.

No doubt some students who have failed to submit completed papers to their community-based editors have simply been operating in a student mode — unaccustomed to their behavior having real consequences, viewing writing as a transaction that ends with a grade. But it is worth considering that they may be baffled by the complex rhetorical demands of a writing task that exists simultaneously in classroom and community contexts. As we work with students on this particularly tricky exercise in audience analysis, we open up a larger set of questions about the functions of writing within and outside the academy.

Outsiders Writing as Insiders

For the writers of *Esperanza*, the most significant reward of the community service writing project was the chance to try on the perspective of the South Bay Sanctuary Covenant. At the outset of the project, they met some extraordinary people, refugees who had given up everything to escape persecution and torture in their homeland, as well as the wonderfully clear-sighted, impassioned director of the SBSC. The student writers were quickly persuaded of the importance of the organization's work and eager to make a contribution. Although they were new to the sanctuary movement, they were happy to articulate its point of view.

Some students are not so lucky. In the winter of the following year, just as President Bush was drawing his line in the sands of Kuwait, I sent a team of three students to write for the Midpeninsula Peace Center. When I learned that all three supported Operation Desert Shield, soon to become Desert Storm, I pointed out that the Peace Center would surely oppose military action in the Middle East and suggested that they consider writing for other agencies. But the students liked their supervisor at the Peace Center and felt the assignment — "fact sheets" on Kuwait and Saudi Arabia — left room for negotiating a middle ground. As long as their facts were accurate, they argued, they would satisfy both the Peace Center and their own principles, and they expected to emerge from the experience with a well-rounded understanding of the issues.

Although the three writers did succeed in producing fact sheets that the Peace Center could use, none was satisfied with the way they finally selected and presented information. Reflecting on the project at the end of the term, one wrote, "I believe that the document was harder to write than, say, a paper for class because I was catering to the needs of a specific group or person, that is, it was writing they would have done themselves if they had the time or inclination. . . . Since [the writing] was not for me, I found I had to try and detach myself from the content and concentrate more on the style and quality. . . . Don't get too attached to what you write. If it's for someone else, let them get attached to it."

For these students, the community service writing assignment provided an authentic rhetorical situation, but it denied them the authenticity of their own opinions, their own voices. In his reflective paper, the student distinguishes between writing for a class and writing for the public, apparently linking this concept to the distinction between writing "for me" and writing "for someone else." Interestingly, when the same student wrote a reflection some weeks earlier about his most recent school paper — an essay about Augustine's *Confessions* for a history course — he reported a similar conflict between his own views and what his reader required. He disliked the assignment, he wrote, "not so much because of the topic or the restrictive nature of the assignment [but because of] a hatred of the classics, especially in a religious context. . . . [Nevertheless,] I succumbed to attempting to please the reader above all else." In both academic and nonacademic contexts, then, this student writes "for someone else."

Every time I ask students to turn in reflections on both their community service writing experience and recent course papers, I find that a small number have suppressed their own voices or opinions in order to satisfy the expectations of community agencies, while a large number have made that choice to satisfy the expectations of teachers. Given students' much more extensive experience of school writing, this finding is unremarkable; it points again to the reality of rhetorical constraints both inside and outside the classroom.

However, the conflict is more troubling when students are writing for the community. Writing for teachers is an academic exercise; its main purposes are to work through ideas and to practice writing. Some writing teachers regularly require students to take positions they cannot sincerely endorse, representing such assignments as opportunities to explore ideas in a context where the writing is private and without consequences. By contrast, a key purpose of writing for a community agency is to advance the agency's work. Community service writing documents are public — they often appear in print, with the writer's name at the top — and they are expected to have real consequences. In this context, students should not be asked to express opinions at odds with their own convictions.

This problem is easily prevented if students have some freedom to choose the agency they write for and better guidance from their teacher than I offered on this occasion. I could have insisted that these student writers choose an organization better suited to their political views, or, as the weeks went by and it became clear that the conflict was not going to disappear, I could have designed an alternative assignment — say, a letter from these students to the Peace Center explaining why they could not complete the fact sheets (for a good example of this approach, see Watters 1991). In this case, however, the problem was not prevented or solved, and I mention it here as a reminder that when we incorporate community service into our courses, we lose not only the artificiality but also the luxury of the academic exercise.

A more common problem is that students do want to assume the voice of the agency but are unsuccessful, or only partially successful, in doing so. I recently observed a student from San Francisco State University who wrote a press packet for a tenants' organization. A very responsible and competent young woman, this student showed every promise of success as a volunteer writer: She wrote willingly and well in her classes, and she immediately recognized the value of the organization's work because of her own experience as a tenant.

The first draft of her press packet, however, was disappointing: It was wordy, its tone and political slant were inappropriate ("Although over seventy-five percent of the residents in this marvelous area are renters/tenants, their voices are rarely heard and the tyranny of the wealthy land owner still continues to reign over its subjects"), and it contained very little substantive information. Recognizing that she needed to know more about her topic, the student attended a counseling session and listened to counselors in conversation with troubled tenants. After a great deal of hard work by both the student and the agency's volunteer coordinator, the paper was revised three times and became nearly usable, though it will be revised again by a staff member before it sees print.

Successful completion of this writing task requires knowledge that the student, predictably, did not have: She was unfamiliar with her genre, barely acquainted with her topic, and uncertain about her audience and purpose. The volunteer coordinator had chosen this task thinking it was easy and had loaded the student down with information about the agency; but, as she observed to me later, there was no way to really prepare the student to do the writing in a few weeks' time. Although her visit to the counseling session made a big difference, she was still an outsider. "I never realized how much background knowledge goes into my writing," the coordinator exclaimed. "Every word — *tenant, tenants' association, affordable, maintenance* — has layers of meaning that you only know if you've been living and breathing this work. You have to know the names of the neighborhoods, the history of the legislative campaigns, what kinds of problems we see every day and which ones we can help with, the politics of the organization. That stuff may never be stated when I write an article, but it's all behind the writing."

Current writing theory can account for the tenants' association coordinator's effectiveness as a writer and the student's difficulty. The writing done at the organization is deeply embedded in its social context; since the coordinator inhabits that context, she can create texts that reflect and sustain the agency's values. Her writing is motivated by communicative purposes characteristic of this community and quite naturally embodies its discursive conventions. By contrast, the student was engaged in the difficult business of crossing discourse communities. Not unlike a second-language learner, this student had to adopt a "fake it 'til you make it" strategy, struggling to create meaning with the concepts and language of an unfamiliar social world.

The question we bump into in community service writing programs is this: Recognizing, even insisting, that texts are embedded in their social contexts, how can we introduce students to a community agency one week and expect them to write in its voice the next? We know that full, productive participation in a discourse community comes with time and practice; it requires a period of apprenticeship that involves not only acquiring topic knowledge and discourse knowledge but also growing comfortable with one's own role in the community (Anson and Forsberg 1990; Chin 1994; Doheny-Farina 1989). As a profession, we have given a great deal of attention to the question of students' acculturation into academic discourse communities. When we ask students to enter community settings and immediately function as writers, are we dismissing the importance of expert knowledge in those settings? Are we undermining our lessons about the particularity of discourse conventions?

As a practical matter, the problem of students' "outsider" status can be addressed in at least two ways. One is to extend students' relationships with the community organizations beyond the limits of the academic quarter or semester. At Stanford, Leslie Townsend has designed a two-quarter course in which students observe and perform direct service at community organizations during the first term (writing some papers about their experiences at the agency and others about the social issues the agency addresses), then serve as volunteer writers in the second term. A similar combination of direct service and volunteer writing is being planned at San Francisco State and may well exist elsewhere.

Another approach is simply to choose writing tasks carefully, avoiding assignments that require a great deal of expert knowledge about genre or about the agency's work (grant proposals, for example, are probably best avoided). Designing community-based writing assignments turns out to be something of an art: While assignments that require too much background knowledge aren't doable, those that require little knowledge (such as editing existing documents) aren't challenging. The ideal CSW assignment is both manageable and meaty. As teachers and staff members at community agencies gain experience with community service writing, they get better at selecting appropriate tasks. The volunteer coordinator at the tenants' rights organization has undergone a learning experience that composition specialists often witness in their colleagues in writing across the curriculum programs: Having become aware of how much expert knowledge she was bringing to bear on her own writing, she is prepared to analyze other writing tasks in terms of the context-specific knowledge they require.

Theoretically, it seems something of a miracle that student writers placed in an unfamiliar social context, asked to produce documents in unfamiliar genres for unknown readers, ever succeed. In fact, they almost always do. While the occasional failure reminds us that texts are indeed embedded in their contexts and that acculturation to a discourse community does indeed take time, the far more frequent successes suggest that both "embeddedness" and "acculturation" are a matter of degree.

As we watch the variation in students' experience with community-based writing, we discover a number of questions whose answers are not provided by current writing theory. What writing tasks are manageable for newcomers to a given discourse community? When we judge that a particular task is or is not accessible to newcomers, how do we know — just what characteristics are we gauging? And how can we account for differences among students? Even faced with what appear to be similar tasks, some students struggle to find a voice appropriate to the rhetorical situation, while others slip into a suitable voice quite effortlessly. Can variation in students' rhetorical flexibility be explained by other differences in their writing abilities? By their personalities or social skills? By the kind of support available to them in the classroom or at the community site? By differences in their own theories of writing or understanding of rhetorical principles? Community service writing programs raise — and offer fertile ground for the investigation of — empirical questions whose answers should be important to composition theory and instruction.

Evaluating CSW Papers, Within Limits

Writing teachers are responsible for evaluating their students' work. Every composition teacher worth her salt is prepared to evaluate academic essays; she can articulate and defend her criteria, and she recognizes whether they are satisfied in a given paper. In community settings, however, students are never asked to write essays. By what criteria does one judge a press release? How do you grade a brochure?

Evaluating community service writing documents pushes us against the limits of our expertise. When I ask other CSW teachers how they determine grades, many describe evasive maneuvers — they give every student a high grade, or they award credit for effort, or they fold the CSW paper into a portfolio and assign a single grade for the whole semester's work. Others face the grading demon squarely. Recognizing that they cannot judge by the textual features they value in essays (clear thesis, well-developed paragraphs, syntactic variety, and so on) and that no comparable list of formal qualities will be relevant to the whole set of community-based documents, they attempt to evaluate each document on its own terms, judging how well it accomplishes its communicative purpose.

In the "real world" of functional writing, there are bottom-line standards for judging texts. If you write instructions for using a new product, they succeed if consumers can follow the instructions and fail if they cannot. If you write a press release urging people to come to a rally, you can judge the release's success first by seeing whether it appears in print and second by counting the people at the rally. Teachers who grade community-based writing on its own terms are essentially guessing what its outcome will be. This is a difficult matter, since we as teachers are outsiders, too; unfamiliar with the community agency's goals, the paper's audience, and the genre, we are ill equipped to judge. Worse, our distance from the rhetorical context may leave us ill prepared to offer useful guidance during the writing process.

The best solution seems to be to call upon the expertise of the site supervisors, encouraging their input in working through drafts and assigning grades. A student working with two writing coaches has the benefit of advice from two perspectives. It frequently happens that suggestions from the classroom and the community agency will overlap and supplement each other in fruitful ways; the student can synthesize the feedback, contextualizing suggestions in light of the teacher's and the supervisor's backgrounds and objectives. In some CSW classrooms, students are encouraged to participate in evaluation, as well. They compare the documents they and their classmates have written, reflect on the feedback and the implied criteria for evaluation, and try to articulate general rhetorical principles that would account for the full range of context-specific criteria.

The opportunity to open up the process of evaluation, then, can enrich the students' learning by making visible the rhetorical justification for teachers' expectations. If a teacher's insistence on clarity, coherence, and correctness is echoed by a site supervisor representing the needs of real readers, it cannot be dismissed as English-teacher fussiness. Community-based editors can lend substance and authority to the teacher's advice.

Except when they don't. Because, sometimes, they won't. In evaluation failure stories, student writers get very different assessments of their work — and different suggestions for revision — from the teacher and the community agency. This happens rarely, but when it does it is confusing to the student and disconcerting to the teacher.

Several years ago I worked with a pair of students who volunteered to write for a recycling center near the university, a well-established organization that accepts materials for recycling and engages in environmental education and advocacy work. The center had been getting a number of telephone calls about backyard composting and needed a four-page informational handout to mail to callers and to keep on display in the office. After gathering information at the center and the campus library, the students wrote an 800-word paper in three sections headed "the landfill crisis," "benefits of composting," and "how to start your compost pile."

When the students brought the paper to a conference, I observed that it made a convincing case for composting: The first section offered dramatic evidence of the environmental risks posed by reliance on dumps and landfills to absorb refuse, and the paper as a whole presented composting as an effective, practicable alternative for organic materials. Some of the claims in the first section struck me as too dramatic to be immediately credible, so I suggested that the students double-check their facts, add supporting information in two paragraphs, and cite their sources. Finally, I praised the clarity of the step-by-step instructions for building a compost bin.

At the recycling center, the paper was less enthusiastically received. The center's director was impressed by the students' effort, but as he made suggestions for the next draft, it became clear that he envisioned a radically different piece. The first section, he said, should be shorter because readers of the "info sheet" would already be interested in composting; while they might like a brief reminder of the relevance of composting to the welfare of the planet, they didn't need to be persuaded. He vetoed the idea of adding more information, then, as well as the plan to include citations (because the paper already sounded "too academic"). The remainder of his suggestions pertained to formatting: He wanted both the benefits of composting and the instructions for getting started in bulleted lists rather than paragraphs; he suggested a photograph of a landfill in the first section, a diagram of a compost bin showing its dimensions, and before-and-after pictures of vegetable scraps and finished compost; he thought out loud about the size of the lettering for the title and headings, the wording of captions, the width of columns, and the color of the paper.

The agency director, in other words, evaluated the paper and recommended revisions based on a different set of criteria than I had in mind. The student writers wisely ignored my suggestions and accepted the director's, recognizing that his criteria were grounded in intimate knowledge of the audience and purpose of the text. In their next conference with me, they presented their revision and explained the rationale for their choices. It was an awkward meeting. All of us felt that my authority had been undermined, and though we finally worked our way into some interesting conversation about the assumptions behind the two evaluations, I had to struggle against the impulse to defend my response. I was embarrassed by what I did not know.

Two kinds of knowledge would have prepared me to offer more useful feedback. First is an understanding of the context, which was more appropriately supplied by the director. Second is an understanding of some basic principles of the organization and design of nonacademic documents. In retrospect, I find it unsettling that I overlooked the possibilities of graphics and layout. The decision to use a photograph, or to present information in a list, is a rhetorical choice; someone who professes to teach "rhetoric" or "composition" ought to be familiar with all the tools, linguistic and nonlinguistic, available to those who compose texts.

In the CSW program's second year at Stanford, we had a joint meeting of instructors and staff members from several community organizations. Asked how the program might be improved, one of the community representatives said he wished the students had access to better desktop publishing software and more guidance about document design. The teacher sitting next to me slumped back in her chair and groaned, "Do we really have to know all that stuff?" The answer is yes, we do. Community service writing gives us a glimpse of writing in the nonacademic world, where standards for the nonlinguistic aspects of texts are quickly rising in response to technological advances. If we teach "writing" — as opposed to "writing personal and literary essays" — we need to learn from our colleagues in Business and Technical Communication, who have long recognized the role of multiple symbol systems in making meaning on paper.

If composition teachers don't know how to evaluate an information sheet, or a brochure, or a press release, that means we don't know much about what goes into writing one. What that means is that we have defined our area of expertise narrowly, bound by theories of writing limited to extended texts and to meaning mediated through words. Whether we embrace more comprehensive theories (such as the "constructivist semiotic" proposed in Witte 1992) depends on how we define the mission of composition instruction. If our job is to prepare students to write successfully in other courses in the liberal arts, then we can be satisfied to know about personal and literary essays. If our job is to prepare students for academic writing across the disciplines, then, as Faigley and Hansen (1985) have observed, we need to build from a broader knowledge base:

> *If teachers of English are to offer courses that truly prepare students to write in other disciplines, they will have to explore why those disciplines study certain subjects, why certain methods of inquiry are sanctioned, how the conventions of a discipline shape a text in that discipline, how individual writers represent themselves in a text, how a text is read and disseminated, and how one text influences subsequent texts. In short, teachers of English will have to adopt a rhetorical approach to the study of writing in the disciplines, an approach that examines the negotiation of meaning among writers, readers, and subject matters. (149)*

If we remember that undergraduate composition courses are, for the vast majority of students, the last opportunity to attend to their writing with faculty guidance — if we then hope to prepare them for the multiple literacy demands that await them in their adult lives — we need still more knowledge. We need to become students ourselves, not only of writing in the disciplines but of the communicative events, genres, and technologies that constitute writing outside the academy.

Community Service Writing and the Goals of Composition Instruction

I hope it's clear that integrating community-based writing assignments into the composition curriculum is a very good idea but by no means a simple one. It creates a number of problems that can be solved only by thoughtful (and labor-intensive) steps on the part of teachers and program administrators: Students may need help accepting the responsibility of writing for a community readership in addition to a teacher and coping with multiple audiences; they need choices among community agencies so they can write for an organization whose goals and politics are matched, or at least reconcilable, with their own; staff members at the agencies need help identifying appropriate assignments, tasks that are neither trivial nor dependent upon deep background knowledge; and teachers need to seek knowledge outside conventional disciplinary boundaries to develop context-sensitive criteria for evaluating students' work.

But even as we create procedural solutions to these problems, it is worthwhile to pause and reflect on what they might reveal about the aims and assumptions that motivate our teaching practices. Of the dozen or so teachers I've known who have experimented with community-based writing assignments, not one has found that these assignments fit easily into her course the first time around; typically, teachers find that the course and the nonacademic writing experience seem to exist on separate tracks, and they struggle to find points of intersection. Our customary lessons about the processes and the formal features of writing are often irrelevant to nonacademic writing, and we are confronted with the fact that as long as we design our courses around personal and literary essays, we are teaching a tiny corner of the world of discourse.

If writing were always and everywhere the same, then studying a tiny corner would be enough: Students could write essays as freshmen, develop skills in choosing words, controlling syntax, and organizing arguments, and employ these skills in their other classes and in the myriad of writing tasks they might face in their adult lives. (This, I believe, is the assumption on which the undergraduate composition requirement, and most composition curricula, is based.) But if writing differs substantially across contexts, then we cannot expect a body of skills and knowledge about writing developed in a single rhetorical context to have universal application.[1]

Our experience with writing across the curriculum teaches us that writing varies; what you need to know to write successfully as a chemist is different from what you need to know to write as a historian. Mostly, of course, you need knowledge about chemistry or history, and this is best taught by experts in those fields. But there is also variation in discourse, which is best understood through rhetorical analysis. Community service writing teaches the same lesson in spades. Like WAC, community service writing demonstrates the enormous variety in written discourse and the degree to which the forms, processes, and purposes of writing are embedded in particular contexts. Like WAC, community service writing enlarges our view of what writers need to know: In addition to mastering the conventions of this discourse community or that one, they need to be able to adapt to new conventions as they move from class to class, from school to work, through a lifetime of shifting writing tasks and roles.

Community service writing finally points us toward a curriculum of textual studies based on inquiry into variation in discourse (for a similar conclusion based on an analysis of poststructuralist literary theory, see Scholes 1985). When students work on both academic assignments and a range of nonacademic writing tasks, their experience raises questions about why texts assume particular forms and functions. What is the relationship between the form of a mission statement, a press release, a brochure, or a newsletter and the aims of the organizations in which these documents are produced? Or between the form of an essay and the aims of academic courses? To what extent does the value of particular textual features depend on the occasion, audience, and purpose of the writing? How does a writer come to know what the occasion requires? Are some features or qualities of texts universally valued? Which features? Can the terms we use when we talk about writing — terms such as "organization," "development," or "clarity" — be defined in such a way that they are both specific enough to be useful descriptors and general enough to apply across contexts?

As they investigate questions such as these, students may develop an understanding of rhetorical variation that prepares them to navigate in multiple discourse communities. As we participate in the investigation, we may extend and refine the theories of writing that inform our work. We may remember why rhetoric was for so many years the cornerstone of higher education.

Note

1. Here I argue that because writing varies, we cannot assume that practice in one context will develop skills or knowledge useful in other contexts. Neither can we assume that knowledge about writing is entirely context-specific: Even when writing tasks are dissimilar, it may well be the case that skills and knowledge developed while performing one task will improve performance on other tasks. The generalizability of knowledge about writing should be investigated rather than assumed. For an overview of the arguments for "general knowledge," "task-specific knowledge," and "community-specific knowledge," see Smagorinsky and Smith 1992.

References

Anson, C., and L.L. Forsberg. (1990). "Moving Beyond the Academic Community: Transitional Stages in Professional Writing." *Written Communication* 7:200-231.

Bacon, N. (1990). "Community Service Writing Program Evaluation." Haas Center for Public Service, Stanford University.

Bartholomae, D. (1985). "Inventing the University." In *When a Writer Can't Write*, edited by M. Rose, pp. 134-165. New York: Guilford.

Bizzell, P. (1982). "College Composition: Initiation Into the Academic Discourse Community." *Curriculum Inquiry* 12:191-207.

Chin, E. (1994). "Redefining 'Context' in Research on Writing." *Written Communication* 11:445-482.

Crawford, K. (1993). "Community Service Writing in an Advanced Composition Class." In *Praxis I: A Faculty Casebook on Community Service Learning*, edited by J. Howard. Ann Arbor, MI: University of Michigan, OCSL Press.

Doheny-Farina, S. (1989). "A Case Study of One Adult Writing in Academic and Nonacademic Discourse Communities." In *Worlds of Writing: Teaching and Learning in Discourse Communities of Work*, edited by C.B. Matalene, pp. 17-42. New York: Random House.

Dyson, A., and S. Freedman. (1991). "Critical Challenges for Research on Writing and Literacy: 1990-1995." National Center for the Study of Writing, University of California-Berkeley.

Elbow, P. (1991). "Reflections on Academic Discourse: How It Relates to Freshmen and Colleagues." *College English* 53:135-155.

Faigley, L., and K. Hansen. (1985). "Learning to Write in the Social Sciences." *College Composition and Communication* 36:140-149.

Harris, J., with L. Brannon, M. Lu, J. Trimbur, P. Bizzell, and T. Fulwiler. (1990). "Writing Within and Against the Academy: What Do We Really Want Our Students to Do?" *Journal of Education* 172:15-28.

Mansfield, M.A. (1993). "Real World Writing and the English Curriculum." *College Composition and Communication* 44:69-83.

Nystrand, M., S. Greene, and J. Wiemelt. (1993). "Where Did Composition Studies Come From? An Intellectual History." *Written Communication* 10:267-333.

Scholes, R. (1985). *Textual Power: Literary Theory and the Teaching of English*. New Haven: Yale University Press.

Smagorinsky, P., and M.W. Smith. (1992). "The Nature of Knowledge in Composition and Literary Understanding: The Question of Specificity." *Review of Educational Research* 62:279-305.

Watters, A. (1991). "Reflecting on Public Service Writing." *Notes in the Margin*. Stanford, CA: Stanford University, Department of English.

Witte, S. (1992). "Context, Text, Intertext: Toward a Constructivist Semiotic of Writing." *Written Communication* 9:237-308.

Community Service and Critical Teaching

by Bruce Herzberg

"Capitalism with a human face," said our new provost, Phil Friedman. This was the way he hoped the United States would model capitalism for the new democracies in Eastern Europe. It was, therefore, a motto for what the students at Bentley College, a business school, should be learning. My English Department colleague Edward Zlotkowski challenged the provost to put a human face on the students' education by supporting a program that would make community service part of the curriculum. Friedman agreed, and Zlotkowski took on the massive job of linking courses with community agencies. At first, the projects were simple: Students in writing courses visited soup kitchens and wrote up their experiences. Later, as the service-learning program developed, students in accounting classes helped revise the accounting procedures of nonprofit community service agencies and audited their books for free. Students in marketing and business communication designed advertising and public relations materials to improve the distribution of agencies' services. And the students in one freshman composition class — mine — learned to be adult literacy tutors and went weekly to a shelter in Boston to offer their help.

There are many obvious benefits, to students and to the agencies and individuals they serve, from service-learning. Many students become eager volunteers after the ice is broken by class projects and they see where they can go, how they can help. A surprising number of the students in my class, for example, did some volunteer work in high school but would not be likely to do so in college — in a new city, without contacts — were it not for the liaison provided by service-learning. Most agencies are eager for new volunteers.[1] And of course, the students perform real and needed services. Faculty members, too, report a new sense of purpose in their teaching. This is, perhaps, most striking at a school such as Bentley, where students not only are majoring in business but often seem to have fallen into the narrowest view of what that means, adopting a gray and jaded image of the businessman, scornful or embarrassed by talk of social justice and high ideals. Edward Zlotkowski (1993) describes his teaching efforts at Bentley in the years before he founded the service-learning program as attempts "to help my students break out of the intellectual and moral miasma in which they seemed to me to wander."

I should interject here that the idea of service-learning did not originate at Bentley. There are well-developed community service projects at several colleges and universities. Stanford has made extensive use of service-learning in freshman English courses. And Campus Compact, an organization of college presidents that promotes public service in education, has been in existence since 1985. The observations I have made about the venture at Bentley are echoed in reports from other schools.

There is a good deal of evidence from our program that service-learning generates a social conscience, if by that we understand a sense of the reality and immediacy of the problems of the poor and homeless along with a belief that people in a position to help out should do so. Students report that their fears and prejudices diminish or disappear, that they are moved by the experience of helping others, and that they feel a commitment to help more. This is a remarkable accomplishment, to be sure.[2] But it is important to note that these responses tend, quite naturally, to be personal, to report perceptions and emotions. This is where my deepest questions about service-learning lie.

I don't mean to belittle the kind of social awareness fostered by service-learning, especially with middle-class students. Students in business courses are discovering real applications of their knowledge in the organizations they serve. More importantly, they are learning that they can use their knowledge not only to get jobs for themselves but also to help others. But what are they learning about the nature of the problems that cause these organizations to come into existence? How do they understand the plight of the people who need these services? I worry when our students report, as they frequently do, that homelessness and poverty were abstractions before they met the homeless and poor, but now they see that the homeless are people "just like themselves." This, they like to say, is something that could happen to them: They could lose their jobs, lose their houses, even take to drink.

Here, perhaps ironically, is a danger: If our students regard social problems as chiefly or only personal, then they will not search beyond the person for a systemic explanation. Why is homelessness a problem? Because, they answer, so many people are homeless. The economy is bad and these individuals lost their jobs. Why are so many people undereducated or illiterate? Because they didn't study in school, just like so-and-so in my fifth-grade class and he dropped out. Community service could, as my colleague Robert Crooks (1993) puts it, "work in a larger way as a kind of voluntary band-aiding of social problems that not only ignores the causes of problems but lets off the hook those responsible for the problems."[3] Campus Compact director Susan Stroud (1992) voices the same kind of concern: "If our community service efforts are not structured to raise the questions that result in critical analysis of the issues, then we are not involved in education and social change — we are involved in charity" (3).

I agree. I don't believe that questions about social structures, ideology, and social justice are automatically raised by community service. From my own experience, I am quite sure they are not.

Such questions can and should be raised in a class that is engaged in a community service project. Here, too, there is no guarantee that students will come to see beyond the individual and symptomatic. But that is what I wish to discuss at greater length. I don't see why questions like these cannot be raised in any course in the university, but if there are prime locations, they would be (and are, at Bentley) courses in economics, political science, sociology, and composition.[4] The connection to composition is by no means obvious. It is all too easy to ask students to write journal entries and reaction papers, to assign narratives and extort confessions, and let it go at that. A colleague reported overhearing a conversation between two students: "We're going to some shelter tomorrow and we have to write about it." "No sweat. Write that before you went you had no sympathy for the homeless, but the visit to the shelter opened your eyes. Easy A."[5] Even for those whose awakening is genuine, there is reason to doubt that the epiphany includes an understanding of the social forces that produce and sustain poverty, illiteracy, discrimination, and injustice. There is little evidence that students spontaneously gain critical self-consciousness — an awareness of the ways that their own lives have been shaped by the very same forces, that what they regard as "choices" are less than matters of individual will. Writing personal responses to community service experiences is an important part of processing the experience, but it is not sufficient to raise critical or cultural consciousness.

Writing about the actual experience of doing community service, then, does not seem to me to be the primary work to be done in a composition course like mine. Instead, we study literacy and schooling and write about that.[6] At this point, I need to explain some of the mechanics of the course, but I will keep it short.

Students are invited to be in this project, and we have had no difficulty raising enough volunteers from the pool of incoming students. I have run the project in a one-semester version, but the two-semester sequence that I will describe here is far better. During the spring semester, the students are also enrolled together in a section of introductory sociology.[7] In the fall semester, the students are trained to be adult literacy tutors, and in the spring semester they do the actual tutoring.

The composition course is not devoted to literacy tutoring, but rather to the study of literacy and schooling, as I have mentioned. This is an important distinction: We do not set out to study teaching methods or composition pedagogy. The students learn some of the teaching methods they will need in tutor-training sessions that take place largely outside of class time. But in the class itself, our goal is to examine the ways that literacy is gained or not gained in the United States, and only in that context do we examine teaching theories and practices.

During the fall semester, we read Mike Rose's *Lives on the Boundary* (Free Press, 1989) and a number of selections from *Perspectives on Literacy*, an anthology edited by Kintgen, Kroll, and Rose (Southern Illinois University Press, 1988). In the spring semester, we read Kozol's *Savage Inequalities* (Crown, 1991) and more of the essays in *Perspectives on Literacy*. The students write many summaries of sections of these books, as well as several essays drawing on what they learned from them. In the spring semester, they write research papers on topics that arise from our studies.

Toward the end of the fall semester, the students have about 10 hours of tutor training designed to sensitize them to the problems and attitudes of illiterate adults, as well as to provide them with some teaching materials and methods. These sessions focus on the need to respond to the concerns of the learners and to understand the learners' reasons for seeking literacy education. The sessions also help the tutors generate ideas about teaching materials and how to use them. While the tutoring is going on, we devote some class time each week to questions about how to handle interpersonal problems or obtain appropriate teaching materials.

In the 1992-93 session, the sociology professor and I took the students to the shelter at the beginning of the spring semester for an orientation session. The following week, the students returned to the shelter without us and started the actual tutoring.

At the start, the students were naturally apprehensive about tutoring adults in a shelter. Most of them had done some volunteer work before, but not in settings like that. They were very nervous when we actually went to the Pine Street Inn. We left Bentley's clean, well-lighted suburban campus and drove the 10 miles into downtown Boston after dark, parked under the expressway, and went past a milling crowd of men into a dreary lobby. We watched the men being checked with a metal detector while we waited for John Lambert, the director of the shelter's education program. The students clumped together around Dave, a football player. Dave wrote in his field notes that he was conscious of this attention and that it made him even more nervous than he already was.

We went upstairs for our orientation, stepping over some sleeping men stretched out on gym mats in the dining hall. Upstairs, we met a number of men who had been working with volunteer tutors. The students later said that they were impressed by the effort that these men were making to try to improve their lives. They did not seem attentive, though, to the analysis offered by the shelter's assistant director, who explained that while the shelter provided critically needed services, it also undermined any sense of independence the residents might have. Their self-esteem seemed to be under constant attack by all the social institutions they came in contact with, including the shelter itself. When I brought it up in class, the students had little memory of this discussion. On their first visits to the shelter, they were simply more concerned with negotiating the immediate physical and psychic environment. Soon, however, they became accustomed to going to the shelter. Two or three of the boys in the class, including big Dave, did not get learners right way, and instead walked around the shelter, visiting with the residents and trying to recruit them into the literacy program. Some of the girls did this on occasion, too. The students were irritated that they did not have learners but eventually realized that their presence in the shelter was a valuable advertisement for the literacy program.

The learners' needs are various: Some are almost completely illiterate, some are schizophrenic, a few need ESL teaching, some read well but need help with higher-order skills. Many of the learners come irregularly; many are easily distracted. One woman is pregnant, another is ridiculed by her boyfriend for needing help with phonics. One young woman is prevented by her mother (who also lives at the shelter) from taking tutoring because, the mother insists, she doesn't need it. But many of the students developed excellent tutoring relationships and all learned how to draw on their own resources both psychologically and pedagogically.

The students tended to see their learners, quite naturally, as individuals with personal problems — alcoholism and drugs, mental breakdown, family disintegration, or some nameless inability to concentrate and cope. It is quite easy to see these problems as individual ones. Very few of the students ever became indignant about what they saw. They hoped to help a few people as much as they were able. They would like to know if there is a "cure," but they don't regard that as a realistic hope. What I want to focus on here is how difficult my students find it to transcend their own deeply ingrained belief in individualism and meritocracy in their analysis of the reasons for the illiteracy they see.

They do become indignant when we discuss *Lives on the Boundary,* which describes the ways that schools systematically diminish and degrade culturally disadvantaged students, or when we read *Savage Inequalities,* which tells about the structural inequities in the funding of public education and the horrible consequences of that inequity. The students are indeed distressed by systemic discrimination against poorer people and disenfranchised groups. In their responses to these books, it is clear that they understand the class discrimination inherent in tracking and the effect of tracking on self-esteem. But they do not seem to see this discrimination in the lives of their learners. One reason, perhaps, is that the learners themselves regard their situations as personal problems. They, too, have imbibed the lessons about individualism and equal opportunity. The traces have been covered over. Thus, in order to understand that they are in the presence of the effects they have been reading about, the students must also understand — viscerally if not intellectually — the nature of what Gramsci called hegemony: the belief that one participates freely in an open and democratic system and must therefore accept the results it produces. They must see, in other words, that the people in the shelter believe the same things that they, the students, do — that there is equal opportunity to succeed or fail, to become literate or remain illiterate. They need to analyze the way that schools and other institutions, like the shelter itself, embody those beliefs.

Here is a passage from *Lives on the Boundary*. We spent a lot of time with this:

> *American meritocracy is validated and sustained by the deep-rooted belief in equal opportunity. But can we really say that kids like those I taught [as a Teacher Corps volunteer] have equal access to America's educational resources? Consider not only the economic and political barriers they face, but the fact, too, that judgements about their ability are made at a very young age, and those judgements, accurate or not, affect the curriculum they receive, their place in the school, they way they're defined institutionally. The insidious part of this drama is that, in the observance or the breach, students unwittingly play right into the assessments. Even as they rebel, they confirm the school's decision. They turn off or distance themselves or clam up or daydream, they deny or lash out, acquiesce or subvert, for, finally, they are powerless to stand outside the definition and challenge it head on. . . . [T]he children gradually internalize the definition the school delivers to them, incorporate a stratifying regulator as powerful as the overt institutional gatekeepers that, in other societies, determine who goes where in the educational system. There is no need for the elitist projections of quotas and exclusionary exams when a kid announces that he just wants to be average. If you want to insist that the children Joe and Monica and the rest of us taught had an equal opportunity in American schools, then you'll have to say that they had their equal chance and forfeited it before leaving the fourth grade. (128)*

Elsewhere in *Lives on the Boundary*, Rose speaks sensitively about the difficulties freshmen have with academic discourse, a discourse "marked by terms and expressions that represent an elaborate set of shared concepts and orientations" (192). Rose himself is a brilliant stylist of academic discourse, as the passage I've quoted reveals. Rose advises that students need many opportunities to become comfortable with this discourse, and I take his advice seriously. There is much that my students cannot fathom in his book, many references to abstractions and complex terms (such as "incorporate a stratifying regulator as powerful as the overt institutional gatekeepers"), so we spend time talking and writing about important passages like this.

"American meritocracy is validated and sustained by the deep-rooted belief in equal opportunity." This sentence is a complete stopper. My students consistently claim that they have never heard the word "meritocracy" before. Once defined, though, the idea is perfectly obvious to them: Of course those who are smartest, most talented, and work hardest rise to the top. What else? "Equal opportunity" is also initially difficult for them — not because it is unfamiliar but because it never seemed to require definition or reflection. This is not the first place in *Lives on the Boundary* that the students have encountered a challenge to the idea of equal opportunity: The challenge is both implied and explicitly stated many times. Yet, even 128 pages into the book, their first reaction is to regard this sentence as a positive statement about a noble ideal, an American virtue. It costs them a great effort to see that Rose is saying that one false idea is sustained by another, that the very words "validated and sustained" carry a negative connotation, that "deep-rooted belief" means self-deception. It costs them more than intellectual effort; it means a reevaluation of the very deep-rooted beliefs that Rose is discussing here. It means seeing that Rose is talking about their beliefs and criticizing them.

When Job, the righteous man, loses his property, his children, and his health, he angrily questions the belief that God is just and gives people what they deserve. He lashes out at his friends, the false comforters, who steadfastly maintain that the good are rewarded and the wicked punished (and thereby imply that Job is suffering for some sin). Yet Job is in a terrible dilemma. He is frustrated and angry, convinced that the comforters are wrong, yet unable to explain his situation — for he believes precisely the same thing the comforters believe. When a belief is deeply rooted, alternatives are inconceivable.

How do my students abandon their comfortable belief in equal opportunity and meritocracy? Did they not deserve, did they not earn, their place in school and society? They have the greatest respect for Mike Rose and want to believe what he says, but it isn't easy. As education critic Colin Greer (1972) says, traditional historians of education "mistake the rhetoric of good intentions for historical reality" (4) and persist in believing, against all evidence, that schools are the instruments of social change. We can hardly fault students for clinging to such a belief. We ran into a similar problem discussing a passage earlier in Rose's book:

> *We live, in America, with so many platitudes about motivation and self-reliance and individualism — and myths spun from them, like those of*

Horatio Alger — that we find it hard to accept the fact that they are serious nonsense. (47)

Here, too, we had worked on the definition of "individualism" and the negative connotations of "platitudes" and "nonsense." The students never heard of Horatio Alger. After I explained about Alger, Lynne told us, without the least self-consciousness and without comment, that her grandfather came from Italy without a cent and became a success in America all on his own, without help from anybody.

In their fall semester papers, the students tested out the ideas they were learning about systemic discrimination through schooling. They are very tentative about this at first. Kyle wrote:

In America today, we find that how an individual will do in school is often dependent upon what economic class they come from. Through studies of literacy, experts have found that there are different levels of success in school among individuals of diverse socio-economic backgrounds. . . . Children of [the] middle- and upper-class are able to attend better schools and have greater access to books and other reading materials. Therefore, they tend to feel more comfortable with the material in school while lower-class children, whose parents are not so well off in terms of money, are more inclined to be insecure. In addition, in situations where parents of poor children have had low levels of education, there is a good possibility that their children will also have low levels of education. While at the same time the situation is reversed with children of well-to-do parents.

These ideas are clearly unfamiliar to Kyle, and so he needs to repeat them and carefully spell out the steps in the process of discrimination, while holding onto the possibility of individual differences. "Experts" have discovered this injustice — it is not immediately accessible to experience. The parents of lower-class children are not so well off "in terms of money" — though they may, I think Kyle implies, have good intentions.

It is difficult, as I have said, for my students to understand these ideas, let alone deal with them critically. In the spring semester, for example, while we were studying Kozol's *Savage Inequalities*, a book that describes and decries the differences between well-funded suburban schools and their decrepit and overcrowded counterparts in the cities, Lynne (who told us about her grandfather) suggested that the students in South Chicago's schools were probably just not personally motivated to do school work, like the kids in her high school who flunked. Several students murmured in agreement, though when I challenged her, several others expressed dismay about Lynne's assumptions. Lynne is not a conservative ideologue. As with the comments about her grandfather, she was simply being unself-conscious here. She is helping us see how hard it is to understand the social nature of experience and to accept the idea of structural injustice.

In an essay called "Critical Teaching and Dominant Culture" in *Composition and Resistance*, a volume of essays on critical teaching, Cy Knoblauch (1991) describes his attempts to bring his students to some consciousness of the injuries of class. He tells how his students were unmoved by "The Lesson," Toni Cade Bambara's story about poor black children visiting F.A.O. Schwartz. Knoblauch quotes a student response that he characterizes as typical: "If you strive for what you want, you can receive it." As Knoblauch cogently argues, the goal of critical pedagogy is to help students see and analyze the assumptions they make in comments like these. Still, it takes a lot of time and work to do this, and Knoblauch is honest enough to say that he did not have the success he wished for.

Time and work were on our side, though, in the literacy-tutoring project — we had two semesters of composition, a sociology course, and the project itself. At the time that Lynne made her comment about Chicago school kids, the students had been tutoring at the Pine Street Inn shelter for several weeks. There was, apparently, nothing automatic or instantaneous about that experience that helped them understand Rose or Kozol. The community service experience doesn't bring an epiphany of critical consciousness — or even, necessarily, an epiphany of conscience. The effect was slow and indirect. In time, the students began to realize that the people at Pine Street were *not* like them. They did not, finally, conclude that "this could happen to me." Though they were not allowed (by the wise rules of the shelter and good sense) to quiz their learners on their personal lives and histories, they had learned enough about the learners' family distress and social isolation, their disconnection from community, lack of individual resources, and reliance on charitable institutions — and the effects of those conditions on their self-images — to realize that "this could happen to me" is a shallow response.

The tutoring, as best we could determine, appeared to be productive for the learners at the shelter. In many ways, the best help that tutors can provide in such a setting is to come regularly and respond sensitively to the learners' concerns. The learners are coming to the literacy program at the end of what is typically a long series of personal and social failures, and though they expect — and often demand — a school-like experience again, the tutors are there to humanize it as much as they can.

The final research papers for the composition course show a growing sophistication about the social forces at work in the creation of illiteracy. Students visited nursery school classes to see how children learn, returned to their own high schools to find out what happened to the kids who flunked, corresponded with convicts in prison-education programs. In his paper, "The Creation of Illiteracy Through Tracking," Dave (the football player) writes, "Tracking tends to maintain or amplify differences in socio-economic status, the opposite of 'equalizing' these differences as schools should." Schools can't be held responsible for prior economic discrimination, Dave argues, but they must be held accountable for reinforcing it. Kevin borrowed several history textbooks used over the last 10 years in the Waltham High School, counted the number of pictures and other references to African Americans and compared them with the number of pictures and similar references to whites, analyzed the images, and tried to imagine what a black student would learn about American culture from an education in Waltham, Massachusetts (Kevin is white). Our friend Lynne asked how school systems with the money to do so were addressing the needs of disadvantaged students. She concludes that "the systems with the extra money to spend on special programs are not facing these types of problems." She points out that there is no lack of information about how to spend this money well and describes the settled and unreflective attitudes about schools and teaching that prevent the adoption of new methods.

Some students referred to their tutoring experience in their papers. Mark, for example, noted the kind of knowledge his learners sought — sentence diagraming and algebra — and commented that their frustrating search for credentials, fostered by traditional (and failed) schooling, had left them without job skills on the one hand and with an artificially low sense of their own abilities on the other. Most of the students did not, however, incorporate the tutoring experience in the research papers they wrote for my class. This was as it should be: The goal of the course was not, as I have explained, to facilitate the tutoring experience but to investigate the social and cultural reasons for the existence of illiteracy — the reasons, in other words, that the students needed to perform the valuable service they were engaged in. In that sense, the tutoring project was constantly present in our class. In the sociology course, the students used their visits to Pine Street more directly as the object of field observations and analysis.

The effort to reach into the composition class with a curriculum aimed at democracy and social justice is an attempt to make schools function the way Dave and my other students want them to — as radically democratic institutions, with the goal not only of making individual students more successful but also of making better citizens, citizens in the strongest sense of those who take responsibility for communal welfare. These efforts belong in the composition class because of the rhetorical as well as the practical nature of citizenship and social transformation.

What the students' final papers show, then, is a sense of life as a communal project, an understanding of the way that social institutions affect our lives, and a sense that our responsibility for social justice includes but also carries beyond personal acts of charity. This is an understanding that has been very rare among Bentley students. Immersed in a culture of individualism, convinced of their merit in a meritocracy, students such as those at Bentley need to see that there is a social basis for most of the conditions they take to be matters of individual choice or individual ability. As Kurt Spellmeyer (1991) says, "the university fails to promote a social imagination, an awareness of the human 'world' as a common historical *project*, and not simply as a state of nature to which we must adjust ourselves" (73). Students who lack this social imagination (most of them, according to the study Spellmeyer cites) attribute all attitudes, behavior, and material conditions to an individual rather than social source. Students will not critically question a world that seems natural, inevitable, given; instead, they will strategize about their position within it. Developing a social imagination makes it possible not only to question and analyze the world but also to imagine transforming it.

Notes

1. A successful program requires a great deal of coordination between the school and the community agencies. Individual teachers working on their own to arrange contacts will find the task exhausting and daunting. While many agencies welcome short-term volunteers, some cannot. Literacy tutoring, for example, requires consistency over time, so that tutors can establish a relationship with the learner. In short, the school-agency ties must be well developed before the students show up. I wish not to discourage such programs but to suggest that good planning can prevent many problems and frustrations (see Cotton and Stanton 1990).

2. The advocates of service-learning assume that values must be taught in college. I'm comfortable with that assumption and won't try to make the case for teaching values or critical consciousness here. The question of whether to teach values at all is by no means settled. It has been raised persistently as a general question in education and it has been a topic of hot debate in Composition Studies. Patricia Bizzell (1993) argues cogently for the teaching of values. Knoblauch and Brannon (1993) is a recent and valuable contribution. Maxine Hairston (1992) dissents. Paulo Freire, Henry Giroux, and Ira Shor have long been advocates of teaching values through the development of critical consciousness. And I have something to say about the issue in "Composition and the Politics of the Curriculum" (1991).

3. Crooks (1993) goes on: "Let me hasten to say that by 'those responsible' I mean all of us, who through direct participation in institutional actions, policy making, ideas, attitudes, or indirectly, though silence and compliance, offer support to pervasive economic, social, political, and cultural systems that produce the kinds of problems that community service addresses."

4. At some universities, the theology department is the primary location for these courses. Georgetown University, Boston College, and Marymount College link community service to theology courses on injustice and social responsibility, for example.

5. I reported this conversation to Zlotkowski, who responded that he believed that many students remained defensive about the fact that they really did have their eyes

opened. In anonymous student evaluations that have no effect on grades, he finds a predominance of sincere reports of changed attitudes.

6. The courses in the Stanford program tend to focus on writing to or for the agency being served. Such projects are undertaken at Bentley by more advanced classes. See "Let 100 Flowers Bloom" (n.d.) for a description of Stanford's rationale. A high school writing course in which students work as literacy volunteers is described by Norma Greco (1992).

7. The benefits of "clustering" courses are described by Gabelnick et al. (1990). When students are coregistered in two or more courses, instructors can develop common themes, draw on material taught in each other's courses, explore shared readings from different perspectives, and have some common writing assignments. While my students were working on their writing with me and doing their tutoring at the shelter, in the sociology course they were learning about the effects of social and institutional forces on the formation of identity. Their final research papers were submitted in both courses.

References

Bizzell, P. (1993). *Academic Discourse and Critical Consciousness.* Pittsburgh: University of Pittsburgh Press.

Cotton, D., and T.K. Stanton. (1990). "Joining Campus and Community Through Service Learning." In *Community Service as Values Education,* edited by C.I. Delve. San Francisco: Jossey-Bass.

Crooks, R. (1993). "Service Learning and Cultural Critique: Towards a Model for Activist Expository Writing Courses." Presentation at the Conference on College Composition and Communication, San Diego, CA.

Friedman, P. (1989). "A Secular Foundation for Ethics: Business Ethics and the Business School." *EDP Auditor Journal* 2:9-11.

Gabelnick, F., J. MacGregor, R.S. Matthews, and B.L. Smith, eds. (1990). *Learning Communities: Creating Connections Among Students, Faculty, and Disciplines.* San Francisco: Jossey-Bass.

Greco, N. (1992). "Critical Literacy and Community Service: Reading and Writing the World." *English Journal* 81:83-85.

Greer, C. (1972). *The Great School Legend: A Revisionist Interpretation of American Public Education.* New York: Basic Books.

Hairston, M. (1992). "Diversity, Ideology, and Teaching Writing." *College Composition and Communication* 43(2): 179-193.

Herzberg, B. (1991). "Composition and the Politics of the Curriculum." In *The Politics of Writing: Postsecondary,* edited by R. Bullock and J. Trimbur. Portsmouth, NH: Boynton/Cook.

Knoblauch, C.H. (1991). "Critical Teaching and Dominant Culture." In *Composition and Resistance,* edited by C.M. Hurlbert and M. Blitz, pp. 12-21. Portsmouth, NH: Heinemann.

——, and L. Brannon. (1993). *Critical Teaching and the Idea of Literacy.* Portsmouth, NH: Boynton/Cook.

"Let 100 Flowers Bloom: Community Service Writing Curriculum Materials Developed by the Stanford Freshman English Program." (n.d.). Stanford University.

Rose, M. (1989). *Lives on the Boundary.* New York: Free Press.

Spellmeyer, K. (1991). "Knowledge Against 'Knowledge.'" In *Composition and Resistance,* edited by C.M. Hurlbert and M. Blitz, pp. 70-80. Portsmouth, NH: Heinemann.

Stroud, S. (Fall 1992). "A Report From the Director." *Campus Compact,* pp. 3-4.

Zlotkowski, E. (1993). "Address to the Faculty of Niagara University." Niagara University, New York, April 16.

Rhetoric Made Real: Civic Discourse and Writing Beyond the Curriculum

by Paul Heilker

Whenever I think about the *where* of teaching writing, I find myself both rehearsing a quote from the film *The Adventures of Buckaroo Banzai* — "Remember, wherever you go, there you are" — *and* reciting what I understand is a tenet of 12-step recovery programs such as Alcoholics Anonymous: "There is no such thing as a geographic cure." Let me begin, then, by acknowledging that simply changing the *where* of teaching writing without concomitantly redefining *who* we are, *what* we teach, *how* we teach it, and *why*, will probably be of little consequence. That being said, my argument here is a simple one: Writing teachers need to relocate the *where* of composition instruction outside the academic classroom because the classroom does not and cannot offer students real rhetorical situations in which to understand writing as social action.

Composition students have suffered for too long in courses and classrooms that are palpably *unreal* rhetorical situations. Their audiences are not real audiences; their purposes not real purposes. In most cases, students are writing to the teacher, to an audience of one, who is required and paid to read the text at hand, who is almost always both a better writer *and* more knowledgeable about the subject matter than the writers, and who is reading primarily to find error and grade the formal attributes of the text. Sometimes students are instructed to write to their classmates as their audience, a group homogenous in strange, manufactured ways, and who almost never get a chance to actually read the *finished* versions of the texts supposedly intended for them. And sometimes students are asked to work within completely hypothetical scenarios and to simulate the kinds of writing they might need to compose outside of the composition class, whether in other courses in the university or "out there in the real world." In this case, a student writer needs to *imagine* an entire rhetorical world, to conjure up an appropriate audience, subject matter, and *ethos* out of thin air. In addition to these unreal audiences, students are almost always writing with an ultimately unreal rhetorical purpose, seeking not to persuade or inform or entertain but to complete an assignment in a required course. Given these conditions, it seems little wonder that so many students are convinced that writing has nothing to do with the "real world." They desperately need *real* rhetorical situations, real audiences and purposes to work with, real people to become in writing.

Similarly, composition courses suffer from a lack of "content" — that is, they lack a specific and elaborated discourse for students to engage with, and thus offer them no particular community to enter. The analytic codes we urge our students to adopt are not particularized, but rather are meta-codes, like rhetoric, cultural studies, or feminism, which cut across disciplinary boundaries. As a result, our students end up guessing at bits and shards of some mythically universal "academic discourse." As Peter Elbow (1991) has pointed out, "The fact is that we can't teach academic discourse because there is no such thing to teach" (138). In like manner, the elaborated discipline-specific discourses that do exist in the academy are too esoteric and too ephemeral to teach in first-year writing courses. Students need to experience an urgency to enter and master a particular code, to write from a position of true authority in a real community, and to use language to recreate the worlds they live in and the people they are.

In order for students to experience writing as social action, we need to move the *where* of writing instruction to some place outside the classroom. For instance, as part of their writing instruction, students could write for some nonprofit, politically active organization of their choice outside the schools they attend, such as the local chapter of the United Way or ACT UP or Operation Rescue or the John Birch Society, composing newsletters, press releases, lobbying materials, and the like. Such groups welcome such inexpensive and specialized help *and* constitute *real* rhetorical situations for students, real audiences, subjects, and purposes to work with, real people to become in writing.

Such a pedagogical practice falls under the rubric of service-learning, a growing educational movement that seeks to take the technical expertise of an institution's teachers and students into the surrounding community. For example, the technical expertise of writing instructors and their students makes literacy tutoring a most common form of service-learning in composition. To be valuable, a service-learning program must, of course, tailor itself to the needs of each community agency involved, to each institution's special kinds of expertise, and to the local student body, accounting for both its strengths and its hindering biases. Effective service-learning also requires a remarkable degree of coordination between the school and the community agencies. And since it can easily overwhelm individual instructors to try to find their own service sites, many institutions now have service-learning centers, which compile lists of interested organizations, determine their needs, suggest service-learning projects, and serve as liaisons — coordinating student placements and facilitating their assessment. Virginia Tech's center, for instance, is even offering seed money to help get such projects started.

A growing body of literature contends that service-learning in composition benefits the local community while giving our students new ways of learning, different ways of seeing things that have been taught in our classes. Robert Crooks (1993), for example, argues that the greatest benefit of service-learning is "the enthusiasm generated in students (and teachers . . .) by the tangible evidence that concepts talked about in the classroom have direct application in addressing problems in the world outside the campus." According to Bruce Herzberg (1994), service-learning helps "put a human face on the students' education" (307). In performing "real and needed services," he says, students discover both "real applications [for] their knowledge in the organizations they serve" *and* "that they can use their knowledge not only to get jobs for themselves but also to help others" (308). Furthermore, he contends, "service-learning generates a social conscience . . . a sense of the reality and immediacy of the problems of the poor and homeless along with a belief that people in a position to help out should do so. Students report that their fears and prejudices disappear, that they are moved by the experience of helping others, and that they feel a commitment to help more." As a result, Herzberg notes, "Faculty members, too, report a new sense of purpose in their teaching" (308). Like Herzberg, Norma Greco maintains that service-learning is a powerful way to remove social barriers, to help students feel the human connection "that ideally bonds diverse groups within [a community] but which socio-economic divisions often sever." Service-learning, she says, fosters students' participatory civic behavior, helps them see themselves as responsible citizens and active agents in their communities, and creates in them a "socially bred, . . . socially conscious and reflective voice shaped by a newfound power to effect meaningful change" (83-85). Greco concludes that service-learning can help students become critically literate — in a Freirean sense — critically conscious about the meaning-making practices and institutions in their society, or, in short, transformative readers and writers of their world (85).

There are several ways service-learning has been construed in relation to composition pedagogy, but we must beware, as Crooks put it, "the danger that community service and learning may [remain] separate, though perhaps equally rewarding, activities for students, connected only superficially by some writing assignment." In the simplest version, as one of my colleagues put it recently, service-learning "seems like a wonderful way to give our students something to write about." In this construction, students write about the actual experience of doing community service, such as working in a soup kitchen. The problem with this version, as Herzberg points out, is that "It is all too easy to ask students to write journal entries and reaction papers, to assign narratives and extort confessions, and to let it go at that." Savvy students, he says, soon figure out that conversion narratives and epiphanies of sympathy for the downtrodden can make for easy As (309). Linda Adler-Kassner (1995) likewise observes that the writing that students produce as a result of this kind of service-learning often amounts to little more than "journals [in which the students lament] the problems of their sites' client communities, or [in which] they simply come to the belief . . . that 'this could happen to me'" (552).

In an effort, perhaps, to avoid such results, a second version of service-learning in composition construes the experience of doing community work as *research* — research to be used as a work consulted or work cited for a term paper or as a basis for criticizing an author's treatment of a given topic. In a third form, as we've already seen, students' community service work is linked to coursework that critiques the systemic inequities and injustices that make service work necessary in the first place. The aim here, in Crooks's words, is to "promote cultural transformations aimed at a more just and compassionate society," because without such critique, students' service-learning experiences serve "only to repair the safety nets that serve as apologies for the inadequacies of late capitalism" (1993). In other words, as Susan Stroud put it, "if our community service efforts are not structured to raise the questions that result in critical analysis of the issues, then we are not involved in education and social change — we are involved in charity" (quoted in Herzberg 1994: 309). Most recently, Adler-Kassner (1995) has argued for a fourth version of service-learning in composition. Rather than focusing on issues about social structures, ideology, and social justice, she maintains, we should instead "concentrate on developing students' acumen with academic writing" and see their service-learning experiences as good places "to start helping [them] frame their ideas in a form that is more acceptable in the academy" (554).

But I am advocating a fifth form of service-learning in composition, one that enables students to understand writing as social action. In this version, a model long employed at Stanford University, the students actually complete essential writing tasks for the nonprofit agencies in which they are placed. At the University of Michigan, for instance, Karis Crawford's advanced composition students have written materials such as a volunteer recruitment pamphlet for a battered women's shelter, a publicity campaign for a children's hospital, and a grant proposal for a hunger relief agency. Crawford (1993) contends that

> *when students write materials that will actually be used by the agency they are working with, . . . [t]hey find themselves seriously considering issues of tone or reading level as these relate to the language chosen for a brochure or letter. They attend [carefully] to grammar and mechanics of presentation. . . . Students who have been accustomed to having the rules of each term paper spelled out for them suddenly find themselves figuring out . . . how to condense seven pamphlets on different kinds of donations into one simple pamphlet or how to organize information on current [gov-*

ernment] legislation . . . into a comprehensible series of articles for a newsletter. (82)

This version of service-learning thus offers students real rhetorical situations in which to work: real tasks, real audiences, real purposes for writing. These writing tasks do not simulate or replicate or ask students to hypothesize about *anything.* They are the real deal. This kind of service-learning also enables students to work with a very specific "content": the mission of the agency. As Adler-Kassner (1995) points out, for students to complete writing tasks for their agencies, they must "understand and be able to reproduce the agencies' philosophies" (554). In other words, this version of service-learning urges students to enter into, assimilate, and effectively "master" an elaborated, community-specific normal discourse and ethos. In this way, students can come to write from a position of true authority in a real community and feel the power of their language to change the worlds in which they live. Moreover, this version of service-learning emphasizes the necessity of what we might call writing *beyond* the curriculum, highlights what Herzberg (1994) calls the "rhetorical as well as the practical nature of citizenship and social transformation" (317), and underscores that, as writing instructors, we have much more important work to do than simply helping students master the conventions of academic discourse. Let us never forget Donald Stewart's excoriation of academic discourse as a "linguistic outrage perpetrated" to make knowledge unintelligible to the general public (1988: 70), as a "disgrace . . . whose purpose is to impede genuine communication with every resource the writer can muster" (68). Having students do an agency's writing as their service-learning can help us refocus our efforts on the teaching, learning, understanding, valuing, and usage of tough-minded yet humane and productive *civic* discourse, which, by all accounts is in serious trouble in this country as we approach the end of the millennium.

Finally, the political aims of this form of service-learning, while significant, are more modest, and therefore more readily attainable, than those versions that strive for cultural transformation to the left. While I completely agree with Sharon Crowley (1989) that a teacher's job is to move students from less-satisfactory to more-satisfactory political positions and thus make them better, wiser people and the world a better, wiser place in which to live, I choose to focus my limited energies on moving students to take what some might call baby steps, but which I consider to be essential and very difficult (if not radical) first steps out of stasis and apathy and into active citizenship and social responsibility. Teaching is, of course, always an act of teaching values, of advocating some political orientations over others — my grade school teachers advocating and teaching me to value democracy over totalitarianism and capitalism over communism, for instance. But our localized institutional settings often make strong claims over what specific values we can and cannot teach, what specific orientations we can and cannot promote. Moreover, I have found that urging students toward a particular political orientation frequently results in many of them moving quickly past resistance — which is productive — and into simply oppositional behaviors, which are not. My response is to allow students to choose which agencies they wish to work with and write for from among a set carefully selected to represent the full political spectrum. Having this choice both increases students' enthusiasm for doing a good job and protects me from Limbaugh-esque charges of indoctrination. Through this kind of service-learning, I *am*, of course, indoctrinating students: indoctrinating them in the values and utter necessity of active, participatory, informed, responsible, rhetorical citizenship regardless of one's particular political leanings.

When I was in 10th grade, we relentlessly badgered and frustrated Mr. Kalman, my geometry teacher, with a whiny, "But when are we going to use this in the *real* world?" While I fervently disagree with the claim that learning must be utilitarian or instrumental in nature to be of value, I still think we need to do a better job of responding to this ubiquitous student lament, a better job of showing students how rhetoric is social action, how writing *is* life. *Within* my composition classrooms, for instance, I have begun to do this by having students engage in the letter-writing campaigns announced in the newsletters of nonviolent advocacy groups such as Amnesty International, People for the Ethical Treatment of Animals, and Greenpeace. But, composed within the classroom, I'm afraid that such documents still amount to calisthenics before the big game. It is time, then, to take the next step, to relocate writing instruction to a different, *real where* somewhere outside the academic classroom.

References

Adler-Kassner, L. (1995). "Digging a Groundwork for Writing: Underprepared Students and Community Service Courses." *College Composition and Communication* 46:552-555.

Crawford, K. (1993). "Community Service Writing in an Advanced Composition Class." In *Praxis I: A Faculty Casebook on Community Service Learning*, edited by J. Howard. Ann Arbor: University of Michigan, OCSL Press.

Crooks, R. (1993). "Service Learning and Cultural Critique: Towards a Model for Activist Expository Writing Courses." Presentation at the Conference on College Composition and Communication, San Diego, CA.

Crowley, S. (1989). "A Plea for the Revival of Sophistry." *Rhetoric Review* 7:318-334.

Elbow, P. (1991). "Reflections on Academic Discourse: How It Relates to Freshmen and Colleagues." *College English* 53:135-155.

Greco, N. (September 1992). "Critical Literacy and Community Service: Reading and Writing the World." *English Journal* 81:83-85.

Herzberg, B. (1994). "Community Service and Critical Teaching." *College Composition and Communication* 45:307-319. [Reprinted in this volume.]

Stewart, D. (1988). "Collaborative Learning and Composition: Boon or Bane?" *Rhetoric Review* 7:58-83.

Democratic Conversations: Civic Literacy and Service-Learning in the American Grains

by David D. Cooper and Laura Julier

A healthy public life is vital in the continuing struggle toward freedom and equality for all people. But that movement does not begin with politics, with the formal institutions of government. It begins with the simple opportunities of public interaction: the chance to meet strangers, to deal with fear and conflict, to realize and celebrate our diversity and the unity that lies beneath it.

— Parker J. Palmer

The Service-Learning Writing Project (SLWP) at Michigan State University is a new program designed to link two strong traditions in undergraduate education at the land-grant university: service-learning, handled through Student Affairs by the highly regarded MSU Service-Learning Center, and writing pedagogy, the charge of the Department of American Thought and Language, with its long American Studies–inspired tradition of introducing first-year students to critical reading of American cultural texts and writing in an interdisciplinary academic context. Like the growing number of other postsecondary programs around the country being developed to forge links between service to local communities and classroom learning, faculty who teach in MSU's program have gained insights into both the practical management of such learning initiatives and the articulation of their philosophical and ethical underpinnings.

A limited number of sections of the general-education writing courses offered by the Department of American Thought and Language are designated to include a community service component. Those courses span a number of topics, including Women in America; The Civic Tradition in America; and Science, Technology, and the Environment. In these sections, undergraduates engage in critical reading and discussion of American literary and historical texts, in writing academic analyses of the ideas raised in these texts, and in practicing peer editing and revision in small workshopping groups. In addition, the MSU Service-Learning Center, in consultation with project faculty, provides students in these sections with a choice of placements in Lansing-area community and nonprofit agencies and organizations, which we describe in more detail below.

Efforts around the country to integrate service-learning pedagogy into a variety of disciplinary courses have yielded generative conversations about the nature of education, the mission of institutions and their commitments to research, teaching, and outreach, but also about the content of education and the applicability of disciplinary knowledge to various workplaces. The Service-Learning Writing Project is informed by two different disciplinary conversations — American Studies, or more particularly the study of public culture in America, and Composition Studies — which merge into a focus on civic literacy as the historical and philosophical linchpin of our pedagogy. As American Studies scholars who also teach writing, our interest in composition research vís a vís service-learning has helped us to renew and revitalize our dialogue with a venerable strain of discourse in American Studies recently supplanted by poststructural modes of inquiry: namely, the putative claim for a national purpose based on a unifying civic culture articulated through shared democratic discourse, a claim accompanied by a philosophical faith in the integrative possibilities of interdisciplinary study that has until recently shaped American Studies pedagogy. Heightened interest among new Americanists in gender, race, ethnic, and multicultural studies has brought that methodological convention in American Studies under radical scrutiny (Lipsitz 1990). In the following sections of this article we describe our course in more detail by grounding our discussion in the disciplinary contexts of American Studies and Composition while using the educational mandate of service-learning to revisit the role of a civic culture in current debates over what Cornel West (1991), Henry Giroux (1991), and others have labeled "the new cultural politics of difference."

Democracy and the Arts of Public Discourse

SLWP-sponsored courses such as Public Life in America invite students to critically evaluate a uniquely American value system of civic commitment that is both uniform and mosaic, reflecting a multiplicity of cultural expressions and practices unmatched by any contemporary society, yet mediated by democratic principles and values ideals embodied in American social and political institutions and the diverse traditions that sustain them. What does it mean, we initially ask our students, to be a member of the communities in which we live and work—school and classroom, workplace, place of worship, neighborhood or nation? What does it mean to be a citizen in a democracy? How well do traditions of American citizenship serve the complex demands and increased diversity of public life in America? What is the relationship between civil rights and civic responsibilities? What does "service" mean and what does it have to do with democratic citizenship? Furthermore, we analyze the heritages and diverse discourses that inform, complicate, and criticize the values of public commitment. We invite our students to explore values issues in their own lives and the relevance of those issues to American life generally, past, present, and future.

Above all, we encourage students to question critically America's civic traditions in preparation for their own service-learning experiences. How, for example, have civic, religious, economic, and social traditions shaped moral life in America? In what ways do those values traditions help to ease, or perhaps even aggravate, the persistent tensions in American life between self-interest and civic duty, individualism and commitment to the common good, entitlements and responsibilities, individual rights and the social contract, autonomy and civic virtue? How do current debates over values — abortion, affirmative action, hate speech codes, gays and lesbians in the military, the Contract With America, the militia movement — reflect longstanding assumptions about how to order social life in America? How are today's communitarian values reflected, or indeed refracted, in the popular media, our educational standards, our role models, our rituals of self-governance, our vocational aspirations, and our tolerance for the growing diversity of American life?

In these courses, students read representative works by those voices who have shaped the communitarian conscience of American civic culture — Jefferson, Jane Addams, Martin Luther King, Jr., John Dewey, Dorothy Day, among others. And students wrestle with topics that continue to energize debates over democratic values in America: civil rights versus civic responsibilities, the tyranny of the majority, and challenges to democratic citizenship such as chronic prejudice, persistent inequality, cynicism, self-enclosure, and mass-media distortion. Along with students in writing programs across the country inspired by a resurgent service-learning pedagogy, Michigan State students also take up major writing projects that meet the special needs of Lansing-area public service agencies — projects that have a direct impact on the lives of people in mid-Michigan. Some students, for example, write public service announcements for a regional youth employment center that offers counseling for young persons their age who don't go to college and are having trouble finding jobs. Another group creates a new descriptive brochure for a nonprofit organization that assists individuals with severe physical disabilities and their families. Other student teams draft public service spots for a local TV station, a newsletter for refugees, and a fact-pack analysis of statistics on domestic violence in the Tri-County area.

Like our colleagues at Stanford University, the University of Minnesota, California Lutheran University, UCLA, USC, Bentley College, and elsewhere, we believe that these community service writing projects help build and refine what Benjamin Barber (1992) considers "the literacy required to live in a civil society" (4), along with the discourse skills necessary for university-level work. Ethically committed students — students engaged, that is to say, in meaningful practices of obligation to others — have enormous opportunity, we've discovered, to develop as more proficient writers. As practices of commitment, service opportunities also carry a strong moral valence for students. Service assignments can be points of connection, as Robert Coles (1993) reminds us in his recent book *The Call of Service*, between self and other, moral moments in teaching and learning that yield, Coles says, "an awareness of the moral complexity that informs the choices we consciously make, as well as those we unwittingly make. . . . [A]ll service is directly or indirectly ethical activity, a reply to a moral call within, one that answers a moral need in the world" (154). The synergy generated from structured community involvement enmeshed in academic work helps remind our students of the importance of public life — that the horizons of personal commitment extend well beyond the sanctuaries of friends and family, beyond even the narrow political meaning, which often associates "public" with government or electoral politics, to encompass the "human community" as an ethical arena of meaningful commitment and personal aspiration.

Most important, the service-learning component of our courses invites students to take a leap of faith from intellectual reflection over public culture in America to an experiential immersion in it. We are finding that only through that journey does the vocabulary of democracy truly come alive for our students. They discover what freedom, responsibility, and participation are all about. Students come to understand how important information, deliberation, and compromise are to the hard work of seeking common ground. Students watch groups apply leverage and seize opportunities to build their communities and achieve hard-won solutions to grass-roots problems. Students often come away from their service-learning experiences with a new understanding of and respect for the ethical application of political power.

One way to describe the SLWP is to talk about its resting on three philosophical foundations of civic literacy: (1) Rhetorical strategies made available to students through service-learning placements in nonprofit civic-minded organizations support effective writing pedagogy. (2) Writing projects assigned to students in conjunction with such community service placements advance higher-order academic discourse skills. (3) The combination of writing for a public service agency and the intellectual experience gained through carefully studying primary cultural source materials is a particularly effective way of advancing civic education. Civic literacy is, then, a craft of social inquiry as well as an important mode of public discourse. Students' "most direct contribution to public discourse," according to J. Donald Moon (1991), "comes in the context of particular issues, when they can use their skills to discover the sorts of technical considerations relevant to an issue, find experts to address it, and assist in the presentation of knowledge so that it can be understood by all citizens" (204).

Moreover, we gratefully acknowledge and through our own work affirm the pedagogical principles shared by service-learning and composition studies as pointed out by other teacher-scholars (Anson and Forsberg 1990; Barton and Ivanic 1991; Cooper and Julier 1995; Crawford 1993; Mansfield 1993; McGuiness 1995; Watters and Ford 1995): (1) Students learn best when they are actually involved in their own learning. (2) Students learn best when the learning project is seen to have intrinsic interest and not merely as an exercise. (3) Writers develop language and discourse skills best by writing for a variety of audiences, not only for the teacher as examiner or evaluator. (4) Experience is educative only if it is structured by the teacher through "the process of problematization and inquiry, and the phases of reflective thought" (Giles and Eyler 1994: 80).

This particular line of philosophical inquiry and practical pedagogy views the writing classroom, in short, as a moral and civic venue, a place where moral sensibility, critical literacy, and the arts of public discourse, leavened by reflective and connected learning, develop hand in hand. Research in language development and composition studies shows, in fact, that language proficiency, critical thinking and reading skills, moral reasoning, and historical and civic literacy develop symbiotically. Linguistic dexterity and virtuosity are now understood to be closely associated not only to cognitive development but to refinements in moral and ethical development, as well (see Cooper 1993, 1994; Gilligan 1982; Kohlberg 1976; Perry 1981; Stotsky 1992). Furthermore, given our footings in American Studies, the writing classroom becomes a locus of democratic processes qua rhetorical practices. The writing classroom, in fact, may be said to be a preeminent site of democratic learning, civil dialogue, and civic training at the university. Teaching the arts of democratic practice and teaching higher-order discourse skills are not, then, parallel pedagogies. They are the *same* pedagogy. As Benjamin Barber (1992) has said of the university at large: Not only does the university have a civic mission, "the university is a civic mission, is civility itself, defined as the rules and conventions that permit a community to facilitate conversation and the kinds of discourse upon which all knowledge depends. On this model, learning is a social activity that can take place only within a discursive community bringing together reflection and experience" (260).

Writing Rights

The SLWP curriculum treats democracy itself as the art of public discourse. The writing assignments that we have shaped in connection with or as preparation for our students' agency placements grow out of classroom discussions and readings that block in a fundamentally rhetorical model of democracy.

That model, simply put, imagines democracy as a conversation. Information in a democracy is disseminated by media — print, broadcast, and increasingly electronic — into the public arena. It is important that the information, notwithstanding its mode of dissemination, remains open and accessible to as broad an audience as possible. Information delivery is the burden of the American press that opens up an important line of inquiry in our courses into how well or how poorly contemporary American media fulfill this function. After all, the purpose of information in the public sphere, we often forget, is not entertainment or even persuasion but as a stimulus to discussion and a catalyst for debate. Whether or not the information circulated in the public arena is sufficient for informed decision making or whether it is colored by ideological or political shadings or whether it is even fit for public consumption is the business of civil debate. That is the burden borne, in turn, by a critical electorate. Such business is conducted in the democratic spaces — the *res publica* — set aside for the cultivation of informed public opinion. Once opinion is shaped in the sprawling marketplace of public debate, it is assimilated by decision makers who redebate the issues among themselves and then make laws and adopt policies that are recycled back into another round of dissemination, debate, and decision making.

When we asked our students last term to list resources of political information available to us today, within a few minutes we catalogued on the blackboard no fewer than 22 easily recognizable media for information transmission that often enter en masse into our daily lives. That list ran the gamut from what one might expect — TV, radio, newspapers, opinion polls — to the slightly more offbeat but no less ubiquitous items we have become habituated to: ballcaps and T-shirts, lawn signs, fax machines, blimps, and, of course, the personal computer upon which we effortlessly hitch rides onto the information superhighway. We then turned to list the venues for public debate and discussion of information. Just as quickly we generated names of 18 such forums: editorial commentaries in local newspapers and town meetings, for example, along with open hearings, public platforms, rallies, roundtables, televised committee deliberations, electronic town meetings, and other media forums that have proliferated into a staggering array, from pamphlets that anyone with access to a computer can readily produce to more sophisticated channelings of public opinion making such as video conferences, electronic bulletin boards, World Wide Web sites, and, for the current student generation in particular, a vast and fascinating underground magazine network largely ignored by adults who teach them English and civics.

What a lush marketplace of ideas! At first blush, one might think that the libertarian model of civic culture — rooted in the fecund Enlightenment principle that an unrestrained exchange of ideas will eventually spawn truth, produce universal reason, and foster civic virtue — is virtually guaranteed by the sheer tidal mass of information accessibility and flow in our free society. Factor into the argument that the seemingly unchecked freedom of expression we enjoy today is a recent and fragile development in our political history, and one is likely to conclude that the spirit of open inquiry, as Whitman might have it, is running afoot, lighthearted and free.

Yet at the same time, one has the uneasy feeling that our democratic feast has degenerated into junk food for a distracted, even cynical, perhaps confused electorate. What are we bringing to the common banquet table of our public life? Some critics warn that our working concepts of "public life" have become so anemic and degraded that even the analogy of the banquet table might seem strained if not broken. "Our concept of public life," argues Parker Palmer (1991), "has become so empty or narrow or deformed that we are unable to see the public accurately" and, as a consequence, "to act in public creatively" (39). This may be especially true for today's undergraduates, who tend to view the public sphere not as a "commons" where people gather on grounds of shared moral community but as an "arena" where individuals or special-interest groups compete — a view often reinforced unintentionally by the politics of diversity played out on today's campuses.

Besides, we may have crossed or we may be crowding another threshold Hannah Arendt scribed in the late 1950s: a point at which the public realm, she warned, disappears altogether and recedes against the ceaseless encroachment of private spheres, spurred by our insatiable appetite for the details of others' intimate lives. Having arrived in the Information Age, are we able to disentangle, Arendt wondered (1958: 50-58), the important from the trivial, the relevant from the irrelevant, the public from the private? Has citizenship, in other words, given way to voyeurism?

In the democratic model described above, for example, an inability to distinguish the dissemination of information from public relations and marketing strategy, the manipulation of feelings, the hard sell, entertainment, or garden-variety propaganda making threatens to disrupt the democratic process just as surely as does a refusal on the part of citizens, reeling from media fatigue, to participate in forums for discussion and debate. Questions of real concern for democracy today may have less to do with First Amendment liberties that have driven 200 years of debate over latitudes of free expression, and perhaps ought to be trained more critically on whether — and why — the average citizen has become disenfranchised as a player in the public exchange of ideas. The question we often pose to our students — What are we listening to? — begs the more fundamental question: Is anyone out there listening?

What we have just described is more than a gloss on policy-making processes and problems in a post-typographic democracy. We have tried to sketch in, rather, an anatomy of argument and an ecology of opinion making in our body politic. We have offered a discourse model that demands its practitioners — citizens, that is to say — apply principles and generalizations to new problems and situations, and think independently while incorporating the opinions and perspectives of others. As a rhetoric, democratic processes bring into sharp relief the importance of analytic methods that are the stock and trade of any language arts classroom: evaluating hypotheses and conclusions, for example, or distinguishing between fact and opinion, or formulating critical questions, not to mention the arts of critical empathy and examined self-reflection that are the particular goals of the Service-Learning Writing Project and the aims of good teaching, more generally, across the humanistic disciplines.

Polling Through Opinion

In an effort to put those aims of good teaching into practice, we endeavor to devise writing assignments and select agency placements that will initiate students into the democratic/rhetorical model that we reflect on more abstractly in our course readings and class discussions. At the same time, we try to capitalize on the advantages of a service-learning pedagogy that makes learning a social activity, as noted earlier by Benjamin Barber, mediated by discussion, reflection, and experience.

In one of our community-based research assignments, for example, we asked our students to follow closely a developing story in the local newspaper involving proposed changes to the City of Lansing's civil rights ordinance prohibiting discrimination in the areas of housing, employment, and public accommodation. At issue was a controversial amendment to a city human relations ordinance that widened protected class status beyond race, gender, national origin, and religious affiliation to cover height; weight; family, student, or handicap status as well as political affiliation and — the hot button issue — sexual orientation. Our students researched and collected information about the proposed amendment from the local press, including newspaper stories and editorials, special-interest group newsletters, and press releases. They solicited position statements from various individuals and organizations that represent the considerable spectrum of opinions over whether the Constitution's guarantee of equal protection under the law extends to classes or groups defined by sexual preference, including a local gay and lesbian rights organization and members of the religious community who had already weighed in on the debate. Some of our students attended an initial public hearing on the ordinance amendment held by the Lansing City Council, where they listened to emotional but generally civil debate among more than 80 citizens who had signed up to speak in council chambers jammed to capacity. Those students later briefed the class. Other students followed the debate as the City Council deferred discussion to the Human Relations Board for further review. Significantly, one group of students set out to research similar civil rights controversies then embroiling other municipalities and states, including the recent overturning of a gay rights ordinance by Cincinnati's voters and a Colorado initiative to amend the state's constitution and similarly prohibit its cities from enacting ordinances like the one being proposed in Lansing.

It is important to note that our students brought to the debate a fairly solid civic vocabulary and the benefit of perspectives gained from extensive readings and discussions in a course that surveyed the history of civic republicanism in America. In particular, we had already examined the germane constitutional articles that guarantee the basic rights of individuals who may encounter hostile democratic majorities that threaten to run roughshod over them: the First Amendment to the Bill of Rights and, as significant, the equal protection provisions spelled out in the 14th Amendment. We tried to figure out, as well, what sorts of issues belonged in the public sphere and were, as such, subject to our democratic model, and which matters were best left, as Tocqueville put it, to the precincts of individual privacy. We discussed stories that treated the theme of tyrannical majoritarianism, such as Shirley Jackson's "The Lottery" and Ursula Le Guin's turgid "The Ones Who Walk Away From Omelas," along with Herman Melville's durable novella *Billy Budd*. We read the American classics of civic conscientiousness and moral conscience: Martin Luther King, Jr.'s "Letter From Birmingham Jail" and Thoreau's ode to moral integrity and democratic responsibility, "On the Duty of Civil Disobedience." In connection with the matter before the Lansing Human Relations Board, we explored the wrenching case of Joe Steffan, a model midshipman expelled from the Naval Academy in his final semester because of his sexual orientation. And with the help of materials compiled by the Center for Media Literacy, we wrestled with the very special problem of what constitutes civil discourse in a media age. How does one distinguish "argument," for example, from indoctrination, sloganeering, marketing, voyeurism, or doctrinaire propagandizing that otherwise clutters the information marketplace and bombards the public mind? And how important are such distinctions to the serious work of citizenship: the forging of opinion in the service of informed decision making?

Against that contextual backdrop, we asked our students to design and conduct a public opinion poll to help the Lansing Human Relations Board decide whether to recommend to the City Council adoption of the ordinance. We urged our students to keep in mind Jay Rosen's characteristics of public discourse as "the sort of talk a democracy needs . . . to illuminate our troubles and connect them to broader issues." Public discourse, more specifically, according to Rosen (1992), is "open and understandable to all." It "deals with major problems affecting society." It is "conducted in a civil fashion." Above all, public discourse "protects private and intimate matters from the glare of the public realm" (10-11). Since polling has become such a widespread and popular source of information gathering, we directed students to carefully design with their study groups four polling questions that could be answered *Yes, No,* or *Don't Know*; then split up, walk around campus, find at least six students, and conduct their poll. After returning to class and tallying answers with others in the study group and evaluating polling trends, students drafted a memo to the Human Relations Board advising it on what decision to make regarding the proposed ordinance.

Before students left class to conduct their surveys, we were careful to review their polling questions with them. We scrutinized questions according to the four criteria of civil discourse laid out by Rosen. Were the questions accessible and respectful? Did the questions connect the particular feelings often evoked by sexual orientation to the broader issue of civil rights? Would the questions, in other words, carry our students' respondents into the arena of public discourse where informed opinion is forged, or sidetrack them into a cat's cradle of theological, ideological, or emotional entanglements? Would our students' polls elicit information, in short, that would illuminate the controversy facing the Human Relations Board? Or further polarize it?

After they had conducted their surveys, compiled and analyzed the results, and later returned to class with their first-draft memos, we asked our students to examine the methodology of their arguments, paying particular attention to the subtle, even invisible links between the questions they initially posed in their student polls and the conclusions they arrived at and explained to the Human Relations Board. We were especially interested in shedding light on ways in which leading assumptions can often skew polling results and thereby misrepresent public opinion. As pollsters, for example, what kinds of assumptions about discrimination against people based on sexual orientation did our students make prior to formulating their polling questions? In what particular ways were those assumptions reflected in their polling questions? By rephrasing polling questions, could students have elicited different responses from the students they polled? As we discussed those rhetorical matters, we encouraged our students to consider what is sacrificed when polls crowd out other kinds of information in political debate. After a thorough discussion and review, we then required students to reconsider their original memos, revise, and resubmit them.

Among the 164 letters stirred into the crucible of public debate by Lansing's Human Relations Board were several written by MSU freshmen, which brought our students full circle in both the civic and the rhetorical processes played out in our democratic model.

Raising Consciousness From Common Grounds

In one of our community placements, students visited a residential health care center for senior citizens and interviewed residents about their quality of life, concerns, and needs. One student came to that experience with a range of questions — about being around the elderly and the reasons "they" were there, about how they would respond to her interview questions (whether they'd be offended, for instance), but also about how she would write the article she had been asked to produce for the center's newsletter. Who was going to read this? How frank could she be? Wouldn't they wonder why she, a mere first-year college student, was writing it?

Our prior conversations about community translated for this student first into questions about how to see these "residents" as part of the community in which she lives, despite the fact that she currently lives in a dorm on a campus that seems miles removed from the surrounding city. She was also pushed, by our discussions of Daniel Kemmis's reminiscences about barn raising in the rural Idaho of his childhood, to look for common ground: She began to see, for instance, that these senior citizens were, like her, consigned to a living arrangement that is essentially a ghetto of similarly aged peers who have come from vastly different life situations, in a location separated from the surrounding community, and were restricted in terms of choices they had enjoyed in their "previous" lives, such as access to a car and decisions about meals. She then brought with her to our class discussions a more complicated sense of community and diversity.

A student in another group had used metaphors of commerce in the third week of the semester to describe his work with an agency that provides medical-care services to low-income people. He announced to the class that he thought the agency ought to be more thankful and helpful to him and his group: They were providing the agency with free services, and if the staff didn't demonstrate a recognition of that, students would not be willing to help. Obligation and the responsibility for polite (civil) discourse rested, in his mind, with the party who got something for nothing. At the reflective stage in a sequence of writings, this student wrote: "The meaning of service has changed somewhat for me. I feel that service is any act that benefits your community, [but] also implies a sense of commitment and obligation to the task or people that you are serving. . . . That feeling of responsibility [for] a position which society values but is not willing to pay for."

When two-thirds of the semester had passed, he was immersed not only in trying to figure out how to learn the software program that would allow him to produce an informational brochure for this agency but also in wrestling with (as another in that group put it) "how to say all that we need to say in this small space." "Every word matters!" exclaimed yet another. Students were struggling with linguistic choices and rhetorical constraints, and also with understanding how to shape those choices for particular audiences. Conversations about the intended audience for this brochure took our discussions back to the issues raised in earlier discussions when we encouraged our students to inquire into the concept of service and what it means to serve. When asked who the audience for the brochure was, this group had answered, "The entire community is a potential audience." In response to a question about what values they shared with the audience, they wrote, "These services are potentially of use to all of us. Any of us may be in a position where we feel we cannot talk to our parents about physical and emotional problems." And when asked how their own values differed from those of the audience, they wrote, "We are better able to afford treatment because of our parents." However, when pressed to consider whether the audience would be interested in the subject and how the writers might reach out to the audience more effectively or explain the subject more convincingly, they answered, "Because of the nature of the document, we do not need to learn more in order to reach them. The brochure is of value to them, costs nothing, and all they have to do is pick it up." In class discussion, we pointed out that information about AIDS and sexually transmitted diseases is readily available for college students, yet the majority of their peers don't use or believe they need that information, which led the students to consider why people ignore or dispute "factual" or "free" information and how social conditions affect the distribution of services, and appropriate or effective rhetorical strategies. Needless to say, it soon became clear to this group of students that "the entire community" was not their audience.

By the time this group neared completion of their writing project, their sense of obligation, community, and service had shifted dramatically. Because our discussions about audience had focused their attention on the agency's clients, they also came to focus on the clients (rather than the agency, as they had earlier) as the "recipients" of their service. And service was no longer something these students conceptualized as a direct exchange of commodity that they were providing for free; it was something more complex and diffuse, a larger tapestry of which they are already a part, if only, as one student said, because "my tax dollars are being spent on the problems generated by the lack of adequate health care for the poor, so I am in a small way working to change that." Their sense of the public realm and their commitments to it had grown.

We often reap similar expansion and conceptual problematizing of the "public realm" accompanied by a deepening of public commitment among our students in other service-learning agency placements and community-based research assignments. Whether inviting our students to enter into a community debate over whether to rename a downtown street after labor leader Cesar Chavez or examine why an animal rights group is so upset over a local Chinese market selling live chickens and turtles for home slaughter, our experience affirms the rationale for service-learning practices in the writing classroom spelled out by Bruce Herzberg (1994): "The effort to reach into the composition class with a curriculum aimed at democracy and social justice is an attempt to make schools function . . . as radically democratic institutions, with the goal not only of making individual students more successful, but also of making better citizens, citizens in the strongest sense of those who take responsibility for communal welfare. These efforts belong in the composition class because of the rhetorical as well as the practical nature of citizenship and social transformation" (317).

Community and Academy: Some Working Conclusions

Our modest experiment over the last three years with a service-learning pedagogy yoked to a democratic/rhetorical model of writing instruction growing out of an American Studies tradition, along with our experience in placing nearly 200 writing students in more than 50 public agency placements, leads us to some reflections and tentative working conclusions.

Through rigorous, real-time writing assignments and exercises such as the memo on civil rights, students actively join democratic processes while practicing the arts of public discourse that communities use to debate controversial issues. Whether tracking through the state legislature a bill proposing cuts in adult education literacy services or adapting tenant information pamphlets to new laws governing tenant/landlord relations, student writers are initiated into dialogue and deliberation strategies for articulating and resolving differences and determining justice. Rather than receding into the background, civic values and democratic aspirations become central to our students' explorations of diversity, commitments to equity, and respect for the difficulties of resolving conflicts within a neighborhood, a community, or a nation.

Through actual writing projects growing out of public service agency placements, students have extensive opportunities to *practice* public discourse — the sort of talk a democracy needs to illuminate its problems and connect them to broader concerns of public life and the common good — and to engage in constructive conversations over American pluralism. Those conversations include often contested and sometimes uncongenial spaces in the public sphere — AIDS awareness, drug abuse prevention, alcoholism, homelessness, teen pregnancy, domestic violence — and thereby promise to forge lasting affirmations of civic reciprocity and ethical obligation for our students.

Conventional wisdom among service-learning practitioners — especially among those colleagues aligned with the critical literacy movement — often stresses the importance of empowering students through what might be called an "empathetic critique" of social problems — that is, training or nurturing students' intellectual, cognitive, and moral talents through direct experience in the service of solving a community problem or rectifying an injustice. We have also found that effective citizenship demands the "immanent critique" of *solutions* to social problems in addition to the empathetic immersion of students into those problems. Our experience teaches us that there is a difference between solving social problems and engaging democratic processes. Sometimes our case studies of local community problems peak with our students' realization that democratic processes are complicated, demanding, frustrating, tentative, and often as messy as they are important. In the civil rights memo, for example, some students learned more about formulating critical questions, gathering information, figuring out the difference between information and doctrinal dissimulation masking as fact, than about how to resolve an intractable social controversy. Service-learning functions, then, at two levels: It helps make students more effective participants in public life, and it encourages them to be more competent witnesses to our troubled times.

Nonetheless, while conventional community service opportunities and internship programs stress the delivery of much-needed care or the important bridging of theory and practice, the justice-seeking assignments and agency placements sought out by the Service-Learning Writing Project still focus more on bringing democracy to bear directly on groups for whom democracy has not worked well. We seek to immerse our students in the pursuits — sometimes successful, often frustrating, seldom triumphal — of equal opportunity and social justice sought by sectors of American civic culture traditionally underenfranchised: the mentally impaired elderly, for example, or economically dislocated single mothers and their children.

Finally, we adopt as a guiding principle the importance of using the language arts to educate our students in the values and deliberative practices of democracy and as a way of meeting what Benjamin Barber (1994) has called the leading challenge to the contemporary university: namely, "whether the need to honor and acknowledge diversity can be reconciled with the need to create a common civic fabric with which Americans can identify." Our curriculum is an introduction — simultaneously intellectual and experiential — into the ways democracy works or fails to work for the sake of training our students to be more effective and articulate participants in the realization of democratic values. Elizabeth Minnich (1991) speaks eloquently about the democratic "conversations" that exemplify processes of civic interaction we should instill in our students:

> *[The public] is not at its best a marketplace, or a battlefield, or a negotiating arena in which "thing-like" opinions and interests are exchanged, fought over, or traded. At its best, the public is where we find — through conversation with others — a deeper level of understanding of our own opinions and a [new] level of understanding of ourselves and others. Such understanding would allow us to work together. That "working together" may mean that we have found a deeper level of common concern and, hence, can agree, although we initially thought we disagreed. It can also mean that we have come to clearer understanding of how we differ, but that we have done so in a way that reaffirms our shared commitment to a vision of the public and of political process that is not only tolerant of but can be responsive to us all, even as we differ. (223)*

References

Anson, C.M., and L.L. Forsberg. (1990). "Moving Beyond the Academic Community." *Written Communication* 7:200-231.

Arendt, H. (1958). *The Human Condition.* Chicago: University of Chicago Press.

Barber, B. (1992). *An Aristocracy of Everyone: The Politics of Education and the Future of America.* New York: Oxford University Press.

——. (February 5, 1994). "Liberal Education and Education for Liberty: Service Learning in a Free Society." Address at the Institute on College Student Values, Florida State University, Tallahassee.

Barton, D., and R. Ivanic, eds. (1991). *Writing in the Community.* Newbury Park, CA: Sage.

Coles, R. (1993). *The Call of Service: A Witness to Idealism.* Boston: Houghton Mifflin.

Cooper, D. (1993). "*Believing* in Difference: The Ethics of Civic Literacy." *The Educational Forum* 57:168-177.

——. (1994). "Moral Literacy." *The Journal of Value Inquiry* 28:297-312.

——, and L. Julier. (1995). "Writing the Ties That Bind: Service-Learning in the Writing Classroom." *Michigan Journal of Community Service Learning* 2:72-85.

Crawford, K. (1993). "Community Service Writing in an Advanced Composition Class." In *Praxis I: A Faculty Casebook on Community Service Learning,* edited by J. Howard. Ann Arbor, MI: University of Michigan, OCSL Press.

Giles, D., and J. Eyler. (Fall 1994). "The Theoretical Roots of Service-Learning in John Dewey." *Michigan Journal of Community Service Learning* 1(1): 77-85.

Gilligan, C. (1982). *In a Different Voice: Psychological Theory and Women's Development.* Cambridge: Harvard University Press.

Giroux, H. (1991). "Critical Pedagogy and the New Politics of Cultural Difference." In *Higher Education and the Practice of Democratic Politics: A Political Education Reader,* edited by B. Murchland, pp. 245-251. Dayton, OH: The Kettering Foundation.

Herzberg, B. (1994). "Community Service and Critical Teaching." *College Composition and Communication* 45(3): 307-319. [Reprinted in this volume.]

Kohlberg, L. (1976). "Moral Stages and Moralization: The Cognitive-Developmental Approach." In *Moral Development and Behavior,* edited by T. Lickona, pp. 31-53. New York: Holt, Rinehart, Winston.

Lipsitz, G. (1990). "Listening to Learn, Learning to Listen: Popular Culture, Cultural Theory, and American Studies." *American Quarterly* 42:615-636.

Mansfield, M. (1993). "Real World Writing and the English Curriculum." *College Composition and Communication* 44:69-83.

McGuiness, I. (1995). "Educating for Participation and Democracy: Service Learning in the Writing Classroom." *The Scholarship of Teaching* 1(2): 3-12.

Minnich, E.K. (1991). "Some Reflections on Civic Education and the Curriculum." In *Higher Education and the Practice of Democratic Politics: A Political Education Reader,* edited by B. Murchland, pp. 221-229. Dayton, OH: The Kettering Foundation.

Moon, J.D. (1991). "Civic Education, Liberal Education, and Democracy." In *Higher Education and the Practice of Democratic Politics: A Political Education Reader,* edited by B. Murchland, pp. 196-207. Dayton, OH: The Kettering Foundation.

Palmer, P. (1991). "The Nature and Nurture of Public Life." In *Higher Education and the Practice of Democratic Politics: A Political Education Reader,* edited by B. Murchland, pp. 38-47. Dayton, OH: The Kettering Foundation.

Perry, W. (1981). "Cognitive and Ethical Growth: The Making of Meaning." In *The Modern American College,* edited by A. Chickering, pp. 76-116. San Francisco: Jossey-Bass.

Rosen, J. (1992). "Making Politics Work." *Media & Values* 58:10-12.

Stotsky, S. (1992). "Conceptualizing Writing as Moral and Civic Thinking." *College English* 54(7): 794-808.

Watters, A., and M. Ford. (1995). *Writing for Change: A Community Reader.* New York: McGraw Hill.

West, C. (1991). "The New Cultural Politics of Difference." In *Higher Education and the Practice of Democratic Politics: A Political Education Reader,* edited by B. Murchland, pp. 136-156. Dayton, OH: The Kettering Foundation.

Partners in Inquiry: A Logic for Community Outreach

by Linda Flower

Why are we here; what are we doing?

Relationships between town and gown have a checkered history. Especially when the gowns speak for the affluent dominant culture, bent on the self-confident transmission of its cultural tools, its knowledge, its discourse. And when the town speaks for those with far less economic, cultural, or social capital, struggling with problems of poverty, racism, broken schools, unbridled streets.

Consider the typical pattern of literacy programs. When town and gown try to work together, the gowns possess the dominant discourse — and typically assume that their language, concepts, and forms of argument are the most effective for understanding these problems and should be learned and used by everyone else. So the gowns deliver expert advice or they set up tutoring programs in school-based literacy for the children of town folks. Some gowns, on the other hand, attuned to the oppressive potential of such literate practices, may position their work (though it usually stays within the academy) as an act of critique and resistance to academic discourse in the name of supporting diverse communities.

In such collaborations between town and gown, then, academics have often chosen among *using* the elite discourse to analyze/advise a community cause, *initiating* at-risk students into that discourse (whether it is computer literacy, math literacy, or standard written English), or, more recently, *resisting* and critiquing that discourse. Hard-pressed communities look for help where they can find it but remain wary of the process and wisely skeptical about the effectiveness of much of what they get. The rarer achievement is a relationship in which all of these partners work in the same room — and on the written page — together.

Historians of community/university collaboration locate some of the problems that trouble these relationships in the logic that has motivated them. Describing this history from 1880 to World War I, Harkavy and Puckett note how

> *progressive period academics pedestaled the expert and expert knowledge . . . [and created a model that] was elitist, hierarchical, and unidimensional, founded on the assumption that the expert's role was to study and assist, but not to learn from the community. (1991: 562)*

Such arrangements, they argue, not only replicate the status quo on an institutional level but perpetuate the learned helplessness that poverty and its enabler — the professionally designed welfare system — teach to urban poor.

Against this historical backdrop, the current enthusiasm for community/university connections is marked by a more collaborative spirit and multicultural awareness, which has spurred rising student voluntarism, community service projects, and service-learning additions to the curriculum. The justifying principle behind many of these projects is a strong ethic of civic service rooted in the ideals of participatory democracy but balanced by an awareness of the competing demands of the individual and the community (Cooper and Julier 1995). Others are motivated by a long tradition of experiential education, and still others by the urgent call to social justice (Watters and Ford 1995; Kendall 1990; Benson and Harkavy 1991). However, this growing enthusiasm for and informed commitment to civic service face two challenges. The first is that such concerns are cyclical. They come and go as educational trends. And unless this enthusiasm for a community connection is rooted in the intellectual agenda of the university, in academic work, and in the educational system, it will soon fade (Zlotkowski 1996). Marginal programs, identified with soft money, student enrichment, and institutional obligation, will not compete with disciplinary agendas when they are no longer news. Will colleges and universities be able to turn the principle of experience-based civic education into a robust, academically sophisticated educational practice?

A second, more insidious, problem is the danger that well-meaning voluntarism can unwittingly replicate the social structures that are part of the problem, defining some people as the knowledgeable servers while casting others as the clients, patients, or the educationally deficient — the served (Herzberg 1994). To succeed, this new ethic must also confront some philosophical and social tensions within the enterprise itself and within the relationships it builds not only between organizations but between college writers and community contacts, between tutors and students. To avoid the repetition of history, this ethic will need a spirit of inquiry that not only can acknowledge some deep-running differences in how people define the problems and goals on which a collaboration is based but can embrace the difficulties of entering a cultural contact zone (Pratt 1991; Minter, Gere, and Keller-Cohen 1995; Long 1994; Goldblatt 1994). As we try to construct new collaborations in the face of these challenges and our past, it may help to think for a moment about some logics that can motivate service and the relationships shaped by those logics. Consider briefly the logic of cultural mission, of technical expertise, of compassion, and of prophetic pragmatism and problem solving. Since most programs contain some element of all of these logics, our purpose is not to make simplistic distinctions but to consider the relationships each logic tends to promote.

The Logic of Cultural Mission

Historically, community service has often rested on notions of philanthropy, charity, social service, and improvement that identify the community as a recipient, client, or patient, marked by economic, learning, or social deficits. While "doing good" by the lights of the service provider, this paradigm maintains a strong sense of otherness and distance, of giver and receiver. It makes no demand for mutuality in analyzing or responding to problems; it maintains the social status quo.

Economist William Julius Wilson targets a case in point in the work of those analysts of inner-city poverty who focus "almost exclusively on the interconnection between cultural traditions, family history, and individual character" of the poor. Perceiving an apparent lack of ambition, self-reliance, and a work ethic in the poor, "some even suggest that ghetto underclass individuals have to be rehabilitated culturally before they can advance in society" (1987: 13). Calling the logic of this deficit model of cultural repair into question, Wilson shows that the number of single-mother households for young African-American women, for instance, is directly connected to the extraordinary and continuing rise of joblessness for inner-city African-American males, starting in the economic shifts of the 1960s.[1] If the "culture of poverty" Wilson analyzes is not a self-perpetuating culture but a response to pressing social and economic forces, then the logic of charity is shortsighted, and the logic of repairing personal deficits (in attitude, life-style, behavior) or demanding mainstream, middle-class habits in the face of chronic economic instability, is myopic.

Literacy work waves the cultural missionary banner when it reduces reading and writing to narrowly school-based skills (Minter, Gere, and Keller-Cohen 1995) or concentrates on replacing community languages, such as black English vernacular, with standard written English. There is no question that literacy work must help its students recognize the advantages of bi-dialectalism, where standard English is the language of power and access in the mainstream community. However, the desire to "help" others be more like oneself often rests on the cheerful arrogance of what van Dijk (1993) calls the "elite discourses," which assume that the cultural tools of the white middle class (the academy, media, business) are the tools to which others do (or should) aspire. How can a literacy program that works with black youth, for instance, balance this presumption with an awareness of the indirect but analytical tradition of African-American vernacular, the logical structures embedded in street talk (Labov 1972), or the richly expressive literate practices such as signifying (Gates 1988; Lee 1993), in which white volunteers find they are the illiterate (Flower 1996). The logic of cultural transmission

— which valorizes the knowledge and values the *giver* intends to share — raises the question of mutuality. It can distort the map of community/university relationships by making cultural sharing a one-way street.

The Logic of Technical Expertise

More seemingly benign and disinterested than the stance of the cultural missionary is the logic of technical expertise, which brings needed skills, knowledge, and resources to the problems of struggling communities. Technical expertise allows people to document polluted water, to test for diabetes, to create a sophisticated, computer-based distribution system for food banks, or to create a professionally constructed (fundable) proposal for youth jobs. But we must also recognize that when service is organized by this logic, the relationship is not only hierarchical, it can smother other kinds of expertise.

John McKnight's analysis of medical and social-service policy, for instance, documents the transition from a community ethos based on care to a social-service system based on the professional management of need. The technology and the tools of the expert not only tend to dictate the nature of conceivable solutions, they structure the relationships:

> As you *are the problem, the assumption is that* I, *the professional servicer,* am the answer. You *are not the answer.* Your peers *are not the answer.* The political, social, and economic environment *is not the answer.* (1995: 46)

Funding for health, education, and welfare supports an enormous middle-class industry designed to deliver services (not jobs) to the poor. But service is not the same as a solution. For instance, the rising technology (and cost) of medicine has had little impact on rates of morbidity or mortality. "The primary cause of physical malady among the modernized poor is distinctly environmental and obviously unchangeable with medical tools. There is no medical prescription to cure poverty, slums, and polluted air, water, and food" (McKnight 1995: 64). Moreover, when this one-way relationship based on professional expertise and "technological" solutions is in control, McKnight argues, the citizen is no longer the problem definer or problem solver, and the power and initiative of the community deteriorates. Service displaces care.

> *Care is the consenting commitment of citizens to one another. Care can not be produced, provided, managed, organized, administered, or commodified. . . . Care is, indeed, the manifestation of a community. The community is the site for the relationship of citizens. . . . If that site is invaded, co-opted, overwhelmed, and dominated by service-producing institutions, then the work of the community will fail.* (McKnight 1995: x)

University-based community service has to worry about a naive complicity in the social structures that put power and prestige on the university side of the ledger while putting passive need and incapacity on the debit, community side. We must be skeptical of this logic, in part because expert, professional, and technological solutions do not have a stellar record of success in meeting urban problems. More than that, the logic of technical expertise can reinforce the power structures and social assumptions that perpetuate problems. It can leave student volunteers with the temporary euphoria of "doing good" for the "less fortunate" but do little to break their sense of distance and otherness, or their assumptions about the necessary superiority of their cultural tools and traditions. When literacy tutors, for instance, build a relationship based primarily on their educated expertise and the transmission of school-based reading or writing skills, they are not likely to confront larger problems, such as how to use these cultural tools for intercultural purposes or how to judge when a hybrid discourse, integrating the literate practices of universities and communities, would be more effective.

The Logic of Compassion and Identity

The logic of compassion tends to restructure the relationships of service around the Latin roots of the word — around "feeling with." It turns service from an act of charity or authority into an act of empathy that grasps an essential identity between the one who serves and the one in need. Less motivated to blame or reform the victim, it is also not afraid to acknowledge the pain, the stress, the sense of dislocation, and even hopelessness that go with poverty, racism, diminished self-esteem, vulnerability. In our culture, the logic of compassion has its strongest roots in the radical messages of the Torah tradition of Judaism and transformational tradition of Christianity, both of which depart from the legal, rule-focused sensibility often institutionalized in dominant strands of these and other religions.

In *Jews & Blacks: A Dialogue on Race, Religion, and Culture in America,* by Michael Lerner and Cornel West, Lerner argues that the Torah tradition was a revolutionary message in the ancient and medieval world as well as the modern: "If we are to stay in touch with the God energy within ourselves, we need to be able to recognize the Other's needs as our own needs." In this tradition, he argues, "Jewish identity consists of being a witness to God as the force in the universe that makes possible the transformation of that which is to that which ought to be. . . . This goal of this transformation is to rectify the oppression of the powerless. *We* were slaves. So now that we are free, our task is to spread that freedom, and to identify with the powerless" (1996: 8-9). Lerner contrasts this tradition of compassion with the cynicism of contemporary intellectuals, which led "to a kind of lonely 'see through everything, believe in nothing' world view that they thought was revolutionary, but actually fit very well into the needs of the dominant society" (39).

Marcus Borg, a member of the revisionist social history scholars known as the Jesus Seminar, places compassion at the center of an equally radical tradition in Christianity. Although this tradition was shaped by its historical, social, and religious struggle against first-century Roman oppression, it is also at the center of an ongoing conflict between the politics of holiness (focused on correct conduct and shaped by the legalism of enculturated religion and its conventional wisdom) and a politics of compassion (guided by a conviction that culture can be transformed by the power of the Spirit) (1987: 155, 196). Borg places Jesus in the tradition of Jewish charismatics who advocated and modeled an alternative consciousness, in which "God and the world of Spirit are all around us, including within us. . . . We live in Spirit, even though we are typically unaware of this reality" (28). And at the center of this alternative consciousness — and in contrast to the vision of religious legalism — was a experiential awareness of graciousness and compassion (100). Paulo Freire argues that this alternative, compassionate consciousness is the foundation for genuine dialogue: "Founding itself upon love, humility, and [an intense faith in man], dialogue becomes a horizontal relationship of which mutual trust between dialoguers is the logical consequence" (1989: 79-80).

The logic of compassion and identity that is grounded in an alternative consciousness — at the same time it is shaped by religious tradition — works to reorient relationships away from cultural imposition, commodified service delivery, or expert, technology-driven knowledge transmission to ones that replace power relations with greater mutuality.

But its strength also poses a problem. How do we translate this intensely individual consciousness into public action — into literate practices, educational agendas, and institutional initiatives? I ask this question not because there are no ready answers but because there are so many — competing — answers. Can we claim that any given literate practice or educational agenda has a corner on compassionate or democratic collaboration as we plan and argue for a course of action? Let me put our dilemma as educators and program developers another way. Given that our moral and ethical commitments are inevitably culturally inflected, given that our best interpretation of what it means to enact service, compassion, or mutuality is itself a hypothesis to be tested and inevitably revised, how do we find the grounds for action? If the business of the intellectual is skepticism, is there a legitimate alternative to the ironic stance of those who "see through everything, believe in nothing"?

So when universities ask the question "Why are we here; what are we doing?" the answers supplied by the logics of mission, expertise, and compassion challenge us to look thoughtfully at the relationships and the practices to which they lead. The next approach tries to build on the strengths of these other logics, but to do so in a way that grounds action on and transforms relationships into a form of collaborative inquiry.

The Logic of Prophetic Pragmatism and Problem Solving

The logic of this fourth approach points to collaborative social action. Community outreach built on problem solving alone could easily turn into a hierarchical association between people who are "the problems" and those who are "the solvers," unless it is wedded to a compelling vision of mutual inquiry. The logic for this alternative could be called prophetic pragmatism. The term, which is borrowed from African-American cultural theorist Cornel West, builds on the work of John Dewey, which has influenced many current experiments in service-learning. And it may offer one answer to the questions posed above: How does one take moral social action without the crutch of dogmatism or even the staff of full confidence about how one *should* act?

The logic of pragmatism is the logic of inquiry. In its vision, communities and universities embark on what John Dewey describes as an "experimental way of knowing." Dewey's experimental way begins by repudiating the "quest for certainty" that has traditionally undergirded the quest for knowledge in science and philosophy. He challenges us to recognize the unsettling alternative that all our knowledge is hypothetical. It is a hypothesis (even though it is based on the best evidence we can muster) that we use to guide our steps. What, for instance, is the appropriate response to the terrible decay of neighborhoods in the inner city if you are a policymaker? What is the response to risk and stress on those streets if you are an inner-city teenager? And what is the right way to interpret or engage with the life of that teenager if you are a college student mentor? These are questions people must and do answer, but how should we regard or evaluate those answers?

Dewey, looking at both academic theories and personal conclusions, urges what amounts to a courageous vulnerability to the reality of our own uncertainty. "All general conceptions (ideas, theories, thought) are hypothetical." Even when they liberate us, they are "conditional: they have to be tested by the consequences of the operations they define and direct." In giving up the quest for certainty we must recognize that the final value of our theories, policies, and beliefs is determined not by the normal academic tests for comfort and certainty (i.e., by their internal elaboration and consistency) "but by the consequences they effect in existence as that is perceptibly experienced" (1929; in Boydston 1988: 132).

Dewey's pragmatic stance recognizes that our standard assumptions, best ideas, and even cherished beliefs are always and only guiding hypotheses about outcomes, built on stronger or weaker bodies of evidence — that is, some hypotheses are much more reliable predictors than others. This stance translates *knowledge* (including the expert knowledge the academy would offer the community) from a stable object into an *act of knowing*, that is, into an urgently ongoing attempt to improve our hypotheses by an intentional effort to reveal new connections and relations. Dewey puts it concretely: "To grasp an unfamiliar object of the mind, we discover its qualities by uncovering its relationships: We turn it over, bring it into a better light, rattle and shake it, thump, push and press . . . for the purpose of disclosing relations not apparent otherwise" (Boydston 1988: 70). The knower is an interpretive seeker and knowing is an act of inquiry.

However, the radical premise of Dewey's philosophical pragmatism is not just that knowledge is interpretation, but that the meaning and value of ideas lie in their enabling *conditions* and their *outcomes*. The meaning of an urban policy lies in the conditions required for that policy (with its unpacked baggage of assumptions) to work, and in the world it would produce as a result if it were enacted. The meaning of a street-savvy teenage strategy for dealing with stress (and a mentor's response to that strategy) lies in the conditions under which it exists (e.g., the street conditions under which a strategy such as acting "hard" or even aggressive may seem the best proactive defense). And meaning lies ultimately in outcomes: The meaning of mentoring (like the meaning of adult "advice") is not in its "truth" or "wisdom" but in its outcome for that teenager and for the relationship it creates.

This connection between conditional knowledge, continued inquiry, and ethical action seems central to a new model of community/university relations. C.I. Lewis puts it simply:

> *Pragmatism could be characterized as the doctrine that all problems are at bottom problems of conduct, that all judgments are, implicitly, judgments of value, and that, as there can be ultimately no valid distinction of theoretical and practical, so there can be no final separation of questions of truth of any kind from questions of the justifiable ends of action. (quoted in West 1993: 109)*

If community/university relations are to be based on the logic of inquiry, the first issue to put on the table is the problem and potential of cultural difference. Difference exists not just in simple distinctions such as town/gown, rich/poor, black/white, but in the alternative discourses, literate practices, goals, and values brought to an inquiry. When the people doing this hypothesis making, testing, and judging live much of their lives in different worlds, talking different languages, they may indeed struggle to be understood at times. But when they come to the table as collaborative equals (where everyone's discourse, practices, and goals are recognized), those differences can produce an explosion of knowledge. Consider Dewey's insistence that the *meaning* of ideas (e.g., of social concepts about youth or urban policies about work) is found in the continuing examination of the situated conditions for and the outcomes of those concepts and policies. It follows that no one group can lay claim to omniscience about all those conditions and outcomes. No one can pretend to take a god's-eye view of how those concepts and policies play out in the daily lives, psyches, and social histories of the people affected or how those hypotheses need to be revised in light of that reality. Intercultural collaboration extends the reach of our knowledge.

Cornel West, cultural critic and professor of Afro-American studies and the philosophy of religion at Harvard, extends the reach of inquiry yet further with the intellectual stance he calls *prophetic* pragmatism. Here the addition of "prophetic" does not carry the popular suggestion of predicting the future; instead it "harkens back to the rich, though flawed, traditions of Judaism and Christianity that promote courageous resistance against, and relentless critiques of, injustice and social misery." To be more operational, it is a stance that "analyzes the social causes of unnecessary forms of social misery, promotes moral outrage against them, organizes different constituencies to alleviate them, yet does so with an openness to its own blindnesses and shortcomings." In the spirit of Dewey and the tradition of American pragmatism, its critical temper "highlights the provisional, tentative, and revisable character of our visions, analyses, and actions." But unlike the distanced, disillusioned, or ironic stance of much cultural criticism, it provides a logic for mutuality in community/university and intercultural relations. That logic is based on what West calls democratic faith — "a Pascalian wager (hence underdetermined by the evidence) on the abilities and capacities of ordinary people to participate in decision-making procedures of institutions that fundamentally regulate their lives" (1993: 139-140).

In building relationships across class and race, democratic "faith" in ordinary, fallible people is probably too weak a word for what West has in mind — which is really a politics of representation. His bolder argument calls for a representation of difference that insistently foregrounds not the deficits but "the agency, capacity, and ability of human beings who have been culturally degraded, politically oppressed, and economically exploited by bourgeois liberal and communist illiberal status quos" (1993: 29). The challenge to universities, then, is not to deny their power, expertise, or agendas. Their technical tools, specialized discourses, and intellectual goals are needed. The challenge is to construct a mutual representation of the intentionality, the communal wisdom, and the evaluative competence of the community partners. The question is not whether such agency is there but whether institutional partners can organize themselves to uncover and acknowledge it.

In short, the logic of pragmatism calls for a rigorous openness to inquiry and the consequences of our actions. Prophetic pragmatism shapes a compassionate commitment to such inquiry in the midst of social and cultural struggles in which "we are forced to choose, in a rational and critical manner, some set of transient social practices, contingent cultural descriptions, and revisable scientific theories by which to live" (West 1993: 134).

What would an inquiry-based community/university relationship look like in terms of actual practices? The literate practice I want to describe below has been shaped by the tradition and logic of a prophetic pragmatism and by concern with the problems of cultural mission and expert transmission. It makes no claims for simply avoiding much less solving those problems. It is, indeed, a model that runs those risks because it is focused on education, grounded in research, and trying to exploit the technological capability of the university. It probably illustrates its ideals most clearly in the continuing revisions toward them. Nevertheless, a literate practice has the virtue of specificity, which makes it a stepping stone in inquiry.

Inquiry as the Basis for Community/University Collaboration

In "Community Literacy" (1995), Wayne Peck, Lorraine Higgins, and I described the practice of community literacy operating in the historical and social context of a university collaboration with a neighborhood community center. We described an attempt to develop a set of strategic literate practices that could motivate learning and support inquiry and intercultural collaboration between college mentors and urban teenagers. In this paper, I want to build on that foundation to explore another literate practice, one I will call *community problem-solving dialogues*, that grew out of those mentoring collaborations and out of the public "Community Conversations" they were working toward. However, here I would like to shift the focus from what is possible in a long-term, stable collaboration, such as the Community Literacy Center (CLC) or in courses dedicated to community experience, to what faculty can do in "ordinary" courses.

This chapter will explore one way faculty might build such a dialogue into a writing course or a disciplinary project. In such a course, students would already be reading, discussing, and writing about educational, cultural, civic, or social issues that involve this larger community. But in the place of (or in conjunction with) standard methods of learning (another assigned reading, a major paper, a group project, logging volunteer hours, writing for an agency), students would enter a community problem-solving dialogue in order to transform community service into an educating inquiry. With the help of the instructor and a community contact to convene the meeting, students hold one- to three-session dialogues, which put course-relevant problems on the table and let students and community members seek out, interpret, and negotiate culturally diverse perspectives on live issues and their human consequences.

Creating a Community Problem-Solving Dialogue

A community problem-solving dialogue (CPSD) operates around a literal and metaphoric table, which can bring together students, faculty, community leaders, and everyday people, as well as the written knowledge of the academy and the oral wisdom of the neighborhood. It is convened around the kind of issue that is both (1) an open question with no single answer, and (2) a problem with immediate and local impact on lives. Consider, for example, an issue that reframes the topic of "gangs and urban violence" by looking at its flip side and asking, what are the apparent possibilities for success, respect, and work for urban youth? Where, *in the experience of teenagers,* are the roads to respect that seem open in the urban community? Where, *in the eyes of teenagers,* are the beckoning avenues that lead to such respect through work? What is the message (and reality) the community is sending *to them* about the possibility of a self-sufficient future? Questions like these are often approached in reading, writing, history, and social science classrooms, through reading data-based analyses such as Wilson's *The Truly Disadvantaged* (1987), ethnographies such as Heath and McLaughlin's *Identity and Inner City Youth* (Teachers College, 1993), educational histories such as Gilyard's *Voices of the Self* (Wayne State University, 1991), or personal accounts such as Rose's *Lives on the Boundary* (Free Press, 1989) or by analyzing print and popular culture. But in a standard classroom, these discourses, and their insights and arguments, are rarely situated for the college student in a complex context of lived experience, nor are they tested and conditionalized by people who know that context best.

Who is at the table? A community problem-solving dialogue tries to bring the voices of academic discourse, *as well as those of the people described by that discourse,* to the table. As a community/university inquiry, such a dialogue would naturally bring whatever academic and professional expertise it could to this table. In our example, it might invite voices that could speak about education and urban schools, about the economics and opportunities of the region, about the street economy and sociology of work in urban centers. If the students were doing a community writing project, their inquiry might also seek out the hypotheses of the community leaders running youth programs or those engaged in economic development and neighborhood renovation, as well as the activists engaged in struggles with encroaching institutions (such as universities, hospitals) that often displace homes and small businesses in poor neighborhoods.

However, in a CPSD this inquiry would not remain a discussion between an agency (needing a report on youth job opportunities) and a college student acting as stand-in expert (doing the report with the help of faculty advisors and the resources of the library). The goal of a CPSD is to go beyond knowledge based on academic research alone or on contact solely with the community's professional representatives or bureaucracies. And it is to go beyond transferring knowledge to community, by moving toward inquiry *with* the community. Therefore, this table would involve everyday people, including the teenagers concerned, who have walked the paths that urban streets offer. Instead of learning about people from distant neighborhoods, the "gowns" at this table would be learning from them, just as the "town" would be looking to see what the "hypotheses" of economics, education, and sociology have to offer in their search for better responses to a problem.

How do you deal with difference? Both philosophical and prophetic strains of pragmatism put a great value on different perspectives, but how do you turn intercultural inquiry into a social and literate practice everyone can use? Dewey describes knowledge as a situated, revisable understanding of the connections between things, people, and ideas. I have tried to argue elsewhere that Dewey's insistence on knowledge as this network of observations calls for a strong rival hypothesis stance to issues, especially to issues of intercultural understanding (Flower, Long, and Higgins, in prep.). By a rival hypothesis stance, I simply mean a stance that starts by posing problems as open questions — too complex for single, or conclusive, answers. As a result, this stance doesn't just tolerate competing hypotheses; it actively seeks alternative interpretations, diverse readings, and multiple perspectives. It has us climbing mountains: "One can not climb a number of different mountains simultaneously, but the views had when different mountains are ascended supplement one another; they do not set up incompatible, competing worlds" (Dewey 1916: 110).

A *strong* version of this rival hypothesis stance (unlike some versions in science and philosophy) is not interested in eliminating its rivals. Rather, it uses them to construct a *negotiated* meaning that attempts to acknowledge and in some way embrace multiple "truths" (Flower 1994). Unlike the protective skepticism of an ironic stance, the rival hypothesis stance asks us to move from committed "rivaling" to committed, revisable, inclusive conclusions and reflective action.

If Dewey has us climbing mountains to discover rival hypotheses, Richard Bernstein, a contemporary philosopher of praxis, brings us closer to an intercultural table:

> *The basic conditions for all understanding requires one to test and risk one's convictions and prejudgments in and through an encounter with what is radically "other" and alien. To do this requires imagination and*

hermeneutical sensitivity in order to understand the "other" in the strongest possible light. (1991: 4)

The idea of "other" is not about simplified, poetic dichotomies between people but about the otherness of the unfamiliar. I would go on to suggest that for intercultural understanding in general and community/university relations in particular, this encounter must be held not only in the imagination (as it is in reading) but in person-to-person dialogue that lets "other" people speak back to our interpretations for themselves (Flower 1996). Such dialogue can lead not only to reflection but to reflective social exchange.

Whose discourse? In envisioning a collaborative inquiry, there is no advantage to being naive. The warm metaphors of "voices," "tables," and "being heard" belie the fact that inquiry, as something more than mere conversation, is a demanding literate practice. A CPSD combines problem analysis with narration; it invites people to tell the human, insiders' story behind the public story and then to rigorously search for rival hypotheses; it asks a group to project multiple options, then to evaluate them in light of probable predicted outcomes based on the expert knowledge of the community. In a typical dialogue, people leave the table as collaborative planning partners, and use writing as a collaborative tool to develop stories, analyses, and arguments they bring back to the discussion. Writing is central to this process, yet producing text is not an end but a means. While such a discourse draws on the kinds of expertise and distinctive literate practices associated with both the university and community, a CPSD is a hybrid that asks everyone to engage in new strategies.

A community problem-solving dialogue is not, for instance, modeled on a free-form town meeting. In our research, the tenor of typical community group meetings is adversarial, driven not by knowledge seeking but by political advocacy (Higgins, Flower, and Deems, in press). Academics don't do well in such forums, but then neither do most of the community people, in a contest in which the loudest or most persistent voice prevails. Moreover, teenagers are almost entirely shut out of such forums, lacking the skills of academic analysis and the community clout of age, status, or power.

The discourse of a community problem-solving dialogue is not going to be anybody's home discourse. Aside from the emphasis on sustained analysis and writing, it cannot rely on the practices that are the property of any one group. It needs to create a hybrid discourse in which there is a collaborative structure that gives everyone a space, and in which multiple ways of talking and writing and representing problems and actions are privileged.

Strategies for Dialogue

The text in Figure 1 (see pp. 108-109) is the overview from a Community Literacy Center *Urban Youth Report on Risk, Stress, and Respect*. It has a thumb-

Figure 1

WHAT ARE TEENAGERS

THREE STRATEGIES TO AN

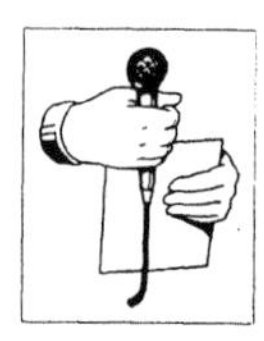

STRATEGY 1: GETTING THE STORY BEHIND THE STORY

Teenagers have expertise—and alternative perspectives—on urban issues that involve youth. They can help us define the problems, describe the hidden logics of youth that adults may not see, and evaluate options. Teenagers in Community Problem-Solving Dialogues use the Story Behind the Story strategy to talk about some critical causes of risk and stress:

- Urban teenagers tell how they cope with a constant sense of risk. When the adult community seems to turn its back, teenagers describe the need for alternative groups (including gangs) that can provide three essentials: safety, understanding, and identity.

- Urban teenagers tell how they are motivated by deep needs for respect. Respect is hard to find in inner cities. Adults relate through authority—teachers, police, parents rarely ask why, don't seem to care, won't listen. The future holds no solution: old paths to economic adulthood look closed; other roads to achieving respect are hard to find or follow. Finding identity and respect is the problem teenagers want to solve.

STRATEGY 2: SEEKING RIVAL HYPOTHESES: BRINGING MORE VOICES TO THE TABLE AND INTO THE PLAN

Complex questions don't have single answers. So Community Problem-Solving Dialogues use the rival hypothesis strategy (rivaling) to seek out alternative perspectives on risk, stress, respect, and other issues. In their writing and videos, CLC teens document surprising rival perspectives that people often don't expect.

- RISK: Stressful and potentially risky situations can be open to rival (alternative) readings by teens and adults. For instance, a group of teenagers standing on the street is often seen as threatening—invested in protecting turf and proving a "hard" identity. A rival reading, however, might argue that, given the options in the inner city, teens are actually seeking a safe and social place to "hang" together. And a third rival reading might see in that group individuals who are struggling with not only social pressure to belong, but practical concerns for safety if they don't join. Adding police to the scene can be read as the arrival of help or of harassment; it can be the imposition of order or the imposition of power without recourse. Rival readings occur every day on the street when women clutch purses at the sight of any young African American male: women see risk; teenagers see racism. And when white adults see black youth dressed in hoodies, cornrows, and baggies, they see signs of antisocial intentions, but urban teens see the mark of "fashion."

CLC URBAN YOUTH REPORT 4

SAYING ABOUT RISK?

INTERCULTURAL DIALOGUE

- STRESS: In trying to cope with the stress of the street, poverty, racism, and adolescence, teen culture often advises its members to "bury" the stress, to just "hang on," or more proactively, to "be hard." The rival wisdom of adult culture, however, urges teenagers to "just say no," disaffiliate with their peer group, or accept adult counsel. Teenagers, facing everyday risk and stress, bring a deep skepticism to the advice of adults who grew up before the violence started—adults who "haven't been there."

- RESPECT: Is respect the obligatory response one must give to those with age, status, or power? Or, the rival goes, is receiving respect also the right of the young, the powerless, the learner? Authorities often use subordinate "respectful behavior" as a way to judge urban youth (and a prerequisite for even listening). But teenagers (who hold the rival view) often look for signs of mutual respect and zero in on signs of "dissing" (disrespect) from adults—including teachers, police, and business people. They see resistant behavior as part of their demand for dignity. **Adults want to manage behavior; teens are trying to manage stress.**

STRATEGY 3: EXAMINING OPTIONS AND OUTCOMES

It is not enough to listen empathetically. A Community Problem-Solving Dialogue tries to weave rival perspectives into a community-constructed plan for action by, first, generating multiple, competing and complementary options. Secondly it subjects these options to the test of local knowledge—it uses teenage expertise to play out probable outcomes under real conditions. Action plans are then judged, not by good intentions, but by predicted consequences.

- When teenagers talk about options that would make a difference, they start with a direct call for respect, compassion, and serious conversation with adults—a change from the familiar outcome in which adults put out advice, give instruction, and rehearse the situations of their time.
- Teenagers also ask adults to take more committed public action: to create safe opportunities for socializing and athletics in poor neighborhoods, too; to create schools that can motivate, encourage, and educate even the children under stress; to create an economic future for us all. But when policy makers focus on youth, they often end up trying to manage behavior, create constraints, and punish. And the outcome of that policy is polarization.
- Teenagers don't stop at suggesting options and outcomes for adults. As you'll see in later sections of this report, they place equal emphasis on the role this strategy plays in the decisions they make on a daily basis.

A Community Problem-Solving Dialogue follows a strategic path that leads from constructing Stories, to seeking Rivals, to examining Options.

Join the table, and read on to see what this three-step strategic process is revealing.

nail sketch of three strategies that were used to structure the mixture of discussion, writing, and public presentation that led to a series of teen-produced documents and videos, which this report tried to summarize.

These three literate practices — telling the story behind the story, rival hypothesis thinking, and examining options and outcomes — lay out a strategy for inquiry and discussion in a CPSD that gives presence to community expertise. They invite different kinds of writing and the kind of hybrid discourses described above. In a dialogue that extends over multiple sessions, partners (such as college students and community teenagers) break off in small collaborative planning sessions to generate a "story behind the story," or to explore "rivals," before coming back to the larger table for discussion. In dialogues limited to one (taped) meeting, these strategies let community members enter the analysis of problems, while giving college students a rich "text" (in the form of a transcript) upon which to reflect.

Our experience at the Community Literacy Center argues that not only inquiry but effective problem solving calls for learning — not only learning *information* about rival positions and perspectives but also learning *strategies* for collaboration, for planning, for naming and exploring problems, for seeking rivals, for examining options, and for using writing to build a collaborative story that communicates to others. Growing out of work with teenagers and with neighborhood housing groups and health clinics, we find it important to start in narration that gives everyone a place at the table. However, these narratives must go beyond simple personal testimony, as people use them to construct scenarios that illustrate significant problems and represent the views of multiple players (Higgins, Flower, and Deems, in press). Moreover, they validate the expertise of people who may feel uncertain, such as teenagers, by asking them to uncover the story behind the story — the logic, the reasons, the feelings, the thoughts, the causes, the experience — that was probably not apparent to adults, outsiders, or to abstract analysis.

"Rivaling" (the name CLC teens quickly gave to rival hypothesis thinking) works in the same way to validate and encourage vigorous alternative interpretations, but not in a sprit of adversarial contest. Rivaling is not a zero-sum game. It is an attempt to invite people with different perspectives to describe the views and the options they see from their particular mountains. And, then, in the spirit inquiry (rather than advocacy), to rival their own ideas.

"Options and outcomes" is a decision-making strategy. Just as Dewey asserts the need to envision the outcomes of our ideas and actions, current research suggests that adolescents tend to see yes/no choices and are reluctant to generate other options or play out possible outcomes unless encouraged to do so. This strategy makes a space for more images of possibility and for the exercise of informed choice.

Figure 2 (see p. 111), also from the CLC's *Urban Youth Report*, outlines

Figure 2

How To Create A Community Problem-Solving Dialogue

Preoccupied with other problems, Pittsburgh has left its teenagers to face risky streets, broken schools, declining jobs, and few roads to respect. Gangs offer protection, respect, and identity. Early motherhood confers adulthood and the promise of love. Can we meet this competition—with better options for forging identity, achieving respect? Can Pittsburgh draw its youth into alternative, intercultural communities?

Are you ready for a breakthrough? Urge the groups you know—your neighborhood council, your business, civic, and religious groups, as well as the schools, youth agencies, and policy makers we support—to create working partnerships around the problems on their tables.

1. Invite urban teenagers to the table with you—as partners.

Bring the expertise of those "in the struggle" into the analysis of problems and the evaluation of options for both adults and teens. Don't let the adults become counselors and the teens become advocates. But train your group to work as problem-focused, collaborative planning partners. Creating partners creates an intercultural community.

2. Explore a problem—strategically.

The problem-solving strategies illustrated in this report use writing and discussion (aided by interactive video and computer tools) to scaffold a substantive intercultural dialogue. Working in pairs, teens and adults sketch problem scenarios that uncover the "story behind the story." They come to the table prepared to consider "rival" readings, to generate multiple "options," and to evaluate possible "outcomes."

3. Envision options and outcomes.

A problem-solving dialogue goes beyond the rhetoric of complaint and blame by building options, using the expertise of teenagers to play out probable (and rival) outcomes. It puts these stories, key points, and conclusions down in writing as a springboard for discussion and action.

4. Bring the larger community to the table.

Make your collaborative planning and writing the basis for a wider community conversation, which invites more people to join the table not as advocates or critics, but as collaborative partners in building their own community.

5. Name a place for action.

Turn talk into action by identifying a concrete situation in which alternatives can be tested and revised.

CLC Urban Youth Report 14

ways an organization (such as a college class) can create working partnerships with the community by creating problem-solving dialogues around their own concerns. It goes on to describe what the CLC calls its "dialogue support system," which includes a workshop, a training video by teens for teens on conducting a dialogue, written guides, and three hypermedia computer programs that use video, writing, and reflection about risk, stress, and sexuality to teach rival hypothesis thinking and to explore life plans.[2]

Community problem-solving dialogues immerse students in a larger, more intercultural space, in more richly represented problems and issues, and in the human reality of those issues. But it is also a challenge to grasp this mix of voices and to somehow integrate this understanding with the very different discourses of school. Is it any surprise that students sometimes wish to compartmentalize their "service" experience and their academic lives? But service needs an intellectual mission to help ensure its future in the university, and academic work and professionalism need to be challenged and shaped by the compassionate spirit of rigorous inquiry articulated within prophetic pragmatism. In the face of such goals, a simple writing assignment seems like a small thing, but in my own classes I have found it helpful to put the problem of multiple voices and competing discourse squarely on the table, and ask students to worry less about producing the kind of assertively certain argument, critique, position paper, or final answer they seem used to writing and to focus on putting these voices in a more direct dialogue. The assignment in Figure 3 (see pp. 113-114) invites a paper that requires a negotiated response to multiple distinct voices.

To What End?

A community/university inquiry creates the one thing a prophetic vision most needs — a public forum for the articulation of "serious hopefulness" (Brueggemann 1978: 65). Not a place to whistle Pollyanna's tune before the darkness falls, but a place to examine and debate our choices, name our hopes and hypotheses, examine the outcomes as we step again. Prophetic imaginations are fueled by the vision of an alternative community. Intercultural inquiry can engage us in progressive, outcome-shaped construction and reconstruction toward that possibility.

Notes

1. In 1982, for example, the pool of marriageable (employed) men (ages 16-17, based on a ratio of men to women) was 13% for blacks (but nearly 40% for whites). In the age 20-24 group, it was still under 50% (Wilson 1987:84-86).

Figure 3

Shaping an Inquiry

You may find that a traditional academic paper -- one focused on making and supporting claims or reporting the results of research -- would make it difficult to convey some of the tentative, experiential, or unresolved aspects of what you want to express. Here is a way to *shape a text* so that it reflects *the shape of a inquiry.* Like any good analysis this approach still asks you to be explicit, but invites you to use techniques you know from creative writing and document design to help people visualize this situation and to capture the conflicting voices that are part of a good inquiry.

Part I:

A. Name and situate a problem you see. (For whom is it a problem? What's at stake?)

B. Find a text/artifact/event that represents this problem or your puzzlement. Using this concrete instance, collect rival interpretations of this problem from teenagers, mentors, and others. Project what the authors of our course readings might say. Here are some examples:

Problem/Question/Puzzle	Text/Artifact/Event That Invites Interpretation
A strain of advertisements seem written to exploit minority teens. How do these ads work?	Selected advertisements
What images does the student you mentor have of everyday college life?	The University's promotional video
A perplexing event or exchange between you and your student or community contact	An account of that event, the dialogue, the setting, the outcome
What should schools do to help students develop a sense of their cultural identity?	Use the debate between Cohen and Greene from *A Hero Ain't Nothin' But a Sandwich*

Part II: In writing your final paper, bring multiple voices to the table to offer rival interpretations of *what's going on*, *why*, and *why it matters.* (In text, you might even set this up as a script, with the various voices responding to one another. However, it must also be accompanied by a running commentary from you, to tell us how *you* interpret them.)

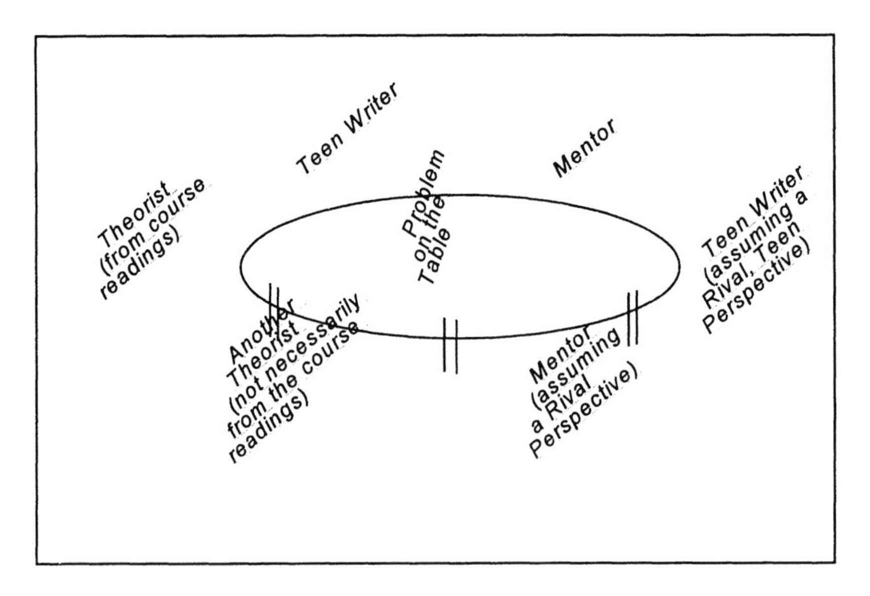

Part III: Analyze these responses and the dialogues you have created to discuss what you have learned. This can be a challenge -- plan on getting feedback on your first draft. You may also feel your conclusions are tentative—so talk about the rivals that exist in your own mind. But pull your insights, intuitions, and discoveries together into a strong, negotiated interpretation of what this means for you from where you now stand.

2. To support intercultural collaboration and problem-solving dialogues, the CLC uses text, video, and hypermedia. **Videos:** *Teamwork: Teenagers Working Through Community Problems*. An interactive training video by teens. A lively community problem-solving team demonstrates strategies for collaborative planning, rivaling, and decision making as they investigate a problem case of urban stress. A manual and additional video problem cases help viewers transfer strategies to other issues. **Guides:** *How to Be Heard. A Handbook for Community Literacy,* edited by Linda Flower and Elenore Long. A practical guide to community literacy strategies for teens. *The Community Literacy Primer,* edited by Linda Flower and Elenore Long. An introduction to theory and practice of community literacy in vignettes of literate social action. *Community Literacy Research*. A series of reports and reprints of articles on community literacy. **Computer Programs:** *Rivaling About Risk: A Dialogue Tutorial*. An interactive HyperCard program that uses video, writing, reflection, and teen-authored texts to teach critical and rival hypothesis thinking and to give voice to teen perspectives on issues of urban risk. *What's My Plan?: Sexuality and Contraception*. Friendly computer support for a dialogue among young women and health workers, using the strategies in teamwork to make (and print out) one's personal plan. *Struggle: A Dialogue About Life Plans*. A personalized computer program that lets teenagers, parents, and caring adults work together to acknowledge struggle, name aspirations, and make committed life plans.

References

Benson, L., and I. Harkavy. (Spring/Summer 1991). "Progressing Beyond the Welfare State." *Universities and Community Schools (University of Pennsylvania)* 2(1-2): 2-28.

Bernstein, R.J. (1991). *The New Constellation: The Ethical-Political Horizons of Modernity/Postmodernity*. Cambridge, MA: MIT Press.

Borg, M.J. (1987). *Jesus: A New Vision: Spirit, Culture, and the Life of Discipleship*. San Francisco: Harper & Row.

Boydston, J.A., ed. (1988). *John Dewey: The Later Works, 1925-1953 (Volume 4: 1929)*. Carbondale, IL: Southern Illinois University Press.

Brueggemann, W. (1978). *The Prophetic Imagination*. Decatur, GA: Fortress Press.

Cooper, D.D., and L. Julier. (1995). *Writing in the Public Interest: Service-Learning and the Writing Classroom*. East Lansing, MI: Writing Center, Michigan State University.

Dewey, J. (1916). *Democracy and Education: An Introduction to the Philosophy of Education*. New York: Free Press.

——. (1929). "Quest for Certainty." In Boydston 1988.

Flower, L. (1994). *The Construction of Negotiated Meaning: A Social Cognitive Theory of Writing*. Carbondale, IL.: Southern Illinois University Press.

——. (1996). "Negotiating the Meaning of Difference." *Written Communication* 13(1): 44-92.

——, E. Long, and L. Higgins. (In prep.). "The Rival Hypothesis Stance and Intercultural Inquiry: Study of a Literate Practice."

Freire, P. (1989). *Pedagogy of the Oppressed*, translated by M.B. Ramos. New York: Continuum.

Gates, H.L., Jr. (1988). *The Signifying Monkey: A Theory of African-American Literary Criticism*. New York: Oxford University Press.

Goldblatt, E. (1994). "Van Rides in the Dark: Literacy as Involvement in a College Literacy Practicum." *The Journal for Peace and Justice Studies* 6(1): 77-94.

Harkavy, I., and J.L. Puckett. (1991). "Toward Effective University-Public School Partnerships: An Analysis of a Contemporary Model." *Teachers College Record* 92(4): 556-581.

Herzberg, B. (1994). "Community Service and Critical Teaching." *College Composition and Communication* 45:307-319.

Higgins, L., L. Flower, and J. Deems. (In press). "Collaboration for Community Action: Landlords and Tenants." In *Collaboration in Professional and Technical Communication: Research Perspectives*, edited by R.E. Burnett and A.H. Duin. Mahwah, NJ: Lawrence Erlbaum.

Kendall, J.C., and Associates. (1990). *Combining Service and Learning: A Resource Book for Community and Public Service (Volume I)*. Raleigh, NC: National Society for Internships and Experiential Education.

Labov, W. (1972). *Language in the Inner City: Studies in the Black English Vernacular*. Philadelphia: University of Pennsylvania Press.

Lee, C. (1993). *Signifying as a Scaffold for Literary Interpretation: The Pedagogical Implications of an African American Discourse Genre*. NCTE Research Report, no. 26. Urbana, IL: National Council of Teachers of English.

Lerner, M., and C. West. (1996). *Jews & Blacks: A Dialogue on Race, Religion, and Culture in America*. New York: Plume/Penguin.

Long, E.A. (May 1994). "The Rhetoric of Literate Social Action: Mentors Negotiating Intercultural Images of Literacy." Doctoral dissertation, Carnegie Mellon University.

McKnight, J. (1995). *The Careless Society: Community and Its Counterfeits*. New York: Basic Books.

Minter, D.W., A.R. Gere, and D. Keller-Cohen. (1995). "Learning Literacies." *College English* 57(6): 669-687.

Peck, W.C., L. Flower, and L. Higgins. (May 1995). "Community Literacy." *College Composition and Communication* 46(2): 199-222.

Pratt, M.L. (1991). "Arts of the Contact Zone." In *Profession 91*, pp. 33-40. New York: Modern Language Association.

van Dijk, T.A. (1993). *Elite Discourse and Racism*. Sage Series on Race and Ethnic Relations, vol. 6, John H. Stanfield II, series editor. Newbury Park, CA: Sage Publications.

Watters, A., and M. Ford. (1995). A *Guide for Change: Resources for Implementing Community Service Writing*. New York: McGraw-Hill.

West, C. (1993). *Keeping Faith: Philosophy and Race in America*. New York: Routledge.

Wilson, W.J. (1987). *The Truly Disadvantaged: The Inner City, the Underclass, and Public Policy*. Chicago, IL: University of Chicago Press.

Zlotkowski, E. (January-February 1996). "A New Voice at the Table? Linking Service-Learning and the Academy." *Change* 28(1): 21-27.

Figures 1 and 2 are reprinted with permission from *Working Partners: An Urban Youth Report on Risk, Stress, and Respect* (Pittsburgh: Community Literacy Center and Carnegie Mellon University, 1996).

Service-Learning: Bridging the Gap Between the Real World and the Composition Classroom

by Wade Dorman and Susann Fox Dorman

"So, whadja do over Spring Break?"

"Man, if I could remember, I'd tell you."

Binge drinking, a pain therapy epidemic on campuses across the country, is only one of many signs we see regularly of student alienation and despair. Surely you have seen them too: Absenteeism. Plagiarism. Lack of preparation. Nonparticipation. Cramming for exams. Obsession with GPA. Facile distraction by such escapist activities as soap operas, televised sports, bar-hopping, substance abuse, and exploitative sex.

Alienated, our students are sightseers rather than explorers; instead of discovering for themselves, they follow the path laid out in text and lecture, taking notes on what the tour guide/teacher points out. So suggests Walker Percy in his stimulating little essay "The Loss of the Creature." According to Percy, "as a consumer receiving an experience-package" (1954: 57), the contemporary student is more likely to settle for certification, "the sanction of those who know" (55), than to seek authentic learning. Students aren't uniquely alienated, says Percy; they merely experience the "predicament in which *everyone* finds himself in a modern technical society" (61, emphasis added). "Everyone" includes teachers, who are "well aware that something is wrong, that there is a fatal gap between the student's learning and the student's life" (57).

Evidence of the gap abounds throughout undergraduate education. We are focusing on writing classes, not only because we know them best but also because the "ability to read and write," or "literacy," as Rudolph Weingartner notes in *Undergraduate Education*, is "the most ancient and most prominent proficiency declared to be a goal of education" (1993: 14). It is a crucial tool for attaining "the level of competency deemed satisfactory for an American citizen near the end of the 20th century" (17). We also believe that writing instruction, because it is isolated in most universities from its integral relationship with the thinking and producing processes *within* disciplines, is especially likely to alienate students. Percy's "fatal gap" may be at its most lethal in a writing class, so as writing instructors, we need to study the gap carefully.

Students who see no relevant connection between learning and life don't try to store the learning for life, but only through the final exam, so they cram it all into their short-term memory. We're not surprised, then, when empirical studies reveal that "50 to 80 percent of what is learned [in college and university] courses is lost within one year" (Bowen 1977: 88). Unaware of meaningful connections between the real world and the classroom, students not infrequently mistake the symbol for the substance, substituting a degree or diploma for the learning it is supposed to represent. As Weingartner (who over the years has been a philosophy professor, department chair, dean, and provost) explains, educators "require what we believe students *need,* what they cannot do without; *fulfilling requirements,* however, soon becomes the whole of education" (3, emphasis added). Echoing Percy's language, he notes that we "take seriously, perhaps too much so, getting grades and graduating — forms of certification" (101).

What students have done, as Percy outlines it, is to surrender their autonomy (he calls it "sovereignty") as genuine learners. They give up being motivated by their own authentic needs and interests as individuals in the world, becoming instead consumers of learning predigested and packaged by well-intentioned experts, whose evaluation translates into dollars on a paycheck. It is an abdication whether or not a student is aware of choosing it. In fact, Percy warns, the "great difficulty is that he is not aware that there is a difficulty" (1954: 57), echoing the Kierkegaard epigraph to his novel *The Moviegoer* (1960): ". . . the specific character of despair is precisely this: it is unaware of being despair." Which is where teachers come in. After all, we are the ones telling students not only what and how to learn but how well we think they have done it.

Teachers contribute to the abdication by using pedagogy that divorces the classroom from the real world, validating "those stern grandfatherly warnings that life is not like school" (Weingartner 1993: 110). Often the divorce is precipitated by apparently laudable concerns such as efficiency and economy. Writing teachers especially, whose discipline tends to be more labor-intensive than many, can see the advantages of having students, for example, use casebooks of sources for documentation. Given teachers' "desire to have things orderly" (98), each course is ideally a neat package in which specified behaviors result in certain rewards. The subjective nature of writing again tempts instructors to be precise about all sorts of imprecise things — e.g., assigning a point value to each mechanical error. But in trying to control the situation so as to isolate those behaviors we are teaching, we reduce multiplicate reality to a classroom devoid of real decision making, placing the student squarely in the passive, consumer role Percy describes as "a receptacle of experience" (1954: 58).

Just such a student sat in Wade's office — the brightest of the bright; graduate of our state's premier, public, college-prep boarding school; intelligent, verbal, and clearly steamed about his research assignment for a history of the Baton Rouge Volunteers of America.

"Look, I don't like this project you've got us doing," he announced.

"What don't you like about it?"

"I've looked through five years of Baton Rouge newspapers on microfilm — that's a lot of hours cranking that machine — and I didn't find the first mention of Volunteers of America, much less any history. Why did you send me over there if I wasn't gonna find anything?"

"But you *did* find something. You found that there was nothing in those five years of newspapers. And since you were looking at a period for which there is no index, actually looking at the newspapers was the only way to determine whether there was any information for us. Remember, we're talking a local organization, so the local newspaper is our primary print source. This is important research."

"No, no," he corrected, "I've done research before, and it wasn't anything like this. Our teacher never sent us to look for something that she hadn't already found out was there."

Here was a "good" student, one who'd done exactly what he was taught to do by exceptional teachers in an elite school, who didn't know the difference between research — genuine exploration and discovery — and an Easter egg hunt — finding more or less artfully hidden but accessible data. Alienated, he saw no connection between what he was supposedly learning and its actual usefulness in the world outside the composition classroom, where no one would precede him compiling the relevant information he would need to solve problems effectively. For this student, who had all the apparent advantages, teaching failed.

But a worse failure, according to psychologist Carl Rogers, is when teaching *succeeds*. Influenced like Percy by Kierkegaard, Rogers came to believe that students surrender their autonomy in a more complicated way when they enthusiastically and uncritically reproduce "what the teacher is looking for." Confesses Rogers,

> *When this happens I find that the results are damaging. It seems to cause the individual to distrust his own experience, and to stifle significant learning. Hence I have come to feel that the outcomes of teaching are either unimportant or hurtful.* (1969: 153)

In other words, teaching is a lose-lose activity. The harder we try — even the more we succeed — the wider the gap between the student and the real world. Percy concludes somewhat pessimistically that "there is nothing the educator can do" to solve this problem; "everything the educator does only succeeds in becoming, for the student, part of the educational package" (1954: 63). What's a teacher to do, faced with such absurdity? Some have seriously suggested that we give up, abandon the classroom. Rogers, for example, recommends that we "do away with teaching," examinations, grades and credits, degrees (1969: 154-155). We would do away, in other words, with certification. And higher education as we know it.

Rather than abandon any attempt for meaningful education, we decided to move our writing classes closer to the messy comprehensiveness of the real world, where problems almost never come wrapped in neat packages with clear criteria and specified rewards for solution. We sought a composition pedagogy that would locate students in complex, unpredictable situations. That's why we had for a long time not assigned students writing topics, but instead given them heuristics for discovering meaningful topics that really existed in the messiness of their lives. And given the reality that people affect each other whether they bowl together or alone, we included the real-world messiness of interdependence. That's why we were already using workshop-style classes, why we stressed the needs and demands of community in our teaching of communication. And why we emphasized self-reflection, cognitive maturity, and ethical appeal in teaching argument, since, as Quintilian asserts, the good rhetor is the good man. Wade's student Laura made that connection in writing about our argumentative assignment series: "The progression from the evaluative viewpoint to the empathic is a path of maturation. In the evaluative perspective, my feelings and opinions (selfishly) were of most importance. The empirical viewpoint broadened the scope to emphasize facts to back my opinions. Then, in the . . . empathic perspective, I had to attempt to understand a view which opposed my own. I think this progress applied to my life." Like Laura, we thought we were creating classroom circumstances more likely to facilitate learning that, to use Rogers's criteria, is "self-discovered" and "significantly affects behavior" (153). Authentic, autonomous learning.

Service-Learning Writing – Version One

Thus we were ripe for service-learning as a site for real-world writing when Ronald D. Whitmer, director of the nonprofit PULSE of Louisiana, walked through our office door in the summer of 1991. Starting with a modest grant from the Baton Rouge Area Foundation, Ron pieced together enough financial support to pursue the potential of service-learning community development. His vision, based on the PULSE (not an acronym) program developed over many years by Boston College, was to link mostly white Louisiana State University and historically black Southern University, by mingling students from both institutions at common community service sites. He sought the involvement of writing classes primarily because writing is an important means for the self-reflection that distinguishes service-learning from voluntarism. Recognizing the potential for connecting our students' coursework to the real world, we quickly signed on. Since then we have experimented with several ways to facilitate this connection, from having students write *about* their service work to writing *as* their service.

Initially, we adapted our workshop-style rhetoric-based composition class to incorporate service work. Students did 30-40 hours of volunteer work each semester, in addition to the usual course requirements. As part of the reflective component, students kept journals on their service work. The service work, performed for the participating community agency of the student's choice, was the subject matter for as many of their essays as they chose, but at least one. Our aim was to facilitate students' exploring situations from their actual real-life experiences in the community outside the classroom: problems the students had firsthand experience with, for a cause they had invested in, seeking solutions that really were needed, addressed to an audience they knew something about. After experimenting with requiring that all and none of the course writing assignments be related to the service work, we settled on requiring only one, the student's choice among seven assignments. Some chose to evaluate their choice of agency or the agency itself. By far the majority of the students focused on their documented paper, combining research statistics with firsthand experiences and quotes from agency officials as they explored some aspect of the community problems their agency addressed.

Did the course reduce student alienation? To answer this question requires a bit of background. Due to problems we have not yet managed to overcome, it has been very difficult to advertise the service-learning composition classes — 2 sections among 60 to 65. The only official notice of the offering (not including various forms of publicity we generated) is in the university's course schedule book, but the students typically register by phone, and the computer does not announce the community service requirement. As a result, we have never, on the first day of classes, had even half a class of students who knew what they had signed up for. Also, because these sections typically filled up last, we seemed to have a higher-than-usual percentage of disaffected students — those who had waited for various reasons until the last minute to register. A tough audience, perhaps unusually alienated. This comment from Kip is a typical reflection:

> *As I walked into my English 1002 class I didn't know what to expect. I was moved from English 1001 and had been out of school for a number of years. I soon found out that I had to do thirty hours of community service as part of the class. Needless to say, I wasn't happy.*
>
> *I would have changed classes but it was too late in the semester so I decided to push on. I commenced my community service at the Bishop Ott Shelter with almost a frown in my heart because I really didn't want to be there.*

Given initial attitudes such as this, we were pleased by the PULSE students' responses to end-of-semester questionnaires at the end of our second year. We believe our students became more autonomous learners, using their writing skills to connect to the community as they reflected on and joined the dialogue about real-world situations. Wrote one, "The C[ommunity] S[ervice] has provided a wonderful link to the outside world." And although evaluating service-learning experiences is difficult, as Rob Shumer, director of the National Service-Learning Clearinghouse, has pointed out (1995: 2), and our sample was too small to be statistically significant, the 1996 first-year report of the Corporation for National Service's Learn and Serve America, Higher Education (LSAHE) initiative seems to corroborate our feeling that we were onto something: that "students who participate in service show stronger gains than nonparticipants in academic achievement, life skills, and civic responsibility" (UCLA 1996: xi).[1] Among the positive results in all of 35 measures of student development across the above three outcome areas, several findings especially reinforce our experience with service-learning in our composition classes.

Life skills. In terms of autonomy, the LSAHE participants reported significantly higher increases in "leadership ability" and "social self-confidence." Though we were of course not using the same instrument, the results from our PULSE students were similar. In response to the item "This experience had an impact on my personal growth (a sense of who I am and my value as a person)," 95 percent marked "very" or "somewhat true." As Wendy, who tutored adults at O'Brien House, a halfway house for recovering substance abusers, wrote, "The day that my student, Cal, read a sentence without any mistakes, I knew I had accomplished as much as he had. I realized that I have the strength to do things I never imagined possible, and I realized this by doing community service." Other students echoed her response in more general terms: "I gained satisfaction in myself and accomplished more than I thought I could." "This semester I feel that I have grown as a person and a student and the community has also grown from my involvement."

Civic responsibility. The LSAHE study found that "students who participated in community service become more interested in effecting social and political change" (UCLA 1996: 50). For us, this area roughly correlated with two survey items. A complete 100 percent of the students we surveyed reported as "very" (78.6%) or "somewhat true" (21.4%) that the experience "helped me better understand some of the problems of the community." And 94 percent agreed that the experience "helped me recognize and want to work with others over the long term to address the deep-seated systemic needs of our communities."

Perhaps most importantly, after their service work, a statistically significant number of LSAHE participants reported *dis*agreeing with the statement "Realistically, an individual can do little to bring about changes in our society" (58). That negative outcome, expressed in its positive inversion — the belief that individuals *can* change society — may be the kernel from which the other outcomes grow. To use Percy's terms, belief that the individual can change society empowers student sovereignty. Learning becomes meaningful when connected to improving the quality of life in the real world. Our students' responses relative to continuing service work after the course was over seem to reflect this confidence. Brian, who was still volunteering at Baton Rouge Green several semesters after he made the following comment, explained it this way: "This experience built me more as a member of community than as a four-year student at the university. I now know what it takes to make our communities better places to live." In a variety of ways, others agreed with Tammara, a volunteer in public schools, that, "Community service is very important to me and I plan to continue volunteering." Kip, who began his service at the Bishop Ott Shelter "with almost a frown in my heart," concluded, "I know that either I will continue to work with the agency now, or another agency in the future."

Academic achievement. We were of course especially interested in academic achievement related to writing, which took two major forms: reflective journals and formal essays (for more on reflective journals, see Anson in this volume). Several students singled out journal writing as of special importance in their evaluations of the class. Wrote one, "The journal writing improved my writing skills." Another said, "I documented what I witnessed and experienced in my journal, which helped me develop as a person and as a writer." A third's poignant journal entry about realizing that the mothers of the children she was tutoring were children themselves led to an essay on teenage mothers that she considered her best writing of the semester. Overall we agreed with Tom, who analyzed the effect of service-learning on him and his classmates this way: "English 1002 Community Service brings real life situations into the students' writing. Doing community service offers the students real life experiences to draw upon when they write, which can only improve their writing. The assignments are more real to the students because they have experienced and are knowledgeable on the topic." Many of the students also commented on an unexpected benefit, the effect of the course on their time-management skills: "This English class will teach you how to balance your time, manage your private life, and put yourself on a schedule. There were times we could not get it together, but the community service obligation helped put our priorities in place."

Did we see better writing outcomes? Yes. Our students increased their investments in the arguments they were writing, they had a greater awareness of audience, awareness more grounded in the realities of the situation they were writing about, they did more thorough research, they used real-life examples. And, like Wendy, they wrote with satisfaction about the ways their learning was meaningful to them.

Such results, suggesting that students were bridging the gap between the classroom and the real world, seem to us an encouraging measure of reduced student alienation. Most of the LSAHE service-learning participants saw the "relevance of course work to everyday life" (56). Likewise, 90 percent of our PULSE students replied that the service-learning "experience had a positive impact on my educational development." Asked to complete the sentence, "Because of this experience, learning has become more . . . ," the three words PULSE students used most often were "important" (38%), "real" (32%), and "alive" (14%).

Service-Learning Writing – Version Two: Real-World Writing

Despite our satisfaction with these results, we still felt the real-world connection to the composition class could be stronger, so we adjusted again what Percy calls "the fundamental placement of the student in the world" (1954: 57). Rather than have students write *about* their service work, we wanted the writing itself to *be* their service work. Such a model, pioneered at Stanford, seemed an answer to the pedagogical question posed by educators from a variety of disciplines: How does the course provide opportunities for the students to actually function in the discipline? Educational psychologists Widick, Parker, and Knefelkamp, for example, ask, "Are courses designed and structured so that students actually experience being an historian, a psychologist, or an engineer?" (1978: 14). And in our discipline, Kenneth Bruffee seems to be proposing the same standard: "How does this course create conditions in which students learn to converse with one another about writing as writers do, and learn to write to each other as do the members of the community of literate people?" (1993: 73).

When we asked whether the students in our original service-learning writing course were actually experiencing being writers, the answer was no. They were, for example, simulating writing for an audience outside the classroom, while actually writing for the teacher. They never faced a truly opaque audience, or an audience ignorant of its conflicting wishes. They never had to meet a real deadline, only the instructor's artificial ones; never had to stay within a budget, choose an ink color or a paper stock.

So in the spring of 1994, having realized that we wanted students writing *for* and *to* and *in* the community, rather than merely *about* the community, we asked the various agencies providing service sites to suggest writing tasks for our students. The Baton Rouge chapter of Volunteers of America responded with a request to write their history in time for the national organization's 1996 centennial. This project ultimately spanned three semesters, involving three different classes: beginning composition, advanced composition, and independent studies.

Two freshman composition sections started researching and writing pieces preliminary to a draft in the spring 1995 semester, essentially duplicating each other's efforts for the sake of coverage and vetting. We divided them into working teams, and assigned writing by and about the teams to fit into the context of an argumentation course. For example, we had team members evaluate themselves and apply for various research or editorial positions on their team.

Students also collected information from available living informants and transcribed their audiotapes.[2] They consulted Louisiana and Baton Rouge histories and paged through decades of unindexed newspaper files. They kept logs of their work hours, and journals of their experience. They wrote progress reports. After they had finished their oral and archival research, we had them do team reports evaluating the material they had collected for inclusion in the final history. And at the end of the semester, we had them individually evaluate their work for the semester and argue for the grade they thought that work deserved.

We learned quite a bit from that first semester, mostly from the mistakes we made. Idealistically, we had avoided starting with a detailed syllabus. Instead, we treated the students like coeditors, laying out for them our deadlines with VOA and inviting their participation in planning our semester's work together. It freaked them right out.

As one of Wade's students wrote in his end-of-the-semester evaluation,

> *We discussed how we should manage our individual groups, how we should divide tasks and research, and other general subjects which should have already been decided and outlined beforehand. This wandering in the dark wasted valuable time, decreased motivation, and frustrated the students, which led to other problems.*

Another assumption proved false was our belief that students would be thrilled out of their alienation by the reality of the project. That disgruntled student researcher we mentioned earlier was, as you might have guessed, disgruntled with his research in the first semester of the VOA history project. His conclusion?

"Our teacher never sent us to look for something that she hadn't already found out was there."

Wade patiently explained, "I know it's frustrating not to have some photocopies of facts to take away from the microfilm, but you really have contributed to our knowledge base. Besides, real research is like that — you sometimes put a lot of effort into tracking down a lead, only to come up empty-handed. But the only way to avoid that is to know ahead of time; except, if we knew ahead of time, we wouldn't have to do the research."

"Well, if that's research, I don't want to do any of it."

But then, he's probably right — he probably doesn't want to do research. That's significant vocational learning. It is equivalent to the learning of a student in one of our early service-learning freshman writing courses. She had come back to school after work with Catholic charities had convinced her she should go into social welfare, but she learned from serving in a children's shelter that she couldn't handle the emotional pain of bonding with them. So she changed her major to elementary education, which would allow her to usefully love the children without wanting to adopt them.

And consider the autonomy of Wade's student coming to the office to complain about what he was being assigned and graded on, about how he was having to spend his time. Especially consider it in comparison with his own past experience with learning — impotently carrying out a task that clearly didn't need to be done, that had in fact already *been* done before he was assigned to "do" it. Or consider his complaining in comparison with the host of students who keep quiet about the meaninglessness of their learning to them, immediately discarding it from short-term memory or numbing the pain of their alienation with alcohol. This student was angry, maybe even desperate. But he wasn't completely alienated. He was engaged and autonomous enough to speak up. We were sure we were onto something.

Real-World Writing – Version Two

The following fall, Wade taught one section of advanced composition, advertised as Real-World Writing, which carried on the project. That course is a requirement for education majors, so about half the class were future teachers, leavened with students majoring in poli-sci/pre-law, mass communications, and marketing. Wade changed the class structure from that of a writing team (all members coequally writers, editors, and planners) to that of a writing shop (students as writers and editors under his management).

Representatives came from VOA Baton Rouge to answer the class' questions about how VOA saw the history, who would read it, and how VOA expected to use it. Near the end of that meeting one student concluded, "So what you want is as much a *spiritual* history as it is a factual history." When Wade asked how the writers could manage to achieve a spiritual history, the class replied, "By using interviews, people talking about what they *believe*, not just what they did."

To establish continuity, the class started by organizing and logging material collected the previous semester, and then visually arranging events on a 13-foot brown paper time line. Constructing the time line was one way the class "conversed," using Kenneth Bruffee's terms ("as literate persons do"), with writers in the preceding semester. While students organized the existing data, they also canvassed for additional information. Students wrote public service announcements, requesting informants or records and addressed to the writer's favorite local media outlet — which included a public radio jazz station, a newspaper community-interest humor column, a nursing home bulletin board, a church bulletin, and an early-morning TV interview program.

By the time everything we knew was on the time line, we had a pretty good sense of what we knew, and what we didn't — in other words, we had pretty clear research and writing assignments. (To the students, of course, that management clarity was nothing like the reassuring order and structure of the typical writing class.) Some assignments were individual; the majority were collaborative. That writing Wade assigned in two formats: one as a stand-alone feature piece for magazine or newspaper publication; another as a piece for direct inclusion in the history. We put intermediate and final drafts in the library so that class members could read, comment, and edit one another's pieces at their leisure — so they could "learn to converse with one another about writing as writers do," that is, "in their own communities" (Bruffee 1993: 73). In the future, we plan to substitute a class online bulletin board for the library reserve.

After everybody had read everyone else's writing, the class nominated an editorial board. From their nominations we chose three people, who agreed to begin assembling the individual pieces from the class into a unified, consistent draft, which they made available in the library for the class to edit. Meanwhile, the other student writers were polishing their stand-alone pieces. The history was complete only to the level of an intermediate draft by the end of the semester. Therefore, even though the class had agreed on paper, ink, and format, we were not able to publish in time for them to hold the final product in their hands. Wade ended the semester with students submitting a portfolio of their semester's writing and research effort for him to assign a grade, with an introductory essay in which they evaluated their own performance.

In anonymous responses not available to the teacher until after grades were turned in, students evaluated the performance of the course: "The most helpful [aspect of the course] for me was the new skills like Research, Public Relations. Most of all, even though I had to do it kicking and screaming, I learned to adjust to other people's styles and them being in control, and I know that's a good thing and not a bad." "We had a lot of say-so on things." "I thought it was helpful, all of us revising all of the draft. Also, revising others' [writing], and letting them revise mine stimulated me, made me realize the mistakes I had made, and that I could help someone with theirs." A lot of the learning they praised, interestingly enough, was also something they had been frustrated by, some messy reality.

In the spring of 1996 we concluded the project. Two independent studies students and a third who worked with us for no course credit (all from the previous semester's editorial board) completed the final draft and prepared camera-ready copy for the printer. These students so thoroughly "owned" the project that they refused to quit until it was done. They drafted and edited repeatedly. They handled the printing order. (One got the printer to search for a paper that was *close* to the one the class had chosen, but didn't have to be special-ordered, saving time and money.) And when the printing was done, the editorial board passed press-hot copies among themselves for a couple of days before one of them thought to tell *us*. Autonomous learners — explorers, not sightseers — they didn't need our certification; the product was their certificate. The product, and the audience response, and how they felt about themselves: the rewards real writing always offers.

We are proud of the resulting history, *Giving Shelter: A History of the Volunteers of America, Baton Rouge, Inc.* It is balanced, reasonably accurate, and warmly human, with a lot of the voices in it of our community's finest citizens. As the national celebration got under way, Baton Rouge VOA's CEO, Bill Coffey, reported, "The history is getting rave reviews, and that makes me the envy of many of my counterparts around the country" (personal letter, June 24, 1996). In the wake of publicity about the project, we received requests from other nonprofits to have students do similar ones.

The shape of the book represents both the method of its writing and the nature of the VOA itself. Its smoothly flowing, loosely connected pieces, for example, result from the large number of writers and the necessity of subgroups and individuals contributing. But that also represents the lives of people as they intertwine with VOA. Thus, the history is a living interface among the forces that gave it being, and it thereby binds the lives of its writers into the lives of the people they know will read it, into the concrete as well as abstract facts of the VOA, and ultimately into the community that both supports and is created by writing. In other words, it is what James Berlin (1988) would call "socially epistemic."

In all but the third of these courses, we still had students who didn't accept sovereignty but continued to "play the game" — interestingly, the education majors were chief among these. But we also experienced increasingly more enthusiastic participation, more successful management of the uncertainty and challenge of reality. More real-world learning. And we attributed continuing lack of authenticity and autonomy at least in part to students' lack of real choice in the project: In the second semester, all the students again worked on the VOA history, and it was ongoing when they took the course.

Real-World Writing – The Latest Version

So we changed the course again. In the spring of 1996, Susann taught a section of advanced composition, also titled Real-World Writing, in which the students' primary requirement was to submit for "publication" a collaborative writing project for a nonprofit group or cause that could not afford to hire the writing done. Five writing teams were established by choice of project, three suggested by students and two from a number of suggestions Susann made. Before the end of the semester, groups had submitted scripted videos on AIDS to the local Friends for Life and on the Vietnam war to a local magnet high school social science department; a video script of an oral history project to the director of the university's oral history center; a brochure of after-school tutoring services to a neighboring community board; and a three-color brochure on South Louisiana's attractions for college students to the tourist commission.

Though there were problems, especially with the collaborative aspects of the work, and we can think of other changes, as well, the course was a positive experience in terms of our objectives. One student valued most "the opportunity to experience what happens in the real world; i.e., meeting deadlines, the editing process, time restraints." Another commented that the class "really brought home to me the fact that the real world is not as structured as a classroom. I wasted a *lot* of time calling and recalling people for information." In terms of autonomy, another wrote, "The best aspect of this class is that it allows you to be in complete (almost complete) control of your own work, both creatively and structurally. This way you can OWN what you do!"

We are convinced that making service-learning an integral part of our composition classes is a challenge worth the effort. At the same time, we have plenty of ideas for further development. Service-learning is not, of course, a wonderland from which alienated students emerge transformed into literate, responsible citizens. But it does provide a site for students to exercise autonomy as writers, in response to real-world complexities, for bridging the gap between the composition classroom and the real world. Students do engage. They do develop a literacy to suit them for citizenship in a democracy. They do develop the confidence that they can make meaningful change. They are more connected, less alienated.

"Whadja do over the break, dude?"

"Interviewed the guy who set up Roosevelt's New Deal in Louisiana then helped start United Way. He's in his 90s, still jogs, and he's gonna carry the

Olympic torch through Baton Rouge. Way cool, man. You?"

Notes

1. Our survey, conducted in the spring of 1993 by Ron Whitmer, included 56 anonymous responses, 27 from LSU and 29 from Southern. UCLA's HERI study is a three-year project that will use both qualitative and quantitative data collected from a variety of sources (students, faculty, institutions, agencies). The first-year report includes data about student outcomes in 1994-95, based on a survey of both participants in service-learning (2,309) and nonparticipants (1,141).

2. We prepared students for this assignment with help from the Williams Center for Oral History and Edward D. (Sandy) Ives's video *An Oral Historian's Work* (Orono, ME: Northeast Archives of Folklore and Oral History, 1987).

References

Berlin, J.A. (1988). "Poststructuralism, Cultural Studies, and the Composition Classroom: Postmodern Theory in Practice." In (1996) *Teaching With the Bedford Guide for College Writers; Vol II: Background Readings*, edited by S. Morahan, pp. 285-300. Boston: Bedford.

Bowen, H.R. (1977). *Investment in Learning: The Individual and Social Value of American Higher Education.* San Francisco: Jossey-Bass.

Bruffee, K. (1993). *Collaborative Learning: Higher Education, Interdependence, and the Authority of Knowledge.* Baltimore, MD: Johns Hopkins University Press.

Percy, W. (1954). *The Message in the Bottle.* NY: Farrar, Strauss, and Giroux.

——. (1960). *The Moviegoer.* New York: Knopf.

Quintilian, M.F. (95 C.E.) *Institutio oratoria, book xii, chapter I.* In (1990) *The Rhetorical Tradition: Readings From Classical Times to the Present,* edited by P. Bizzell and B. Herzberg, p. 347. Boston: Bedford.

Rogers, C. (1969). *Freedom to Learn.* Columbus, OH: Merrill.

Shumer, R. (Fall 1995). "An Update on Information." *The Server* 3(1): 1-2.

University of California-Los Angeles, Higher Education Research Institute. (May 1996). "Evaluation of Learn and Serve America, Higher Education: First Year Report, Volume I."

Weingartner, R.H. (1993). *Undergraduate Education: Goals and Means.* Phoenix, AZ: Oryx.

Widick, C., C. Parker, and L. Knefelkamp. (1978). *Erik Erikson and Psychosocial Development.* Applying New Developmental Findings: New Directions for Student Services, no. 4. San Francisco: Jossey-Bass.

Systems Thinking, Symbiosis, and Service: The Road to Authority for Basic Writers

by Rosemary L. Arca

In the movie *Mindwalk*, Sonia, a "recovering" physicist, passionately details a shift in our world view. She suggests that our world is moving from a mechanistic, Cartesian perspective, which separates all elements into individual components, to a view of the world and society that sees all biological, psychological, social, and environmental phenomena as interdependent (Capra 1982). Although she is grandly general in her discussion of our "global interconnectedness," she argues that we must necessarily see ourselves as part of a system, an ecological view that emphasizes our interdependence. It plays out in all facets of our existence — in our global connections, in our social and political arenas, and in our schools and communities. Such interdependence also encourages us to develop clear symbiotic relationships with one another in all aspects of our lives. When we acknowledge our interconnectedness, we recognize how we can effect change, and then we seek to serve. When we serve, we realize that our service is changing not only the focus of our service but also ourselves. At the end of *Mindwalk*, all of the characters — the physicist, the poet, and the politician — have profoundly changed their views of themselves and the parts they play in the world. When they walk off into the sunset with a heightened sense of self and of the authority of their roles, they are challenged by their responsibility to serve.

When basic writers enter our classrooms, they arrive with a diminished view of themselves and of the power they have to effect change. They often come with no sense of authority — the power to influence or persuade — in their lives, in their expressions in written text, or their participation in class discussion. One of the fascinating outcomes of using community service writing in a basic skills writing class is the synergistic effect it has on the writers, their texts, and their communities. Although historically service-learning has not been a part of most developmental writing programs, perhaps because of the perceived disparity of student writing skills and community agency standards, I would argue that community service writing can be a powerful agent for change in basic writers' thinking, writing, and interactions with their communities. And although there are admittedly potential problems inherent in asking basic writers to produce flawless documents for the public arena, I would also argue that there are major benefits to creating opportunities for basic writers to compose for real audiences and giving them real responsibilites for public texts. In this essay, I would like to explore these issues by sharing some of the writing from my community service writing class for basic writers.

When I sit down to develop curriculum for my basic writing students, I am reminded of the characters from and the plot of *Mindwalk*. Am I not, in my basic writing skills class, trying to help my students locate themselves in "the system"? Do I not encourage them to develop a series of symbiotic relationships within our writing community, relationships that will help them develop not only their writing skills but also their sense of authority? Because, in fact, these are my goals for basic writers, for the past two years community service writing has been the curriculum of choice in my basic writing classes.

After many years of teaching developmental students, I am convinced that they come to my classroom overworked, time-impacted, disheartened by their sense of powerlessness in communities that challenge them in a multitude of ways. So, when I sit down to develop curriculum for these students, I need to consider not only their academic needs but also their social and personal needs, as well. This is where a community service writing curriculum serves the students well.

First of all, a community service writing class is predicated on the notion that our students *are* already knowers and thinkers, capable of responding to a call to serve. Second, a community service writing curriculum challenges our students beyond paragraph- and sentence-level exercises and gives them opportunities to be makers of meaning and agents for change. Such a curriculum provides more "nourishing food for thought" for the students, welcoming them into the academy, acknowledging their diverse voices, and re-creating them as "authorities" in all senses of that word.

Ann Watters and Marjorie Ford, in *Guide for Change,* a text on community service writing, suggest that "service-learning experiences provide unique learning opportunities for student writers to learn about our increasingly varied and changing world, to develop resourcefulness, a stronger inner self, [and] a clearer sense of personal identity" (1995: xi). These are powerful experiences for any student, but they are essential ones for the basic writer. Community service writing and service-learning experiences are powerful pedagogies for developing writers because they challenge students to "think clearly and creatively in unanticipated situations" (xii). Such classes provide what Paulo Freire calls the means for authentic thought (1970: 71) This curriculum addresses the skill needs of the developmental writer, skills that are essential to clear communication, within the context of writing assignments focused on a real audience, written with a clear purpose, requiring interaction with a text — the stated objectives of our basic writing skills course. Such a curriculum, I believe, when carefully scaffolded, can build bridges between the students' community and the academy, transcending boundaries between basic writing and writing for change, creating writers, knowers, and thinkers who become agents for change within themselves and change out in their communities.

In the community service learning class I taught at Foothill College, in California, students were asked to explore an ever-expanding circle of responsibility relationships — the family and community, self and community, society and community, and ending with a rather philosophical discussion centered around the systems thinking elaborated on in the movie *Mindwalk*. Each ripple in the ring of relationships became the focus of the class reading and discussion, and then the source of an essay. Each essay carried the students further along on their journey of self-discovery and persuaded them that, as Freire suggests, "to exist, humanly is to name the world, to change it" (1970: 76). Each leg in that journey convinced them of their power to effect change. As one student suggested, "I learned about the power of one; that one is me!"

Although some teachers have questioned the wisdom of involving basic writers in community service writing, arguing that writing for the public requires a strong grasp of grammar fundamentals and unified and coherent prose, I would argue that basic writers especially need to recognize the immediate connections with readers, the purposeful intent, the clear communication of ideas that service writing requires. But beyond the actual written act itself, I would argue that community service writing prompts basic writers to think of how they are "connected" to their world and creates opportunities for students to operationalize those connections. Whether they are writing *for* an agency or nonprofit, as is usually the case in most community service writing courses, or they are writing *about* the community service they have observed or performed, as is the case in my class, these students are engaged in analysis and expression that engages and challenges them in their real world. These effects may seem theoretical, until we review the students' own reflections in response to the assignments.

The students begin the basic writing class with an incredible diversity of perceptions about themselves, their communities, and their writing. If they have any thoughts on community service at all, these are usually grounded in their experiences with high school community service requirements or, for many of the older students, in their experiences as the recipients of service. They recall the former with a sort of resigned resentment, at best; the latter with cynicism or exasperation at the "do-gooder" mentality that sometimes characterized the interaction. Ironically, the very demographics of my basic writing classes create a subtle confrontation between those who have done service and those who have experienced it. Their ages, income levels, years of work experience, and ethnicities are literally all over the map.

Our early discussions must therefore locate community service writing in the abstract, focusing on the nature of community, service, and writing as concepts before we can explore specific service learning experiences.

We begin by talking about our "villages," those communities to which we belong by choice and whose rituals and experiences we share. These discussions are especially illuminating because basic writers often feel marginalized from many of the communities that society values. We must necessarily, then, create the opportunity for basic writers to consider and explore the notion of community as a first step to creating lives within the boundaries.

Writing in response to the first essay prompt, which asked her to observe the interplay of family and community and also to come to a personal definition of a strong community, Jesille Kuizon, a very quiet student, wrote movingly about her observations of her friend Clarissa's neighborhood. (Some students named in this text are composites and/or named by pseudonym at their request.) Someone knocks on the door to borrow some tortillas and beans. The neighbor down the street is pulling weeds for an elderly shut-in next door. A boy in the next apartment is getting car repair pointers from the man in the apartment above. Jesille notes that the little "services each of them render surely affect the behavior of the community." She concludes:

> *To me Clarissa's community was that one small candle that could light up others. The neighborhood did not have much to offer but the greatest gift of all was the helping hand they gave to one another. The love and kindness that the neighborhood shared inspired me to reach out to others. . . . It made me strong as a person because I realized that I should not be scared of people different than I. I should be grateful to know that these people are here so I can help them and in return they help me. . . . These activities made me realize that my good behavior does affect others and my setting an example I made them stronger. . . . To me it does not matter if you are the volunteer or you're the reason why the volunteer is there. All that matters is that you have made a difference in someone's life or that someone has made a difference in your life. Good behavior does really strengthen communities. The services we all render creates this behavior. As we strengthen the community, in the process we strengthen each other.*

What Jesille and the other basic writers found while writing on community was that they could observe a phenomenon they took for granted, apply some analytical tools to the observation, identify the underlying assumptions that shaped the event, process the implications of those assumptions and behaviors, draw some conclusions, and then write all this up in a coherent text. Quite a piece of work for students who are usually held to writing paragraphs of classification and description! Such writing, by its very process, engaged the students in a dialogue with others, creating a sense of ownership and power. Jesille began to see her own place in a system she herself had identified, described, and analyzed. She was able to see that the day-to-day courtesies she observed in Clarissa's neighborhood created a reciprocal tie among the neighbors. This symbiotic relationship at once created a sense of belonging to a community, as well as the responsibility to respond to its needs.

After the students personalize their definition of community, they consider the notion of service. Basic writers, some by the very complexity of their lives, are often stuck in a cycle of powerlessness that shapes the students' thinking about what they can do and what they can be. For many, the mere notion of service is laughable, a luxury of time, opportunity, circumstance, and skill. For others, the idea of service brings uncomfortable memories of their being the recipient of service or charity, thus rekindling feelings of isolation and insecurity. In my basic writing class, I have found it best to suggest service-learning as an option for those whose lives and circumstances allow them to participate, and I encourage them to consider working at one-time events or job-sharing service opportunities, which means that at least half of the class is engaged at one time or another in service-learning. Regardless of whether a student is actively involved in the actual performance of service, or is observing and reflecting on the idea of service, I find that the students in the class profit from the thinking they do about service. What they find, both about their place in their communities and about themselves, is a redefinition of the nature of what service is and a reconceptualization of their roles in the world. For example, Carol Arthurs, one of my older reentry students who was resistant to adding a "service commitment" to her busy school-work-family calendar, later became one of my most articulate writers on the nature of service. She writes:

> *When I look at myself and ask what I do, in a voluntary manner, that contributes to the community, my first thought is that I do nothing. I do not got to soup kitchens to feed the poor nor bring in a homeless person when the cold weather hits, nor go into a poor inner city school to help teach. And I would not do any of these things, because, like Rhonda [her focus for the interview assignment], I am not disposed to these forms of service. Then I realized that if I took away the stereotyped vision of the noble self-sacrificing volunteer as the only kind of person who serves the community that I do indeed give to others but in my own way. I am a blood donor and I am registered as a bone marrow donor and I do this because I can save a life with very little trouble to myself. Not a very self-sacrificing motive but I am sure the person receiving the donation does not think less of the gift because of my lack of altruistic behavior.*

She goes on to list the other kinds of "service-like" contributions she makes

— to the Goodwill, to the recycling dump, to certain charities — and she wonders if all these things "count" because she is actually doing them for herself — to spring-clean, to save the environment, to assuage her conscience. Carol asks:

> *So are duty and responsibility the only correct motives for volunteer work? Does the motivation have to be noble to make the service worthwhile? I say no to both questions and I think Rhonda and her work as a member of CARDA (a dog search and rescue team) proves it. And if you were indeed buried alive after an earthquake . . . I do not think you would find her work less valued because it is the byproduct of her hobby.*

Although some might argue that such conscious behavior with such a self-serving goal is not the characteristic nor approved model of community service, Carol might respond that her wrestling with the notion of service is a positive first step toward living a productive and focused life. Through her writing about community service, Carol discovered a sense of new-found satisfaction in her place in her community, as well as a new sense of herself as a contributor and an agent for change. She learned that she can redefine herself, that she can be more than a "remedial" student who needs help; she can be a helper and a doer.

Laura, another student in my class and a single mother of a two-year-old, would agree. She is angered by society's assumption that she is a drain on community resources rather than a contributor to them. She resents the automatic corollary that equates single-mother/teen college student with welfare mom/flake. She has argued that community service gives her a chance to transcend the stereotypes her circumstances seem to conjure up and allows her to re-vision her public self as productive member of society, thus reinforcing her private sense of self-worth. In her "community" essay, she wrote about the community of single mothers, and her analysis of the issues facing these women helped her understand her own situation and redefine her goals. One of her classmates, Forrest Mock, was so moved by her articulation of these issues and reminded of his sister's situation that he chose to research the topic of subsidized day care for his problem-definition assignment. He summarized studies on child development and the effect of educational day care on preschool children. He concludes:

> *As we see, preschool plays an important role in an individual's development, but it is not always readily available for everyone. Preschool is very expensive. Many middle class and poverty-stricken families cannot afford pre-school or daycare. For example, my sister Shirlee was paying $250.00 per month for sixteen days of daycare. Little Forrest [her son] was not learning physical or cognitive skills at this daycare, but was being placed in a home without a structured learning environment. Instead of coming*

home and showing Uncle Forrest his Dental Care Bear Hygiene Techniques, he was biting and spitting at me as if this was normal. Although he was being cared for, the financial burden was tremendous. My sister and her husband would have to call in sick three or four times a month to cover the days they couldn't afford.

Forrest continues with a description of existing subsidized day care programs and the process for applying for them. He ends with an appeal:

Our government should re-think its values and pay our teachers what they are worth while making [preschool] education an obtainable reality for all people. . . . [A]n early educational background beginning at age two, as we would say "getting your foot in the door," could help a child begin a prosperous and more fulfilling life.

Forrest's essay on subsidized day care, sparked by Laura's concerns and shared in the class, became the catalyst for a grass-roots directory of subsidized day care centers to be written by the students. Clearly, these basic writers saw community service writing as intrinsically useful and they created a writing experience that met their needs. In this class, in this and many other instances, community service writing gave these students the opportunity to shape their community, define their service, and focus their writing on their own experiences. They defined community service by the questions Sonya Siyan, one of their classmates, asked:

Where does it all start? Everything starts from the bottom level to the top just like a new building starting up from the basement and up to the top floor. Here, in the society, the bottom level is the individual. He has the potential to influence the community and make a change. Self-confidence and self-belief are the major aspects of doing so. As long as an individual believes in himself and is determined to do something. There is nothing impossible.

For basic writing students, many of whom circumscribe all of their worlds with a boundary of the "impossible," such thinking is revolutionary. For other basic writing students, some of whom default to complaints of "bad breaks" or "lost chances," such thinking is empowering. David Kolb, author of *Experiential Learning: Experience as the Source of Learning and Development*, suggests that "the dawn of integrity comes with the acceptance of responsibility for one's own life. For in taking the responsibility for the world, we are given back the power to change it" (1984: 230). Community service writing seems to give basic writing students a curriculum of change, responsibility, and power.

Whatever the impact of community service learning on the students themselves, I, as basic skills teacher, must necessarily consider its effect on their writing. What have I found? In my two years of teaching community service writing, I have noted that my basic writing students are writing far more complex, thoughtful papers than before. The papers contain a rich mix of sources — student observations, recalled experiences, interviews, texts — and a wide range of interesting and locally focused topics. I have read papers on gang intervention, search and rescue dogs, gay and lesbian youth groups, wetlands preservation, domestic violence, subsidized day care, youth ministry, care for the elderly, after-school activities, spiritual isolation, and arranged marriages. Each of these papers resulted from a student's identification of a local problem, an investigation of existing resources, and a suggestion of other possible volunteer solutions. Each of the papers was written with passion and authority, in the student's voice of authentic concern. Each of the papers sparks with the vitality of a human engagement in a human issue. Consider Aaron's introduction to his paper on gangs:

> *It's 7:30 AM, had my breakfast, got my hat, got my books, got my gun. Okay I'm ready for school. In our communities we face problems everyday from every direction. It might be health issues such as AIDS, high school dropouts, homelessness, domestic violence, unaffordable housing, drugs, teenage pregnancy, suburban crimes. The problems appear never ending. Today gangs are a principal problem in many communities. . . . Out of all the issues that our communities face I feel very strongly about the growth of gangs and how it impacts all of us. This issue is on the move to take our communities into a destructive environment. I feel that my community is already trapped, similar to being in a dark alley. So how do we reverse this direction? How do we educated our youth about the trappings of gang life? What do we need to do to prevent our communities from this territorial gang obsession? . . . We must adopt programs which will provide a wide range of structured activities and classroom instruction for all kids who are at risk. Programs such as the Boys Club and the Girls Club whose philosophy is to help youth become more responsible members of their communities are not widely available. To reduce gang involvement, we need to increase these types of programs and that requires commitment from local government, education, businesses, churches and above all families.*

Aaron's essay outlines the underlying causes of gang obsession and describes a clear, realistic program of interventions that might alleviate the problem. Aaron's passion for this topic is apparent in the questions he asks, and it reflects his recent experiences wrestling with his own gang membership and the consequences of his actions. His writing is strong because it is grounded in the real. His writing is competent because he cares deeply about the topic and he recognizes that in the act of writing his essay he is discovering both the implications of his actions in the past and the possibilities for change making in his future.

Whatever the pedagogical impact of community service on the writing of the students in my classes, I am convinced that it is the personal impact that most profoundly changes them. When one considers that basic writers come to the academy via, as Mike Rose suggests, an almost medical triage of placement tests, after years of intervention, diagnosis, and prescription, it is no wonder that basic writers come to my classes feeling weak in more than English skills (1989: 210). Through their experiences in service-learning, or their conversations with volunteers, or their observations of effective advocacy groups, these students grow to appreciate their fundamental role in the system and the nature of their authority. They begin to understand the symbiotic nature of service and its capacity to give power to those who serve. A Samoan proverb says, "The road to authority is through service." Isn't true "author-ity" — that sense of potency as a writer who not only has something important to say but also has the skills to say it well — what we want our basic writers to realize? Perhaps, then, the road to authority for basic writers is through community service writing. Perhaps, it is through this lens that basic writers can become makers of meaning and agents for change, viewing their communities from a proactive vantage point. Ultimately though, in a truly symbiotic relationship, it is basic writers who most potently transform community service writing. Through their insights and their experiences, service writing becomes not a product of the basic writing class but a process of discovery, a journey of the heart, a road to authority, a mindwalk of their own.

References

Capra, B. (director), and F. Byars and F. Capra (screenwriters). (1990). *Mindwalk: A Film for Passionate Thinkers*. Paramount.

Freire, P. (1970). *Pedagogy of the Oppressed*. New York: The Seabury Press.

Kolb, D.A. (1984). *Experiential Learning: Experience as the Source of Learning and Development*. Englewood Cliffs, NJ: Prentice Hall.

Rose, M. (1989). *Lives on the Boundary: A Moving Account of the Struggles and Achievements of America's Educationally Underprepared*. New York: Penguin Books.

Watters, A., and M. Ford. (1995). *Guide for Change: Resources for Implementing Community Service Writing*. San Francisco: McGraw-Hill.

Combining the Classroom and the Community: Service-Learning in Composition at Arizona State University

by Gay W. Brack and Leanna R. Hall

The Service Learning Project at Arizona State University (ASU) was developed in 1993 to help solve two problems that, at a first reading, seem to have little in common: ASU's Department of English and its Writing Across the Curriculum program were attempting to overcome the "empty assignment syndrome" common to many composition departments across the country. At the same time, the university was committed to assisting a local school district find a way to help an overabundance of children whose environments put them at risk of academic failure. Following is a description of these university and community problems and an overview of the partnership that is enabling us to find joint solutions.

The University: Coping With the Empty Assignment Syndrome

One of the major problems confronting teachers in English composition courses is students' lack of engagement with the material.[1] Too often the "research" done in such courses is seen by students as an empty exercise, a means of learning how to use the library or how to use correct citation, not as an avenue for changing someone's mind or making a difference in the world. A service-learning[2] focus for selected ASU composition classes allows students to combine academic and service experiences as they address the specific concerns of at-risk[3] children and youth in a culturally diverse environment. Educators such as Richard Morrill view this structured integration of service and academics as necessary for the complete education of our students, arguing that, in addition to the information acquired in the classroom, learning to be a "literate citizen" also includes developing a sense of personal responsibility and commitment to a set of social and ethical values. Such values and the sense of responsibility necessary to turn them into constructive action are instilled through structured participation in service to the community (Stanton 1990).[4]

Describing the positive effect of service on learning, University of Washington professor Edward E. Carlson states, "Community service experiences are a nearly inexhaustible resource for innovative teaching and active learning. By placing students at the intersection of people and ideas, service-learning pedagogies illuminate their prejudices, challenge their assumptions, and help them understand the connection between broad political, social, and economic forces and the life situation of real people" (n.d.). It is their work at this intersection that has impelled ASU composition students to research real problems, struggle to find solutions, and to articulate the challenges they face and the solutions they find in the papers they write. The academic impact of this project on students is largely a function of its basis in experiential learning. Students in first- and second-year composition classes are able to learn firsthand about the meaning of social responsibility, while students in a third-year composition class are given an opportunity to apply principles and theories from their own fields in the real world.

The Community: Academic Assistance for At-Risk Children

Many children who attend school in the Roosevelt School District (RSD) score below the 30th percentile on national standardized tests, putting them, in most cases, more than a year behind their peers nationally. All 18 schools and more than 86 percent of the more than 11,000 children and youth in the RSD are considered at risk of academic failure.

The principal reason for the children's lack of appropriate academic development is an environment that puts them at great risk of failure. The area is characterized by a high incidence of poverty and crime. The South Mountain precinct of the Phoenix Police Department, which includes the RSD, reports the highest incidence of drive-by shootings and the highest homicide rate in the state of Arizona. The district averages a 16 percent drop-out rate (approximately 1,700 students) and a 19 percent rate for juvenile detention referrals (approximately 2,200 students). Without significant one-on-one help, it is virtually impossible for many of the children and youth in the RSD to achieve grade-level performance.

Recognizing the need for early intervention to promote academic success, in 1992 the Salvation Army Youth and Family Center, located in the RSD, began informal after-school tutoring. Many of the children with whom staff members worked had fallen behind in classes or had been held back because they had only minimal reading skills. In addition, the preschool children in the center's day-care program needed assistance to become learning-ready, while a growing number of high school dropouts who wanted better jobs and/or higher education needed help with reading development to prepare for the GED examination. While the center was eager to assist these groups in reaching their academic goals, it lacked the human resources necessary to accomplish the task. Most of the students who requested tutoring actually needed in-depth subject-matter and reading help rather than basic homework assistance. For example, many math failures occur because students cannot read word problems. Students cannot successfully answer multiple-choice science questions because they cannot read the chapters that provide the information. The center's staff members, already stretched thin, were not able to provide the support required for an effective and sustainable tutoring program. In order to provide students with the supplemental education that would allow them to succeed, the center recognized the need to develop a formal program of tutoring and learning readiness with emphasis on reading development.

The Partnership: Developing Academic Success for At-Risk Children and ASU Students

In 1993, representatives from ASU, the center, and the RSD worked together to develop a plan that would deal with both the community's and the university's educational concerns. This collaboration led to the Supplemental Education Partnership, which has now grown to include three school districts and five agencies. The chief component of the Partnership is a cadre of ASU students in composition classes linked to service internships whose focus allows them to combine academic and service experiences as they address specific concerns identified by the community. Each agency/school district acts as a funding partner and funds the graduate interns who supervise and mentor the undergraduate interns. Each school district provides support services and training for the project. The mission of the Partnership is (1) to motivate and assist at-risk children from kindergarten through high school age to develop the academic skills and the self-esteem that will allow them to succeed in school, and (2) to assist university students to enhance their academic skills and to develop lifelong civic commitment.

Internship Design Overview

Service-learning sections of regular composition courses are linked to internships that carry three hours of upper-division elective credit. First-, second-, and third-year composition courses provide structured academic components for ASU students who contribute one-on-one homework tutoring, reading development, educational enrichment workshops, and learning-readiness programs for children and youth from the RSD. Each ASU student works with two children/youth for eight hours each week throughout the semester. These children range in age from 3 to 14. Students prepare a customized lesson and activities plan for every tutoring session for each child. When our students begin work with new children, they engage in a three-step process designed to ensure that the children have successful learning experiences. The steps are (1) building trust, (2) developing the child's self-confidence, and (3) opening the learning process. This is a challenging task — most of the children with whom we work are far below grade level. It is a common occurrence to find fourth, sixth, even eighth graders who do not have even the most rudimentary reading skills and have, at best, a hazy idea of how to do the most basic of math problems. The degree of progress the children exhibit is astonishing — and a tribute to our students, who spend a great deal of time in researching the best way to solve specific learning problems faced by their children.

Supervision

All undergraduate student intern activities are supervised, monitored, and assessed by graduate student interns. This aspect of the program is critical; without such supervision, the program could not function effectively. While the undergraduate interns are unpaid, the graduate students each receive a small stipend of $1,000 per semester, paid by the agency where the supervisory activities are carried out. In addition, most graduate interns receive tuition waivers from the ASU Graduate College.

Recruiting

Undergraduates. Students self-select for service-learning projects. Our experience indicates that students who are committed to the ideals of service to the community tend to enroll in these courses, courses whose nature is more challenging than are many classroom-only experiences.

We use an open recruiting strategy for service-learning composition classes. Recruiting visits take place in appropriate classrooms — English 101 and University 100 classes for English 102, for example. For Writing for the Professions, an upper-division composition class, our emphasis is on recruiting students who can benefit from field experience in their major areas of study while providing benefit to the community. Recruiting for this course focuses on classroom visits in discipline-specific courses. Our purpose is to recruit students majoring in areas meeting the predetermined needs of the community's youth population. For example, because the community has identified health screening and nutrition clinics as needs, we recruit in nursing, speech and hearing, and nutrition classes; because all the partners in the project need program assessment, we recruit students in the College of Business. Other target majors include (but are not limited to) bilingual, early childhood, elementary, and secondary education; exercise science; and recreation management.

Additional recruiting takes place through contacts with advising centers across campus, presentations to clubs and other university organizations, as well as through informational meetings with incoming and continuing students.

Graduate students. Our graduate mentor/supervisors are selected from specific disciplines. While not all graduate programs provide credit-bearing internships, we have ongoing recruiting activities in several programs relevant to our mission. We regularly recruit graduate students from bilingual education, early childhood education, reading development, media computer-based instruction, English education, and social work. We also recruit in the College of Public Programs and in the American Humanics Program.

Intern Training

Undergraduate formal training. Initial tutor training consists of a series of two-hour workshops provided by the RSD and ASU. The workshops begin two weeks before ASU students meet the children they will tutor and continue for six weeks thereafter. RSD training focuses on strategies of tutoring for reading development. ASU training workshops, provided by the College of Education and the Division of Undergraduate Academic Services (DUAS), consist of the following:

- planning effective lessons and activities;
- motivating children to learn;
- using the "joint inquiry" tutoring method[5];
- dealing with discipline issues; and
- presenting effective workshops (for Writing for the Professions students).

Undergraduate informal training. While it is important to provide continuing formalized instruction, it is also critical to ensure that students learn how to deal with tutoring issues that surface between workshops. In order to meet this need, 30-minute post-tutoring meetings are held daily at each site to train and debrief. Because all students tutor three times a week, they continually receive informal training and current information. The graduate interns are responsible for this ongoing training.

Graduate intern training. Graduate intern training is provided by the College of Education and DUAS, where the project is housed. Graduate intern supervision is provided by DUAS-trained site managers.

Reflection

One important tool used to promote reflection and communication is Electronic Forum, an asynchronous communication network developed at Glendale Community College. Students from each tutoring site share a dedicated forum where they share mutual concerns, discuss practical matters, and work on issues related to discipline, motivation, and self-esteem. In addition, they grapple with larger social and educational issues, such as gang intervention, preschool funding, and the roles of educators today. The Forum is monitored regularly by composition instructors, graduate interns, and project administrators, who pose questions and join in brainstorming to resolve issues. While they are required to write the equivalent of a one-page essay for each entry, students quickly begin writing longer entries than required.

Assessment

Assessment of the Service Learning Project is an ongoing process conducted in part by assessment teams of undergraduate and graduate interns, along with project administrators. These teams focus on four key areas of assessment: (1) the progress of the children being tutored, (2) the progress and effectiveness of the ASU undergraduate and graduate interns on site, (3) undergraduate students' development as writers, and (4) the effectiveness of the program overall.

To assess these areas, the project has developed portfolio systems to track the progress of the children and of the ASU interns. These systems involve compiling a database on the children and the interns by using a variety of methods. For each child in the after-school program, for example, files created contain progress reports from every tutoring session, texts produced by the child, questionnaires, observation reports, and other relevant documents. These portfolios are reviewed weekly to evaluate the effectiveness of the tutoring methods and procedures, and to make any necessary adjustments. Similar systems have been developed for the assessment of the preschool children and of the ASU interns, except that the databases are slightly different; ASU students are assessed on the quality of their activity planners, tutoring, progress reports, and Electronic Forum entries.[6]

While tutoring and mentoring the children is our primary mission, we realize that the commitment of parents to the program is vital to its success. Tutors and children fill out progress reports together after every session. These reports are kept on file at the tutoring site so that interested parents can examine them whenever they wish. In addition, parents complete pre- and post-semester questionnaires related to their children's progress and the effectiveness of the program.

Composition Results

We believe that linking service-learning with composition is achieving both the pedagogical goal of overcoming the empty assignment syndrome and the university goal of assisting children whose environments put them at risk. In the Service Learning English 102 class, for example, students engage in seven writing assignments, five of which are based on shared readings related to effective reading and tutoring strategies, building relationships with at-risk children, and enhancing self-esteem through education. Students begin by summarizing readings on effective strategies, then critiquing an argument on self-esteem issues. These assignments lead to two synthesis assignments based on multiple sources. The first synthesis incorporates summary assignment readings, new readings, and students' tutoring experiences in an informative paper designed to advise future tutors about effective tutoring strategies. The second requires students to draw on primary and secondary research to develop arguments on the role of schools in developing children's self-esteem. Our students are especially interested in this topic; their deep concern over the low self-esteem of many of the children they work with informs Electronic Forum entries throughout the semester.

Along with the five shared-topic assignments, students conduct semester-long research on topics relevant to their specific tutoring situations, such as working with children who suffer from attention deficit disorder or fetal alcohol syndrome, raising self-esteem among children with an incarcerated parent, or motivating children to value reading.

The research papers especially encourage students to consider their experience as it relates to their research and to demonstrate effective analysis and synthesis of both. Such synthesis is evident, for example, in Kate Davis's informative research paper on tutoring children with fetal alcohol syndrome, a topic that grew out of her experience with Alisha, her tutee. She begins this paper, specifically, with how she strives to help Alisha:

> *Monday and Friday from 11:30-2:30 I tutor a precious little girl named Alisha at the Salvation Army. This amazing child always gives me a new challenge or surprise. Minute after minute and hour after hour I struggle to teach this little girl everything I can. There comes a period in the day in which I become emotionally and physically exhausted, yet I continue to feed her information that will hopefully make her life a little easier. Alisha is not only a precious little girl, she is also a child who struggles with an awful disease termed as Fetal Alcohol Syndrome (FAS).*

As Kate presents secondary research on the different characteristics of FAS children, she continually refers back to her experience with Alisha:

> *Alisha is a four-year old . . . who like many other children with Fetal Alcohol Syndrome has a difficult time paying attention. Compared to other children around her she is developmentally delayed. . . . She struggles with questions I ask her and rarely can sit through an entire lesson. It is very typical for Alisha to become overly stimulated. Everything in the room distracts her . . . including other people in the room, music, voices, and myself. The best way to teach her is to remain in a quiet, calm, and orderly room.*

Many ideas that she covers in the papers were originally discussed on the Forum. Most of Kate's Electronic Forum entries, in fact, focus on the difficulties and successes she encountered with Alisha, outcomes that were apparent from her first entry about the preschoolers. Kate also stressed how her research on FAS informed her tutoring, noting on the Forum, "My child is doing good, my report is really helping to familiarize [me with] everything that that little girl is going through."

Another example demonstrates how much another student, Cindy, learned from her research on identifying and reporting child abuse. This topic came out of her personal experience with William, as she describes in the introduction of her informative research report:

> *So there I was, enjoying my second week of tutoring. The graduate student heading the service-learning program at my school had made an executive decision to switch my fifth-grade student with another tutor's first grader, putting two first graders together with me. William was my new student. He had erupted into tears every day of tutoring so far, so I knew the challenge that lay ahead of me, or I thought I knew. It was on the first day of working with William that he made me aware of the bruise on his forehead. I just assumed it was a playground accident, for I had experienced many when I was a child. It was not until I spoke to his teachers that I began to feel uneasy about my experiences with him. . . . I decided that I needed to report his continuous behavior to a school official. My graduate students went along with me to the office. This is where I was awkwardly asked questions about what I thought to be a private matter, in front of anyone who was strolling in or out of the office at that time. The school secretary wrote down what I had to say and sent me on my way. I did not feel as if the school was taking appropriate actions to protect William from whatever awaited him at home. Therefore, I began my own research. I found that child abuse is a serous issue today that needs to be acknowledged. I discovered that there exist warning signs to look for in children, and that I, as a tutor and caretaker, am obligated to report any suspicion of child abuse I may have.*

While Cindy never brainstormed on Electronic Forum about her concerns, for reasons of confidentiality, she worked collaboratively with teachers, administrators, and case workers to help find solutions for William's situation. This experience helped her greatly, and she was pleased at the end of the semester to feel that she had produced a text that could benefit others in similar situations. As she stated in an interview, "The argument will probably be useful to other people, I hope, if somebody is ever in those circumstances I was in, with the whole child abuse thing. . . . If they read my paper, I think they would be informed enough to make the appropriate decision, whereas I wasn't."

Service-Learning Composition Benefits

While the benefits to the children with whom we work are obvious, our project would not be successful unless it were equally beneficial to the ASU students who participate in it. The following are what we see as the major academic and social benefits to our students.

The major impact on our students should be — and is — improvement in their writing and research skills. Composition instructors are finding that service-learning students are more motivated to write because they are writing with a purpose; students are dealing with issues of literacy, social justice, and other topics related to their community experiences. Students uncover, both through research and observation, community problems and develop solutions to those problems. Teachers are discovering that students not only engage in more research activities but eagerly share this research with classmates. Instead of the usual "invention heuristics," students keep electronic journals in which they discuss real and immediate issues. Students' research papers are ultimately derived from this shared discourse.

In the context of this project, students begin developing their research papers from the moment they start their tutoring. And the final audiences for their papers are members of the community, future tutors, and the project's administrators, not just their instructors. Students are charged to link their experiences with the research they have done, to make recommendations, for example, to future tutors about coping with specific social and health problems that lead to learning difficulties: parental imprisonment, child abuse, fetal alcohol syndrome, and attention deficit disorder. They are also encouraged to recommend ways in which the project can be improved. While writing in such a real-world context will not guarantee more engaged writing from every student, such a context is for many students a necessary condition for engagement.

Cultural Diversity

A primary social benefit to our students is the opportunity to interact with culturally diverse populations. The RSD has a highly multicultural student population: 68 percent are Hispanic and 24 percent are African-American. The remaining 8 percent of the district is Anglo, Native American, and Asian. The student population at Desert Eagle School, on the Salt River Pima-Maricopa Indian Community, where composition students will begin tutoring in Spring 1997, is 100 percent Native American.

By combining the composition classroom and the community, the Supplemental Education Partnership is creating an environment that enhances the learning of the community's most in-need children, while providing ASU students with genuine and meaningful writing experiences.

Notes

1. See, for example, Joseph Petraglia, "Spinning Like a Kite: A Closer Look at the Pseudotransactional Function of Writing," *Journal of Advanced Composition* 16(Winter 1995): 19-33; Nora Bacon, "Community Service and Writing Instruction," *National Society for Experiential Education Quarterly* 19(Spring 1994): 14, 27; Sharon Crowley, "A Personal Essay on Freshman English," *Pre/Text* 12(1991): 156-176; James Britton et al., *The Development of Writing Abilities (11-18)* (London: Macmillan Education, 1975).

2. The Service Learning Project at ASU has developed a model of service-learning that is closely aligned with the Campus Compact concept. We define service-learning as a method by which students learn and develop through active participation in thoughtfully organized academically based service that is conducted in and meets the needs of a community and is coordinated with community agencies; helps foster civic responsibility; is integrated into and enhances the academic curriculum of the students; and includes structured time for the students to reflect in writing on the service experience. (Adapted from the Campus Compact service-learning definition.)

3. Factors that the Arizona State Department of Education uses to assess an at-risk environment include: *poverty* (calculated by enrollment in the Free and Reduced Lunch program); *mobility* (the average RSD child moves a minimum of five times during each academic year); *lack of English-language proficiency*; *low achievement on standardized tests*; *absenteeism*.

4. In *An Aristocracy of Everyone: The Politics of Education and the Future of America* (New York: Oxford University Press, 1992), Benjamin Barber argues that more than having a civic mission, "the university *is* a civic mission" (260).

5. Joint inquiry is a method that makes the child more accountable for his/her learning. ASU tutors help the children with whom they work learn how to find answers and resolve problems for themselves, rather than telling them how to do tasks.

6. On a scale of 100 points, attendance at the tutoring site=25%; quality of tutoring=30%; Electronic Forum entries=25%; commitment/overall performance=20% (performance includes positive attitude and concern for children's performance, cooperative team-building skills, leadership, courtesy and respect toward site personnel).

References

Carlson, E.E. (n.d.) "Leadership & Public Service Office." Seattle: University of Washington. Brochure.

Stanton, T.K. (1990). "Liberal Arts, Experiential Learning, and Public Service: Necessary Ingredients for Socially Responsible Undergraduate Education." In *Combining Service and Learning: A Resource Book for Community and Public Service*, edited by J.C. Kendall and Associates. Raleigh, NC: National Society for Internships and Experiential Education.

The Write for Your Life Project:
Learning to Serve by Serving to Learn

by Patricia Lambert Stock and Janet Swenson

> *Students must be enabled at whatever stages they find themselves to be, to encounter curriculum as possibility. By that I mean curriculum ought to provide a sense of occasions for individuals to articulate the themes of their existence and to reflect on these themes until they know themselves to be in the world and can name what has been up to then obscure.*
>
> — Maxine Greene

Charged to provide writing workshop support to students and assistance to faculty interested in integrating writing instruction into their courses, the Writing Center in Michigan State University (MSU) has conceived its task broadly, in keeping with the mission of a research-intensive land-grant university. Mindful that literacy is learned through use across contexts and over a lifetime, in addition to working to improve the quality of literacy in MSU, to developing new knowledge, and to serving the public good, the center has reached out to involve itself in the teaching and uses of literacy in both the communities and schools from which MSU students come and the communities and workplaces that students enter when they leave the university.

In one of these outreach projects — the Write for Your Life Project (WFYL)[1] — we are collaborating with students and teachers in California, Georgia, Massachusetts, Maryland, Michigan, Minnesota, New York, Oklahoma, Pennsylvania, Texas, Virginia, and Wisconsin to develop a literacy curriculum that invites students to learn to read and write by reading and writing about issues of concern to them. This effort — which invites students to use their literacy to turn their preoccupations outside school into the occupation of their studies in school — is developing within a constellation of interrelated and overlapping peer consultancies in the Writing Center that we call Project CONNECTS (COnsultative Network of New and Experienced Collaborating Teachers and Students).[2]

In Project CONNECTS, we are making productive use of the synergies that exist when individuals with different but related goals teach and learn from one another for their mutual benefit. With a combination of collaborative learning, peer tutoring, and service-learning practices that we call *consultative teaching,* we hope not only to expand the academy's definition of research by conceiving our teaching as scholarship (Boyer 1990) and to enrich the academy's understanding of service by refusing to separate it out from other academic work (Coles 1993) but also to contribute usefully to three perplexing social problems: the crisis in teaching in the post-modern academy, the crisis in public education, and the redefinition of citizenship in a society that is thinking globally as it acts locally.

Developing within this program of activities in the MSU Writing Center, the Write for Your Life Project is also taking shape alongside work, such as that of Deborah Protherow-Stith, dean of the Harvard University School of Public Health, that is designed to enable young people to better understand the root causes of the social problems that affect their lives and to protect themselves from these threats. One of the best and best-known educational programs available to students and teachers interested in studying the threatening challenges that face young adults in our society, the curriculum Protherow-Stith has developed begins when students brainstorm lists of threats to their well-being, often in customarily coined formulations; proceeds as they study those issues; and is realized when students develop strategies for avoiding those threats (Protherow-Stith 1991).

The dialogic curriculum advanced in the Write for Your Life Project begins differently, not with the general and the abstract but with the local and the particular. Moved by our observation that students learn more easily and better when they undertake a new study in terms of the images and experiences they bring to it from their home communities (Stock 1995), the Write for Your Life curriculum begins with the personal narratives that students compose in the English classrooms in which they typically study imaginative literature.

After they have written their way into a topic of inquiry, students in the Write for Your Life Project define issues that concern them, not by brainstorming lists of problems others have named for them, but by identifying the themes imbedded in the stories they have composed for one another. When students have "articulate[d] the themes of their existence," their teachers guide students' reflections on those themes in order that they may "know themselves to be in the world and can name what has been up to then obscure" (Greene 1978: 18-19). In this process, students transform their preoccupations into the occupation of their studies. They translate the conditions and circumstances they wish to study — and sometimes to change — into topics of inquiry, subtopics, if you will, of the broader course of study in which they are engaged, a course that might itself be named "American Adolescents: Challenges to Their Health and Well-Being."

After Write for Your Life students have identified subtopics for study, their teachers introduce them to both imaginative and nonfiction literature, film, mass media, and Internet resources they can use to expand their initial understandings of these topics. For example, when students in several Write for Your Life classes wrote their initial narratives about their own and their peers' uses of alcohol and drugs, about car accidents, and overdoses, about untimely deaths of friends with whom they sat in classes and cafeterias, with whom they played on ball fields, their teachers asked them to read and view a variety of texts that explored the nature and consequences of substance abuse.

Having written personal narratives about an issue, an issue that might have seemed abstract and distant to them had it been labeled "substance abuse" at the outset, students were able to relate the conditions that made for problems in their experience to the body of discourse that now became a subject for study. Approaching their studies from the perspective of their lived experience motivated students not only to read published fiction dealing with the theme that concerned them but also to read media reports, medical reports, and sociological studies that might be considered particularly difficult — even uninteresting — reading material for young adults. Students wanted to compare their own experiences with those of characters in books and individuals in case and interpretative studies of adolescent alcoholism and drug abuse; they wanted to know how their experiences compared with others'.

After composing stories about their concerns, analyzing those stories, and researching the issues imbedded in them, special-interest groups of students in Write for Your Life classrooms (groups interested in substance abuse, teen pregnancy, gang violence) typically become local "experts," capable of informing their peers about their expertise and of documenting their learning in monographs and pamphlets and in collections of interviews, reports, short stories, poems, and essays that present their developing understandings of the issues they are studying. The MSU Writing Center publishes these writings and distributes them in students' home communities and across Write for Your Life classrooms.

At the outset of the project, we defined these student publications to be the social action toward which their work was directed. Based on our work with other students in other settings, we knew that students' publications can draw communities' attention to problems within them that need to be addressed, we knew that in this way students' writing can accomplish beneficial social work.[3] For example, when her family doctor reproduced a copy of one student's descriptions of her anorexia and placed copies of that description in the waiting room of his office, we recognized this piece of writing not only as evidence of the student's learning and literacy development but also as a service to others who might benefit from her experience and her learning. But as the WFYL Project developed, we found students' individual and collected writings — substantial as they were — failed to satisfy project directors, teachers, and students' expectations for what the end products of the Write for Your Life curriculum should be.

We began to reconceive our expectations when one teacher, Kevin LaPlante, reported in the spring of 1994 that he and his eighth-grade students in the Dewey Center (Detroit, MI) were spending less and less time on their Write for Your Life research projects because he believed his students were becoming despondent as they explored the problems they had identified for study: physical and sexual abuse, AIDS, babies having babies, crime, dropouts, homelessness, poverty, substance abuse, suicide, violence.

We shared Kevin's concerns. His students' work was running counter to the espoused goals of the Write for Your Life Project: to enhance students' literacy in the course of helping them explore ways to live healthier, happier lives. The statistics these eighth-graders were discovering as they conducted their research caused all of us to feel more than a bit depressed. Consider, for example, statistics such as these documented in Joan Kaywell's *Adolescents at Risk: A Guide to Fiction and Nonfiction for Young Adults, Parents, and Professionals* (1993):

- In 1989, 1,849 children were abused in America daily (Edelman 1989); 14 percent of children between the ages of 3 and 17 experience family violence (Craig 1992).
- 25% of the reported cases of AIDS in the United States involved persons under the age of 29, suggesting that most were infected in adolescence (Tonks 1993a).
- AIDS is the sixth-leading cause of death for 15-to-24-year-olds (Tonks 1993b).
- In 1988, the Children's Defense Fund estimated that 488 babies were born every day to girls younger than 18 years of age (Rogers and Hughes Lee 1992).
- Half of all first teen pregnancies occur within the first six months of the young adult's sexual encounter (Kennedy 1987).
- Every day in America, 1,372 teenagers drop out of school (Edelman 1989); high school dropouts between the ages of 18 to 24 earn an average of $6,000 per year, and those dropping out of school now have only one chance in three of finding a full-time job (Hayes 1992).
- The U.S. Department of Education estimates that there are 322,000 homeless school-age children (Crosby 1993).
- Adolescents who begin to smoke or drink during their teens are at particularly high risk for developing drug dependencies (American Academy 1992).
- Gunshot wounds to children ages 16 and under have increased 300 percent in major urban areas since 1986 (American Academy 1992).

Convinced that the work of gathering, reading, and interpreting imaginative literature, statistical data, reports, and case studies dealing with the problems they were researching was leading his students to conclude that the problems were not only inevitable but also insurmountable, Kevin wrote a letter to us in which he said:

> *No matter how much we try to shield them from the cruel realities of this world, most [of our students] will be forced to confront the rotting seams of society head-on. It is up to education to equip them with the skills and wisdom to be able to mend this fabric before it all unravels.*

The day we received Kevin's letter, Janet Swenson proposed what became the solution not only to the concerns that he expressed but to two others, as well: (1) While WFYL students were reading and writing powerful narratives and reading powerful expository/persuasive writing, at this point in the project's development, most were not composing powerful expository arguments, the kind of writing they will be required to compose on local, state, and national writing assessments; and (2) while students were doing extensive research of a variety of kinds, what they were making of that research seemed piecemeal. We were not providing students occasions to synthesize their learning and to present that learning in multiple spoken and written genres.

Janet addressed all three of the stumbling blocks we had identified in our curriculum when she proposed that we ask students to do three things we had not yet asked them to do: to imagine projects they might undertake to "do something" about their concerns, to write grant proposals that would allow them to carry out their imagined projects, and finally to undertake those projects. In response to Janet's proposal, project directors allocated funds to support the work of students who would now shape their developing expertise about troublesome issues into community service projects they believed themselves capable of fulfilling.

Learning to Serve

One Saturday in November 1994, this new development in the Write for Your Life Project saw 200 WFYL students from across the state of Michigan gather with undergraduate, graduate, faculty, and teacher consultants associated with MSU's Writing Center on the Michigan State campus to share and respond to students' narrative writing and to conduct thematic analyses of that writing for the purpose of identifying issues of concern to adolescents. After a morning in which this work was accomplished, the provost of Michigan State University and the dean of the College of Arts and Letters urged Write for Your Life students to use their developing literacy "to make a difference in the lives of those in your communities, in our state, and in our nation."

Following these remarks, students serving on advisory boards of non-profit community foundations in Flint, Lansing, and Saginaw (MI) encouraged Write for Your Life students to work carefully and critically to identify their community's needs regarding the issues that concerned them, and not simply to assume that they knew those needs just because they had conducted general studies of the issues. For example, one 14-year-old student member of a community foundation board asked her audience who among them would vote to provide funding to give teddy bears to young children who had been involved in car accidents. Hands shot up across the room. She asked further how those who raised their hands knew the youngsters would want the teddy bears. Could they offer the children something that children would find more comforting? Did they know whether there was already a community program offering the service? How much did they think it would cost? Were there more critical uses of this money in their communities? Another student board member explained why colleagues on her advisory board were unlikely to fund a poorly written proposal, or one peppered with surface errors, or one that was unprofessional in appearance. The last student speaker charged her audience to make a difference in their communities. She painted a picture of the bleak future that young adults face if they do not learn now the competencies that will allow them to rebuild ailing communities and act to shape a world worth living in through their actions.

Encouraged by a community of teachers, college students, university faculty and administrators, and by student members of community foundation boards — all of whom had modeled the beneficial effects of collaboration, cooperation, and service-oriented citizenship — Write for Your Life students returned to their home classrooms and began work that resulted in grant proposals such as the following ones that were funded in 1995 and 1996: *Reduce, Reuse, and Recycle* (to establish a school recycling program), *Painting a New Attitude* (to paint over gang graffiti on school walls and in a school playground), *A Love of Learning* (to establish a cross-age tutoring program), *Building Our Future* (to establish a quiet study space for children when school is not in session), *Revive Detroit* (to investigate how students might take part in various Detroit Empowerment Zone projects), *Peer Mediation* (to establish peer mediation services in a high school, including a speakers' program, training for students interested in becoming peer mediators, and means of advertising — both within and beyond the high school — the availability of these services), *Reducing Landfill* (to make a video to encourage students to become active in a community recycling program), *Choose Your Own Adventure* (to encourage and enable students to learn statistics about such threats to their well-being as drug and alcohol abuse and sexually transmitted diseases), *Substance Abuse* (to develop and distribute an informational pamphlet about substance abuse in the high school), and *Sports Violence* (to survey coaches and players to learn about the quantity and severity of sports-related violence and to report the results of this survey to a state high school athletic association).

In addition to planning and conducting public service projects such as these, Write for Your Life students are currently also continuing to serve their peers and their communities with individual and collaborative published articles and books that explore the health and well-being of America's youth. While these publication projects allow individual students opportunities to work in genres they find most generative, the grants that students write require them to work collaboratively to compose in genres typically required in school and the workplace. Grant writing in the Write for Your Life Project also allows teachers to function as consultants, as model teachers-as-students who work side-by-side with their own students to inquire, collect, explore, analyze, synthesize, and shape information for genuine audiences and purposes and within clearly specified generic constraints.

Learning to Write

The Write for Your Life request for proposals asks student grant writers to compose the following kinds of writing: an abstract identifying applicants as well as the focus, aims, method, and cost of their proposed project; an introduction explaining why and how the project will be undertaken and expressing a commitment to its fulfillment; a definition and description of the problem in context; a statement of the goals and objectives of the project; an explanation of how students will fulfill, evaluate, and reflect on the project; and a glossed budget.

Excerpts from the writing they composed to fulfill the requirements of their grant proposals illustrate how students' personal investment in projects aimed toward broader purposes enabled both their learning and their ability to serve their communities. For example, consider this introduction that a group of high school students from Belleville (WI) composed to a proposal to reduce homelessness in their community:

> *One in every five homeless persons today is a child. This statistic is so staggering that something must be done to combat the problems. [This class has] committed themselves to aiding the homeless and poverty stricken, particularly children. With the guidance of three adults, and the support of the administration, the 32 students involved will actively take part in trying to make a difference in the community by specifically addressing the issue of homelessness.*

Elaborating on the need for the project, the Belleville students describe how they hope to accomplish it and the benefits they hope to achieve from it:

Although 30-35% of families in Wisconsin cannot afford a two-bedroom apartment (Scientific American, Dec., 91), *few people acknowledge that homelessness is a problem. Educating the public through newspaper articles and photographs will help the community better understand the problems and accept the difficulty in addressing them. As students of Belleville High School, we are prepared to approach this issue and take steps to increase awareness regarding homelessness.*

The problem of homelessness is too great for one group of high school individuals to solve. However, education being a main objective of this project, we will expand our knowledge and pass this information along to others. Educating our youth is the key to solving the problem for the future.

For another example, consider a description of problems in their high school that students in Saginaw (MI) compose to explain why they wish to establish peer mediation services:

The problems we are trying to solve are to cut down on suspensions and referrals. Some of the violence we are encountering are fights, verbal abuse, stealing, vandalism such as locker damage, writing on walls and car damage. We believe the help from Peer Mediation will lower if not stop a lot of the violence happening here at Arthur Hill High School.

Having described a set of problems, these Saginaw students go on to name peer mediation as a potential solution to them and identify how they prepared themselves to establish a peer mediation program:

Our activities commenced with surveys, which were targeted at various audiences. They included Arthur Hill High School students, staff, and the general public from Saginaw's community. Through this activity we concluded that the majority of those surveyed favored peer counseling. After which we immediately focused our attention on the plentiful resources surrounding us. They included attending seminars and teleconferences, hosting a multitude of speakers as well as appearing on a local television program [focused on identification of teen issues].

Explaining their goals for peer mediation in their school, these students also suggest the potential benefit of their work beyond the local level:

The goal of our group is to reduce the number of conflicts at Arthur Hill High School that escalate into violence. We believe that Peer Mediation will reduce the number of frequent referrals to the office for peer conflicts. We also believe that peer mediation will reduce the number of students being suspended from school. Our research indicates that currently peer mediation is being used in over 5000 public and private schools across the United States. . . .

The publishing group [described in the proposal] will take all of our information, all of our surveys and pull it together to form a manual for other schools and local organizations trying to accomplish the same goals [that we are]. This is a worthwhile manual because it will help others who want peer counseling to begin their own program. They will not have to start from scratch and this will save them valuable time and energy.

Consider also how students in Montrose (MI) argue the need for their proposed project to address problems of peer pressure in terms that are equally grounded in their personal experience but quite different from those of their peers in Saginaw:

Our project will address the following aspects of peer pressure: drugs, pregnancy and violence. In our community, our peers are greatly influenced by the need to be accepted. We fear that our school's definition of "cool" and "normal" is drinking, taking drugs, and engaging in pre-marital sex. A student from Montrose said, "Once a leader of the school starts, other people think it's okay and follow." Through our Choose Your Own Adventure book, we will work to change this problem so that our school is a safe learning environment.

We learned that peer pressure was a topic important to teens. We arrived at this conclusion because in the third survey that we conducted, 67% of the 230 students [of a high school student population of 498] said they felt peer pressure to be an influence in their lives (See Appendix D). Mr. Frank Szybala, Hill McCloy's guidance counselor stated that "based on the number of teen pregnancies in our school [13 — some second pregnancies — in a student population of 498], it's obvious to me that something has to be done."

Consider finally, how middle school students in Detroit (MI) describe the goals and objectives of their proposal to establish a recycling program in their school in terms that make sense to them; to their peers, to the undergraduate and graduate writing consultants in the MSU Writing Center, and to the students who serve on community foundation boards who read and responded to drafts of their work; and to project directors who granted them the $455 they requested:

Our [group] wants to start a recycling program in our school for the lunchroom and the middle school classrooms. It is our goal to reduce, reuse and recycle much of the waste in our school. We recognize that this environmental danger is a major problem for our generation, and we want to do something about it. Our plan would require $455. There are eight members in our group, but the program would service the entire school. Our group plans on producing a brochure describing our work, the total amount of *waste we recycled, and give tips for people to recycle at home. In fact, our program will service the entire world that we all must treat with respect and protect.*

Making Words Work in the World

When grant proposal writing was added to the Write for Your Life curriculum, we discovered that it enabled goals such as the following ones we had for our students' learning at the outset of the project:

- to understand that learning does and always will depend on learners' ability to bring their prior experiences and prior texts to bear on their new endeavors;
- to shape the issues of their lived lives into questions for inquiry;
- to see the interrelationships between their lives in school and the community;
- to engage in primary, as well as secondary, research, as that research is practiced in a variety of disciplines and fields;
- to construct new knowledge that depends on their absorbing existing knowledge;
- both to survey subjects of study and to use the English language arts of reading, writing, speaking, listening, viewing, and designing to explore subtopics of study in depth;
- to practice a variety of discourse styles and genres;
- to imagine their lives as service-oriented citizens in the variety of communities in which they will live;
- to see that their writing can work in the world for their own and the common good;
- to recognize the values of collaborative, cooperative, and service-oriented learning and action.

While our goals, enhanced by the grant writing that we enfolded in the Write for Your Life curriculum, can be expressed in the general terms we have just outlined, our experience of the Write for Your Life curriculum — like our students' — has depended on how it works in particular places, for particular students, teachers, and communities, at particular points in time. We have continually evaluated the project, we have done so by examining the extent to which it has allowed students to relate their lived lives and their school work to each other for their mutual improvement.

At the end of the year, when students in the project began to write grants, Kevin LaPlante reflected on the project in terms quite different from the ones he shared with us at the end of the previous year:

Many of my students come from a world surrounded by poverty, but as you read these grants you will see that there is no poverty of spirit here. These students are rich with desire and ideas. The students and I spent over a month working on these grants, and as far as the ideas are concerned, they have grown out of a year long inquiry into improvement of the individual, family, and the community. The students have written needs assessments and personal essays, researched provocative topics in their I-Searches, spun moving tales of their experiences in poetry and prose, read various genres related to this unit, and participated in lively discussions that drove the investigations and mental scrutiny to deeper levels than I could have imagined. Trying to summarize our course load is as foolish as trying to tally up our national debt, but if these students stay on track, they will be an asset to this country in due time.

In their own words, Kevin's students speak about their work in the Write for Your Life course in terms that are not despondent but hopeful. They speak in the voices of young people who see themselves not as victims of conditions that surround them but as agents for change. Consider, for example, the visions of the world they wish to inhabit that one group of Kevin's students composed in a summary statement about their proposal to build a model of a revived Detroit:

For this project we will build a model of a "Revived Detroit." We plan on showing this model to the city's highest officials, at which time we can present our ideas for an improved Detroit.

The goal that we hope to achieve from this project is to reduce crime in our community and put hope in its place. . . . We want to show [other Detroit citizens] that kids really do care about their environments and the well-being of ourselves and others. . . . This project will also help us become better students and people, too. We will do all kinds of writing that goes with the building of a plan for our city: Proposals, research papers, essays, explanations of the new city, and poetry that will move others to take action. . . . However, probably the most important goal of this project is that we, the students of Room 212 will become better problem solvers. Today it is [directed toward creating] a model of Detroit in Mr. LaPlante's class, tomorrow it is the actual city.

Conclusion

As we have reflected on the growth and development of the Write for Your Life Project, we have done so not only in terms of students' growth as learners, writers, and citizens but also in terms of the work we are doing in the Michigan State University Writing Center. Reflecting on that work, we have been mindful of the long-standing debate about the appropriate work of the academy that Derek Bok, former president of Harvard University, reopens in *Universities and the Future of America* when he argues that America's current economic and social problems not only should "be profoundly troubling to those who devote their lives to higher education" but also should provoke us to ask if "our universities are doing all that they can and should to help America surmount the obstacles that threaten to sap our economic strength and blight the lives of millions of our people" (1990: 6). Finding both Cardinal Newman's image of a university unencumbered by worldly agenda and more utilitarian visions of the university wanting, Bok argues that the division between pure and instrumental inquiry in the university is exaggerated:

> *It is possible to explore a subject out of a keen desire to understand it better, and a belief that such understanding may be of use to humankind, just as it is possible to understand oneself more deeply even while learning to practice a profession. One would suppose, therefore, that the true mission of universities would be to nurture a healthy balance between applied intellectual pursuits and the search for truth and meaning for their own sake.* (9-10)

We have also been mindful of the post-modern debate about the possibility for and potential of human beings to work together for their common good that Benjamin R. Barber, professor of political science in Rutgers University, reopens in *An Aristocracy of Everyone: The Politics of Education and the Future of America* (1992). Finding both Jean Paul Lyotard's denial of the possibility for human community and William Spanos's insistence on the totalitarian nature of all human communities wanting, Barber argues that productive human communities — while possible — depend on the "extraordinary and rare contrivance[s] of cultivated imagination" (5). Invoking Tocqueville and Dewey, Barber indicates that citizens in societies that would think of themselves as communities of cooperating individuals must learn to be free and cooperative. For Barber, this learning is best realized within a dialectical model of education in schools that nurtures democracy by teaching and practicing it. He writes:

> *I am arguing not that the university has a civic mission, but that the university is a civic mission, is civility itself defined as the rules and conventions that permit a community to facilitate conversation and the discourse upon which all knowledge, and thus all community, depends.* (222)

With our work in the Write for Your Life Project, we would extend Derek Bok's and Benjamin Barber's arguments. We would argue that schooling in the United States — kindergarten through the university — is a civic mission, a mission that invites teachers and students in schools, colleges, and universities to collaborate, cooperate, and teach one another for our mutual benefit. Quite obviously, we consider the work we have undertaken in the Michigan State University Writing Center as a civic mission. As undergraduate, graduate, and faculty writing consultants in MSU and teacher and student consultants in schools work together, we not only teach and learn from one another, but we also serve one another's self-identified needs. With our work, we hope to demonstrate the accuracy of Derek Bok's observation that individuals can undertake topical inquiries in order to learn more about them and in order to serve the common good.

Notes

1. Following a conversation with David Schaafsma (then on the faculty of education in the University of Wisconsin-Madison; now on the faculty of Teachers College, Columbia University), Dixie Goswami (professor emeritus, Clemson University, and director of the Breadloaf School of English, Middlebury College) encouraged four of us (Schaafsma; Jay L. Robinson, University of Michigan; and Patricia Lambert Stock and Janet Swenson, Michigan State University) to build upon work we had done previously to develop the Write for Your Life Project. We began our work to do just that, sponsored by the Bingham Trust and Michigan State University.

2. Among the peer consultancies to which we refer are an *Undergraduate Writing Consultancy* and a *Graduate Student Writing Consultancy* in which MSU students, prepared in coursework and field experiences in the center, not only assist their peers in the center and online with brainstorming, drafting, revising, and editing writing for courses across the disciplines but also conduct workshops in classrooms and residence halls and provide sustained assistance in courses in which faculty are using writing extensively in their teaching; a *Faculty Writing Consultancy* and a *Teacher Writing Consultancy* in which faculty (in the MSU Faculty Writing Project) and teachers (in MSU's chapter of the National Writing Project) teach one another their own best practices for integrating writing instruction into their courses and respond to one another's writing for publication; a *Student Writing Consultancy* in which elementary, middle, and secondary school students in mid-Michigan, prepared by teachers and faculty in the Writing Center, learn to provide writing workshop support to their peers and assist their teachers in the effective teaching of writing in Michigan's schools; a *Writing Centers Consultancy* in which directors of writing centers across the state of Michigan teach one another their own best writing workshop practices; and a *Community Writing Consultancy* and a developing *Business Writing Consultancy* in which MSU undergraduate and graduate students assist mid-Michigan service agencies and small businesses compose documents that advance their work.

3. Among the publications to which we refer are *Breakwall*, published by students in the Huron Shores Summer Writing Institute (Rogers City, MI); *The Bridge*, published by students in the Public Schools of the City of Saginaw (MI); and *Corridors*, published by students in the Dewey Center (Detroit, MI).

References

American Academy of Child & Adolescent Psychiatry. (1992). "Facts for Families."

Barber, B. (1992). *An Aristocracy of Everyone: The Politics of Education and the Future of America*. New York: Ballantine.

Bok, D. (1990). *Universities and the Future of America*. Durham, NC: Duke University Press.

Boyer, E.L. (1990). *Scholarship Reconsidered: Priorities of the Professoriate*. Princeton, NJ: Carnegie Foundation for the Advancement of Teaching.

Coles, R. (1993). *The Call of Service*. New York: Houghton Mifflin.

Craig, S.E. (September 1992). "The Educational Needs of Children Living With Violence." *Phi Delta Kappan* 74(1): 67 ff.

Crosby, E.A. (April 1993). "The At-Risk Decade." *Phi Delta Kappan* 74(8): 598 ff.

Edelman, M.W. (May 1989). "Defending America's Children." *Educational Leadership* 46(8): 77 ff.

Greene, M. (1978). *Landscapes of Learning*. New York: Teachers College Press.

Hayes, F.W. (1992). "Governmental Retreat and the Politics of African-American Self-Reliant Development: Public Discourse and Social Policy." *Journal of Black Studies* 22(3): 331-348.

Kaywell, J. (1993). *Adolescents at Risk: A Guide to Fiction and Nonfiction for Young Adults, Parents, and Professionals*. Westport, CT: Greenwood.

Kennedy, A.M. (1987). "Teen Pregnancy: An Issue for the Schools." *Phi Delta Kappan* 68(1): 732 ff.

Prothrow-Stith, D. (1991). *Deadly Consequences: How Violence Is Destroying Our Teenage Population*. NY: HarperCollins.

Rogers, E., and S. Hughes Lee. (1992). "A Comparison of the Perception of the Mother-Daughter Relationship of Black Pregnant and Nonpregnant Teenagers." *Adolescence* 27(107): 555 ff.

Stock, P.L. (1995). *The Dialogic Curriculum: Teaching and Learning in a Multicultural Society*. Portsmouth, NH: Boynton/Cook.

Tonks, D. (December-January 1992-1993a). "Can You Save Your Students' Lives? Educating to Prevent AIDS." *Educational Leadership* 50(4): 48 ff.

——. (December-January 1992-1993b). "How Teenagers Are at Risk for HIV Infection." *Educational Leadership* 50(4): 52 ff.

On Reflection: The Role of Logs and Journals in Service-Learning Courses

by Chris M. Anson

As an educational movement, service-learning has appealed to a wide variety of courses across the disciplines. From psychology to political science to composition, service-learning initiatives span many curricular emphases, community connections, and teaching methods. But in spite of this educational diversity, the concept of *reflection* appears again and again as a widely recognized strategy for students' learning. In many service-oriented courses, reflection is encouraged through two often overlapping media: class discussions and personal writing. It is the domain of personal writing, usually in the form of "reflection logs" or journals, that is the focus of this chapter.

Theories of service-learning value reflection for helping to create the connection between academic coursework and the immediate social, political, and interpersonal experiences of community-based activities. Reflection is supposed to encourage a movement between observation and intellectual analysis or consciousness-raising, and conversely to apply abstract concepts (such as citizenship, public ethics, or social justice) to contexts beyond the classroom. Perhaps because journal writing has a long tradition in the teaching of composition, however, we need to examine its purposes in service-based writing classes. How does this unique type of writing fit into courses often aimed at the production of more formal papers? How does our understanding of journal writing (typically as a vehicle for planning formal papers) influence the way that reflection is taught and/or used in a service-learning composition course? This chapter will try to shed some light on these and other questions while offering some practical advice for teachers who may include reflection in their courses.

The Need for an Understanding of Reflection

Carrie, a 20-year-old undergraduate student enrolled in a service-learning course, wrote the following journal entry after her first few sessions tutoring a young boy at a local community center:

> *After tutoring today I was slightly overwhelmed. As I have said, I tutor a child from Bosnia that speaks no English. It is so difficult. We communicate a lot through sign language to get the basic idea across but I really wish I*

could talk to him. He always looks so lost. I talked to the head of the ESL about him and she told me to help or guide him through his homework. But he has a really short attention span, so sometimes it is quite difficult. Another thing that was shocking or interesting is, that he has been picking up some English words — and one word I noticed he has picked up is shut-up. He knew exactly how to use it also. I figured he picked it up by listening and observing the kids around him. I just found it interesting.

Students enrolled in Carrie's course volunteered for several hours a week at local community centers or public schools, tutoring disadvantaged children or immigrants, or older nonnative speakers or GED seekers. All the students were required to record their observations in a course journal, whose entries they would share from time to time during class sessions. In many college courses involving a service component, students keep similar sorts of records, using them to make observations about their work and to connect these with the more academic material in the classroom.

At first glance, Carrie's journal entry may seem to be playing an important role in recording her thoughts and experiences: She is struggling to communicate with a young refugee from a war-ravaged country, and is both interested in and puzzled by how quickly he learns an idiomatic and, to Carrie, somewhat offensive expression. Her entry shows signs of careful observation and a concern for the progress of her tutee. It is also rather unquestioning, lacking the critical, exploratory edge we often privilege in sophisticated journaling. Yet it is written early in what is for Carrie a unique educational experience, and she may be trying to find the intellectual linchpin that connects her undergraduate class to the unpredictable, messy world of her tutoring.

But after nine weeks, Carrie is writing in much the same way:

Some days I really wish I could understand and speak his language. English is so hard to learn. When we read together it is really hard because in his language he pronounces everything totally different. So when he trys to pronounce a word it usually is wrong, so I try to help him and correct it but he probably isn't learning anything. He doesn't understand why we pronounce things the way we do and how we pronounce them, and I can't explain it to him because he wouldn't understand it all. It really can be difficult some days but it is a good learning experience.

In the context of many service-learning courses that include reflection, the lack of change in Carrie's journal writing over the weeks of her volunteer work is entirely acceptable. A typical service-oriented course, for example, includes the following requirements for students' reflective journal writing:

In order to document your volunteer experience, you will keep a regular journal in the course. The journal is designed for you to record and think about your experiences "on the job." Occasionally you may want to tie your experiences with our class discussions or the readings, when there is a special connection between them. You should write at least three pages per week in your journal for full credit.

While such an open-ended requirement can lead students to think in more principled ways about their experiences, perhaps even connecting them to the ideas and concepts in their course of study, sophisticated reflection is by no means guaranteed without a good deal of intervention, modeling, and response. Journal writing in many service courses may serve the purpose of creating a log or record of experience, but fall far short of encouraging the critical examination of ideas, or the sort of consciousness-raising reflection, that is the mark of highly successful learning. For example, in an entire book focusing on the concept of reflection in service-learning, Silcox (1995) devotes only a few pages to journal writing as a genre of reflective discourse. Filled with both theoretical and practical insights into the concept of reflection, the text nevertheless fails to explain how journals, "one of the most valuable and commonly used reflective activities" (119), actually encourage students to engage in intellectually rich reflection, beyond helping them to "notice what is happening, think about experiences and reflect on their meaning and, from that, to grow" (119). In short, the very process of reflective teaching advocated by Schön (1983; 1987), Brookfield (1995), and other theorists of higher education seems conspicuously absent from much of our thinking about reflection itself as a tool for students' development.

Adding a service component to a writing course greatly increases the complexity of the learning situation. The "content" of a usual academic course — readings, classroom discussions, and library or electronic research — is infused with daily, beyond-the-classroom experiences. The subjects students write about are limited by the domains of their service work, but also greatly enriched. Issues of citizenship, public ethics, social responsibility, and participatory democracy blend into the more concrete topics of the students' experiences: homelessness, battered women, drug and alcohol intervention, neighborhood revitalization, AIDS awareness, church-related outreach, crime prevention, companionship for the aged and infirm, housing for the poor, literacy for the undereducated, and a host of other areas that need and attract voluntarism.

In this context, journal writing becomes especially appealing. Unlike more static courses in which students may gather information on a controversial topic and write an argumentative paper, service courses place students in a physically different setting where they must negotiate complex roles and behaviors, define themselves relative to others who may have very different lives and backgrounds, and visit areas of their communities where they may have never set foot before. Journals, for many years theorized as sites for personal and exploratory writing (Elbow 1981; 1989), offer students in such courses a rhetorical space to express their feelings and write about their new experiences.

But the added dimension of service also pressures us to reexamine the functions of journal writing. The use of journals in classroom instruction often borrows, sometimes tacitly, from three traditions (Anson and Beach 1995). The *expressivist* tradition, with roots in 19th-century Romanticism and the rugged individualism of American pragmatism, emphasizes the expression of an individual voice and the development of identity and self-awareness. In writing classrooms, this tradition takes the form of journals that exist for their own sake — sites for experimentation and the free expression of ideas (see Berlin 1988). The *scientific observation log*, exemplars being Darwin, Edison, or Mead, has affinities with the expressivist journal in its emphasis on associative, exploratory writing, but it has developed into a more clinical space for jotting down empirical data from close observation. This tradition often appears in writing classes where students are asked to record sensory data, perhaps for later use in a formal paper. The *prewriting* journal, with antecedents in the world of art and creative writing, is a repository of ideas, musings, doodlings, freewriting, and other kinds of brainstorming preliminary to a formal paper. The journal becomes a place for blueprints or rehearsals of refined writing. In contrast to the expressivist journal, it appears immediately useful, always looking ahead to a finished product.

In classes that engage students in reflective writing, these traditions may blend together, leading to a confusion of purposes in students' writing, or a directionlessness that ends up filling space without creating new ideas or insights. Carrie's entry, for example, mixes the observational quality of a clinical log with the self-disclosure of a freestanding expressivist journal, but does not move her thinking forward very far. Instead of adopting common practices for journal writing in standard, self-contained composition classes, we need to create a genre of the academic journal for service-learning courses that deliberately, creatively, and effectively brings the concept of reflection into sharp focus.

In the field of literacy studies, we have much rhetorical work to do describing the characteristics of successful reflection in students' writing. Dewey, in what has become for many scholars the genesis of the concept of reflection, describes reflective thinking as a

> *special kind of intellectual activity different from other kinds of thinking; it begins with a question, hypothesis, or "perplexity" and leads a person to an inquiry to resolve it. Experience, relevant knowledge, and reasoning ability are all important in this activity. In contrast to routine or impulsive think-*

ing, reflective thinking, according to Dewey, is disciplined and orderly. (Centra 1993: 177)

Reverberating with Dewey's emphasis on intellectual puzzling, most definitions of reflection stress the process of learning through *experience*. Reflection involves accommodating the unfamiliar into the familiar in an effort to make sense out of what is personally observed or experienced. Morton (1989) adds that "the point of reflection is, in some ways, focused inward: What does this mean to me? How do I make sense of it? What am I going to do with what I think or feel? . . . I believe the most important outcome of reflection is that participants can answer the question, 'What has your experience taught you about yourself?'" (128).

A favorite model driving certain kinds of verbal, discussion-based reflection is the Kolb learning cycle (Kolb 1981). In Kolb's theory, learning is best promoted when it begins with concrete experience, in which learners involve themselves fully and openly. In the second stage, called "reflective observation," the learner observes the experience from many perspectives. In "abstract conceptualization," the learner then creates concepts and integrates observations into logically sound theories. Finally, the learner engages in "active experimentation," in which the theories are used to make decisions and solve problems. In a typical service course, students may work through the cycle methodically, providing information in class discussions that then leads to reflection and abstract conceptualization. In journal writing, a simplified version of Kolb's cycle is seen in the typical two-part process of "writing down observations" and then "thinking about/reflecting on them." (Some types of reflection logs, called "double-entry journals," ask students to split their paper down the middle for this purpose, writing facts on one side and reflections or analytical statements on the other.)

Another important way to conceptualize the reflective journal is to place it *against* more rigid academic forms, allowing students to break from the "unequal relationship between the writer and the audience, and between the writer and the subject under scrutiny" (Spellmeyer 1989: 264). As Gannett (1992) claims, the discursive properties of journal writing can become, themselves, the object of reflection: "Having students keep journals . . . can be used to initiate discussion of dominance and difference in discourse itself. Students can consider the nature and relative power of public and private discourses, the relation between canonized forms of writing and marginalized forms, the relation between writing and life, writing and thinking, and certainly, gender and discourse" (204).

In spite of these and other useful ways to think about or practice reflection, there is little consensus on either its general properties or its specific discursive features. As Brookfield (1995) points out, "the terms *reflection* and *reflective practice* are now so overused that they are in danger of becoming buzzwords denuded of any real meaning — of taking on the status of premature ultimates, like *motherhood* and *democracy*" (216). Instead of trying to provide an easy definition of reflection, Brookfield prefers to look at the social and cultural contexts in which reflection occurs. Our "usual" thinking processes are already culturally formed or imposed, so that reflection can become phenomenologically circular, ideas trapped within the realm of already formed ideologies. Brookfield focuses instead on change: "Reflection in and of itself is not enough; it must always be linked to how the world can be changed" (217). To some extent, the concept of change requires that students conceive of their journal writing not as a place for idle contemplation or the passive recording of feelings, moods, or new experiences but as a place to actively explore difficult problems in which they, as members of their culture and community, may be implicated, if only by their inaction.

Encouraging Reflection in Journal Writing

While there is no end of possible practices to encourage reflective journal writing, the concept of *frames* offers us a helpful way to begin. New theories of organizational systems suggest that we can understand the functions of these systems more clearly by seeing them from various alternating perspectives, or frames. To take one example, students enrolled in courses that provide literacy tutoring can, early in their experience, read Sylvia Scribner's article "Literacy in Three Metaphors" (1984). In this piece, Scribner proposes three common ways that literacy is constructed: as adaptation (for real-world survival), as power (for cultural and economic advancement), and as a state of grace (for the virtues of aesthetic or spiritual self-knowing). As students write about their tutoring experiences, this article can have profound effects on their thinking, compelling them to recognize that they bring into their experiences ready-made educational, social, and cultural assumptions, and then contesting those assumptions in productive ways. (See Slattery 1994 for an account of students' journaling in response to this reading.) The result is a kind of internal contestation that seeps slowly, and therefore without psychological violence, into the students' consciousness.

To take another example, Peck, Flower, and Higgins (1995) propose three ways of developing a discourse to deal with difference. In *cultural literacy,* a discourse is created that "seeks to minimize or eradicate difference." In the *literacy of social and cultural critique,* issues of power are addressed openly, "defining social relationships in terms of economic and ideological struggle." This oppositional critique is not unlike Knoblauch's definition of "critical literacy," whose agenda is to "identify reading and writing abilities with a critical consciousness of the social conditions in which people find themselves, recognizing the extent to which language practices objectify and rationalize these conditions and the extent to which people with authority to name the world dominate others whose voices they have been able to suppress" (1990: 79). Finally, *community literacy* seeks an alternative discourse that supports social change, intercultural conversation, strategic decision making, and inquiry (Peck, Flower, and Higgins 1995: 205). Having studied these distinctions as a kind of frame, students can return to the sites of their work and write reflective journal entries examining the assumptions enacted in the kinds of discourse used and the kind of attitudes toward language and literacy they are asked to assume.

Frames for reflection can also be constructed at much higher levels of experience. In asking students to reflect on the concept of citizenship, for example, I have used frames by Boyte and Farr (1996), two political scientists who have worked extensively in the area of service-learning. In these frames, citizens are described in three historical ways in connection with the concept of service. Citizens are understood as

> 1. *rights-bearing members of a political system who choose their leaders . . . through elections;*
> 2. *caring members of a moral community who share certain values and feel common responsibilities toward each other; and as*
> 3. *practical agents of a civic world who work together in public ways and spaces to engage the tasks and try to solve the problems that they collectively face.* (3-4)

As the students experience their volunteer work, these concepts give them a way to think about their own roles and responsibilities relative to the mission they are serving. Who are they "being" as citizens? What attitudes are they instilling in others about involvement in the stewardship of their community? Once they identify various problems, what does each frame say about the possible solutions to those problems?

In contrast to Carrie's entries at the start of this chapter, the following entry by Vivian, a student in another service-learning course, may suggest some of the differences between "routine or impulsive thinking" and the special kind of intellectual activity Dewey — and theorists after him — have in mind when they write of reflective thinking. Vivian's class was given the frame for their journaling during a long discussion focusing on the concepts of class, privilege, and difference. On the board were various statements, written as quotations someone might make, relating to these concepts: "I work hard for a living; why should I bail anyone else out?" "Everyone should give according to their ability and take according to their need." "Let's face it: The poor and uneducated are that way mostly because they are lazy and prefer to be fed off the system instead of feeding it."

Characteristically, Vivian wrote long, complicated, often unresolved entries in which her observations led to philosophical speculations. These speculations then provided her with a kind of intellectual template that she often returned to in later entries, testing it out and modifying it with new experience.

> *In class on Monday I tried to make a point about privilege and humility and the approach we are taking to this type of service oriented work. . . . I was reacting in my response to this amorphous feeling I got from people who spoke of their experiences — this feeling of conflict between their place, their lives, their upbringings and educations, and those of their tutees.*

In a long continuation of this entry, Vivian then recounts an experience riding the bus to her apartment in a downtown area of Minneapolis. She observes a poor, young woman with a pale face and small eyes, very thin, cradling a baby, and listens as the woman tells another passenger about her life. Vivian hears that the baby's first birthday is the next day; the mother works two jobs and hasn't seen the baby's father since he moved away to another city. Vivian "steps down off the bus into the streets which silently throb" around her and walks home. Later that evening, she goes to see her boyfriend, a "wonderful and sensitive" man. As she stands over the sink telling him about her day — her tutoring, her class session, and her experience on the bus — her experiences converge into a sudden burst of emotion.

> *And as I told him, water on my hands, dirty dishes all around, listening to Coltrane, I started to cry about this woman on the bus who is so much me — in her youth, in her sharp-eyed awareness, in her cradling arms — and so much not me in her poverty, in her loneliness, in her motherhood. It struck me all at once: privilege, illiteracy, humility, poverty, womanhood. On the bus. There are countless ways in which I lead a privileged life — from a university education . . . to the man who stood beside me with his hand on my neck, understanding why I couldn't stop crying. I am so glad that that happened because that is what it's about — not desensitizing and looking objectively all the time (articles, write-ups, words spoken and argued), to the point where I look at her, not without empathy like a subject in a research study, but finding human connections and using the privileged access to knowledge that we have to comprehend those emotions, to personally learn and grow from them. That woman will never remember seeing me on Monday. It is not my job to make an effect on her; her life is her own. We can only connect in these basic, human ways and learn what we can, to the greatest degree we can.*

Like the tutors in Stuckey and Alston's "cross-age" program (1990), Vivian recognizes the reality of the poor woman's life (and the lives of her tutees) "as people, not as blighted parts of the social landscape" (249). Like Carrie's, this entry contains astute observations, but they weave like threads in and out of a kind of reflective fabric in which things *mean* or have significance for belief, and ultimately action. In spite of its tentativeness and lack of resolution, Vivian's writing seems to create her ideology just as her ideology is partly creating her writing. It is this quality of reflection — not simply "mental concentration" or "careful consideration," but something akin to the Latin root of the word, *reflexus*, "to bend back" — that seems to best capture the essence of the concept in journal writing.

The Role of Response in Critical Reflection

While frames and other methods may encourage students to think in intellectually challenging ways, as teachers we also need to develop more strategic and critically reflective ways to *respond* to students' writing. In my early experiences teaching service-learning courses in the late 1980s, I was surprised when some undergraduates began to contest the assumptions and methods at the community service centers where they volunteered as tutors. At one point, for example, a student complained that the methods used at the center for tutoring children encouraged boredom and passivity:

> *I'm frustrated with the Crane reading system that we're using. It is BORING! It bores both Heather and me. I've found some ways to make it a little more interesting. . . . I try to come up with other things to do. Sometimes she reads and other times I read to her, or we trade off page by page. She likes to play games, such as hangman or wordfind puzzles. Sometimes I have her write stories. (quoted in Anson 1992: 38)*

In class discussions about this and other students' related experiences, we learned that some of the community centers used reading and writing methods that mirrored those used in the area public schools the tutees attended. The class wondered why this was the practice. We soon learned that there was a relationship between the centers' funding sources, accountability for children's improvement, and educational methodology. To get continued funding, the centers had to show that their services were working. The preferred model of accountability came from comparisons of school-based outcome assessment and parallel assessments in the centers. To deviate from the school curriculum, the centers would run the risk of testing something they were not teaching, the scores would fall, and their funding could disappear.

When these issues emerged, I was at first worried that too public a questioning of the centers' methods could lead to conflict; the leaders of the service programs might think that my course was trying to undermine their work or their credibility. My wish for students to have a "good" tutoring experience and for the entire program to "run smoothly" militated against the kind of response to their journal writing that could push them to critically examine the underlying educational assumptions at work in the university, in the public schools, and in the center for educational outreach where they worked.

Another time that I recognized my resistance to critical reflection happened when I began questioning the ideology of altruism that drives some service-learning programs. I was midway into my first service-learning course when someone sent me a copy of a speech by Ivan Illich, titled "To Hell With Good Intentions" (1968) and urged me to share it with my students. In it, Illich questions the real motives of the American students in the 1960s who swarmed south of the border to help with the international service mission. Illich says,

> *You, . . . like the values you carry, are the products of an American society of achievers and consumers, with its two-party system, its universal schooling, and its family-car affluence. You are ultimately* — consciously or unconsciously — *"salesmen" for a delusive ballet in the ideals of democracy, equal opportunity and free enterprise among people who haven't the possibility of profiting from these. . . . Ideally, [the American altruists] define their role as service. Actually, they frequently wind up alleviating the damage done by money and weapons, or "seducing" the "underdeveloped" to the benefits of the world of affluence and achievement. Perhaps this is the moment to instead bring home to the people of the U.S. the knowledge that the way of life they have chosen simply is not alive enough to be shared.*

Having just established good working relationships at the schools and community centers where they tutored, my students were daily sharing their enthusiasm and their positive feelings of voluntarism. At the time, I felt very reluctant to introduce this rather vitriolic piece of writing: Would they suddenly question their roles and motives? Would this dampen their spirits and lead to a less-active, energetic quality in their tutoring? I decided to keep the article to myself. Naive to the higher-level implications of service-learning, I felt responsible to the logistics of the outreach experiment: It all needed to go smoothly, and we all needed to feel good.

It wasn't long, however, before the issue came up in the context of the students' own work and journaling. Two students who volunteered in a youth program for African-American children in a poverty-stricken area of the city initially felt the effects of being themselves, for once, in the minority, the only white, middle-class people in a busy community center crowded with people of color. A few weeks later, however, their feelings of intimidation turned to frustration as they conjured up images of themselves as the deliverers of knowledge and truth to the "noble savages" they served. As the class discussed their plight, it became quickly clear that the learning was happening precisely because most of the students were *not* "feeling good" about their volunteering. Why couldn't there be more minority tutors, some of them asked. Indeed. That difficult question sustained our discussion for several hours, eventually taking us beyond their own experiences and into the political, cultural, and educational intricacies of the urban American landscape.

I have since realized that, like students' learning, teachers may experience service-learning initiatives through a series of developmental stages. Although it is not my purpose here to explore such stages in detail, they may proceed from initial enthusiasm and commitment (even religious zeal), to a preoccupation with logistics and programming, to the experience of conflict and ideological puzzle, to a realization that the entire enterprise requires ongoing critical reflection and commitment balanced by intellectual skepticism. As teachers, we need to approach our service-learning courses with a critically reflective stance that models for students the kind of discursive explorations they should take in their journals and reflection logs. This requires, I believe, a fundamental shift from providing knowledge to participating in the creation and exploration of knowledge *with* our students, ready for the many intellectual surprises that service-learning courses bring to our classes — if we let them in. It also requires us to delve deeper into theories of student learning, which give us frames for understanding and reflecting on the processes at work in service-learning initiatives (see Delve, Mintz, and Stewart 1990 for a useful synthesis of such theories in the context of community service).

Instead of simply endorsing students' journal entries, or writing positive phatic comments ("great idea!" "right," "wow!" or "interesting observation"), we need to develop ways to respond that encourage students' ideas while pushing them into higher domains of critical reflection. If we introduce and model the concepts of frames, for example, we have already developed a language and a conceptual apparatus for our own response. In the case of Carrie's early journal entry, we might ask her to think about her observation from various structural, social, linguistic, or political perspectives. We might ask Carrie why her tutee learns some terms, such as "shut up," so easily, but is bored when she tries to teach him other words. We might ask her some questions from a social and educational frame: Symbolically, he is learning to utter a word meant to deny utterance. What educational conditions might she explore that relate to children being quiet? What else could she learn in this context about attitudes toward talk that could give her insight into the conditions of this young boy's difficulty learning to speak English? We might then shift to a different frame, perhaps a political one that helps her to explore her frustrations. Why is it so difficult for a middle-class, educated person to connect with a young child from Bosnia? What are the roots of her frustration — is it only a sense that she is not making progress? If this difficulty exists on this small, interpersonal scale in a relatively supportive environment, what does it tell us about more global problems of education, culture, and economics?

As students become more used to critical reflection, it is likely that our own responses to them will become more sophisticated. While we may struggle to move Carrie beyond simple observations of complex phenomena, Vivian's entry offers us a richer, more thoughtful analysis for engagement and commentary. Does her own privileged education really allow her to experience emotional insights — *reflection* — denied to working-poor, abandoned mothers? Is what she hopes to give back to her tutees some version of this privileged compassion? What does she think about the wealthy man, stopped at the light in his Mercedes, who contemplates his own privilege as he watches the poor, thin woman struggling along the dark street cradling her infant in her arms? In our own reflective practice, we also need to be sensitive to the timing and context for such questions, as well as what we know about particular students. At this moment in Vivian's journaling, even gentle contestation may be inappropriate, and could end up denying Vivian what is, to her, an emotion-laden philosophizing, pushing her toward just what she is trying to reject (a clinical stance that objectifies the woman on the bus and turns her into an intellectual experiment).

In "Literacy and Citizenship: Resisting Social Issues," David Bleich (1990) analyzes some shared journal writing of students who wrote both "private" journal responses to their teacher and public responses to members of small, peer study groups. In many cases, the entries themselves express feelings of anger and frustration as the students explored dimensions of their identities relative to other students' statements or self-disclosures. Reading the entries is difficult because they are so tense, at times even combative. Yet as Bleich points out, what students want to write about is

> *complicated by the matter of how ideology determines what people want. In the process of teaching language and literacy, we teachers are bringing new language to the classroom. This new language urges on us new values and makes us all somewhat uncomfortable. However, I don't think we have a choice anymore; the discomfort of studying language with and for other people and other interests is far less than the suffering created by learning language as isolated individuals.* (1990: 169)

As we continue to explore the concept of reflection in service-learning courses, the sort of collective discourse Bleich encourages, ideologically charged and interpersonally meaningful, will surely push us toward strategies that, when carefully adapted to our courses through our own processes of reflection-in-action, will produce of our students better learners, more sophisticated thinkers, and more engaged participants in the world they must shape for themselves.

References

Anson, C.M. (1992). "Academic Literacy Meets Cultural Diversity: An Analysis of Ideological Change Among Student Tutors in a Service-Learning Program." In *Academic Literacies in Multicultural Higher Education*, edited by T. Hilgers, M. Wunsch, and V. Chattergy. Manoa: Center for Studies of Multicultural Higher Education, University of Hawaii.

——, and R. Beach. (1995). *Journals in the Classroom: Writing to Learn*. Norwood, MA: Christopher-Gordon.

Berlin, J. (1988). "Rhetoric and Ideology in the Writing Class." *College English* 50:477-494.

Bleich, D. (1990). "Literacy and Citizenship: Resisting Social Issues." In *The Right to Literacy*, edited by A. Lunsford, H. Moglene, and J. Slevin, pp. 163-169. New York: Modern Language Association.

Boyte, H.C., and J. Farr. (1996). *The Work of Citizenship and the Problem of Service-Learning*. Minneapolis: Center for Democracy and Citizenship, Hubert H. Humphrey Institute of Public Affairs.

Brookfield, S.D. (1995). *Becoming a Critically Reflective Teacher*. San Francisco: Jossey-Bass.

Centra, J.A. (1993). *Reflective Faculty Evaluation*. San Francisco: Jossey-Bass.

Delve, C.I., S.D. Mintz, and G.M. Stewart. (1990). "Promoting Values Development Through Community Service: A Design." *New Directions for Student Services* 50:7-27.

Elbow, P. (1981). *Writing With Power*. New York: Oxford University Press.

——. (1989). "Toward a Phenomenology of Freewriting." *Journal of Basic Writing* 8:42-71.

Gannett, C. (1992). *Gender and the Journal: Diaries and Academic Discourse*. Albany: State University of New York Press.

Illich, I. (April 1968). "To Hell With Good Intentions." Address to the Conference on Inter-American Student Project, Cuernevaca, Mexico.

Knoblauch, C.H. (1990). "Literacy and the Politics of Education." In *The Right to Literacy*, edited by A. Lunsford, H. Moglene, and J. Slevin, pp. 74-80. New York: Modern Language Association.

Kolb, D.A. (1981). "Learning Styles and Disciplinary Differences." In *The Modern American College*, edited by A.W. Chickering, pp. 232-255. San Francisco: Jossey-Bass.

Morton, K. (1989). "First Steps in Doing a Reflection Component." In *Digging Deep: A Guidebook for Developing a Campus Service-Learning Initiative in Your City, State, or Region,* edited by M. Langseth, p. 128. Roseville, MN: National Youth Leadership Council.

Peck, W.C., L. Flower, and L. Higgins. (1995). "Community Literacy." *College Composition and Communication* 46:199-222.

Schön, D.A. (1983). *The Reflective Practitioner.* New York: Basic.

——. (1987). *Educating the Reflective Practitioner.* San Francisco: Jossey-Bass.

Scribner, S. (1984). "Literacy in Three Metaphors." *American Journal of Education* 93:6-21.

Silcox, H.C. (1995). *A How-to Guide to Reflection: Adding Cognitive Learning to Community Service Programs.* Philadelphia: Brighton.

Slattery, P.F. (1994). "Teaching for Various Literacies." *Journal of Teaching Writing* 13:15-31.

Spellmeyer, K. (1989). "A Common Ground: The Essay in the Academy." *College English* 51:262-276.

Stuckey, J.E., and K. Alston. (1990). "Cross-Age Tutoring: The Right to Literacy." In *The Right to Literacy,* edited by A. Lunsford, H. Moglene, and J. Slevin, pp. 245-254. New York: Modern Language Association.

Annotated Bibliography

Community Service and Composition

by Nora Bacon and Tom Deans

Adler-Kassner, Linda. (1995). "Digging a Groundwork for Writing: Underprepared Students and Community Service Courses." *College Composition and Communication* 46:552-555.

A response to Bruce Herzberg's 1994 article "Community Service and Critical Teaching" (reprinted in this volume) observing that the function of community service assignments, and the questions they raise, will vary with the student population. For Herzberg at Bentley College, an important problem was to push students beyond the observation that "this could happen to me" toward an analysis of the political and economic roots of injustice. By contrast, Adler-Kassner taught underprepared students at the University of Minnesota's General College, who already "had a pretty good handle on the idea that American culture is fundamentally inequitable." For them, the challenge was to master a discourse for expressing their critical consciousness. They were best served by a pragmatic course, helping them articulate their perspective in language that will be heard.

Albert, Gail, ed. (1994). *A Service Learning Reader: Reflections and Perspectives on Service*. Raleigh, NC: National Society for Experiential Education. (ph. 919/787-3263)

An anthology of 36 essays and excerpts, broadly addressing issues of service, community, social justice, and fieldwork. The readings range from a two-page excerpt on democracy and individualism from Alexis de Tocqueville's *Democracy in America* to a full chapter from Paulo Freire's *Pedagogy of the Oppressed*. The collection is divided into eight chapters, each containing two to five selections. They include: "Orientation Skills and Getting Started"; "Selfhood and Society"; "Interaction, Reflection and Dialogue"; "Roots of Service"; "Community Service"; "Community"; "Ethics, Decision-making and Social Justice"; and "Global Awareness."

Anson, Chris M. (1987). "The Classroom and the 'Real World' as Contexts." *Journal of the Midwest MLA* 20:1-16.

Examines composition curriculum in terms of its underlying ideology. Argues that the two most widespread conceptions of introductory English classes — as a step toward "cultural literacy" and as practice in basic skills — are irreconcilable because they are motivated by conflicting ideologies, one privileging the study of literature as a context for writing, while the other seeks to equip students with general skills they can use in any context. The emerging ideology, with its focus on the social context of writing, provides a different view of composition courses: as the core of a writing across the curriculum program, encouraging inquiry into the communicative practices of discourse communities. Although Anson's discussion of WAC pushes non-academic writing into the background, he suggests a direction for curriculum and pedagogy consistent with community-based writing assignments.

——, and L. Lee Forsberg. (1990). "Moving Beyond the Academic Community: Transitional Stages in Professional Writing." *Written Communication* 7:200-231.

Anson and Forsberg analyze the experience of six students enrolled in a writing workshop for college seniors; their subjects were competent academic writers majoring in English or journalism with internships in business and public service settings. Anson and Forsberg identify a pattern in the students' transition from academic to nonacademic writing: They began with confidence and high expectations, experienced disorientation as they struggled to perform unfamiliar tasks with little explicit direction, then moved toward a resolution of their frustration as they grew more familiar with the social context of the writing and more comfortable with their own roles. The researchers conclude that "becoming a successful writer is much more a matter of developing strategies for social and intellectual adaptations to different professional communities than acquiring a set of generic skills." Their findings have relevance to service-learning projects in which students are asked to write in unfamiliar discourse communities.

Barton, David, and Roz Ivanic, eds. (1991). *Writing in the Community.* Written Communication Annual: Volume 6. Newbury Park, CA: Sage.

A collection of nine empirically based essays, by both British and American scholars, on the social functions of writing and how writing practices in the community relate to the domains of education and employment. The most pertinent essay to community service writing is Roz Ivanic and Wendy Moss's "Bringing Community Writing Practices Into Education," which notes the differences between writing in everyday life and writing in traditional English classes, and suggests ways for better aligning classroom writing practices with community writing practices. Also helpful are essays by David Barton on "The Social Nature of Writing" and Joanna and Brian Street on "The Schooling of Literacy."

Bizzell, Patricia. (1993). *Academic Discourse and Critical Consciousness.* Pittsburgh: University of Pittsburgh Press.

A collection of 14 important essays, ranging from Bizzell's earlier work on academic discourse, initiation to discourse communities, and composing processes, to more recent critiques of "cultural literacy" and advocacy of rhetorical approaches to literacy, the disciplines, and writing instruction. Although Bizzell never directly addresses service-learning, her Afterword makes a compelling plea for foregrounding civic virtue in our teaching practices, including helping students to "discover heretofore unrealized points of contact with the interests of groups to which they do not belong, and moral commonalties with other positions." Also of particular interest are the chapters "Academic Discourse and Critical Consciousness: An Application of Paulo Freire" and "Arguing About Literacy."

Brodkey, Linda. (1989). "On the Subjects of Class and Gender in 'The Literacy Letters.'" *College English* 51:125-160.

Beneath a thick layer of poststructuralist jargon lies the story of an exchange of letters between six teachers and six adult basic writers. Although the correspondence is not a community service project, it raises issues relevant to service-learning programs and adult literacy programs, especially the miscommunication that can result when class differences go unacknowledged.

Brooke, Robert, and John Hendricks. (1989). *Audience Expectations and Teacher Demands.* Carbondale and Edwardsville: Southern Illinois University Press.

An excellent introduction to the pedagogical problem that many community-based writing assignments are intended to address: the difficulty of teaching students to write for an audience when their real audience is a teacher. Brooke and Hendricks describe a first-year composition course at the University of Minnesota in which students were asked to make decisions about their texts based on the needs and expectations of fictive "real world" readers. They report the students' frustration in trying to discern what their teacher wanted, as well as some students' belief that the course did not prepare them for other academic writing tasks. The authors do not consider the possibility of writing for audiences outside the classroom; they conclude that "teaching 'writing to an audience' always presents real conflicts to students in writing classrooms" and consider how students' response to these conflicts was conditioned by their effort to establish their identities as college students.

Coles, Robert. (1988). "Community Service Work." *Liberal Education* 74:11-13.

In this short article, Coles advocates student involvement in community service and highlights the potential of literary works and discussion in helping students to intellectually and morally process their experiences. For more Coles on community work, see *The Call of Service: Witness to Idealism* (Boston: Houghton Mifflin, 1993), which gathers narratives from several contexts of service and includes the syllabus for his popular Harvard course, A Literature of Social Reflection.

Conniff, Brian, and Betty Rogers Youngkin. (1995). "The Literacy Paradox: Service-Learning and the Traditional English Department." *Michigan Journal of Community Service Learning* 2:86-94.

Beginning with Mike Rose's observation that "the atomistic model" of literacy instruction — with its emphasis on teaching "basic skills" and eliminating error — separates developmental reading and writing instruction from the study of literature and literary theory, Conniff and Youngkin describe an effort to unite basic composition instruction to "the generative struggle with ideas." The Dayton Literacy Project introduces undergraduates to literacy and developmental theory, then brings them together with adults from the community — women reading at a fifth- to eighth-grade level working toward a GED — with whom the undergraduates discuss selections of poetry and short fiction. They work on individual and joint writing projects, with the undergraduates serving as literacy mentors. Conniff and Youngkin assert that the project challenges current conceptions of English as a discipline; they suggest a broader conception that would comprehend both literacy and literature, highlighting the natural link between them.

Cooper, David, and Laura Julier. (1995). "Writing the Ties That Bind: Service-Learning in the Writing Classroom." With annotated bibliography by Martha Merrill. *Michigan Journal of Community Service Learning* 2:72-85.

Cooper and Julier argue that "higher-order discourse skills" and "the arts of democratic practice" are essentially identical, so undergraduate writing courses appropriately emphasize analysis of and practice in public discourse. They describe Michigan State's Service-Learning Writing Project, which integrates community-oriented language into the composition curriculum in a number of ways: Students discuss the use of language in public debate over community issues; contribute to the debate by writing such documents as polls and letters to the city council; serve as volunteer writers at community agencies;

study short stories and essays about the concept of public life and community; and are encouraged to conceptualize their own language use as a citizenship skill.

Crawford, Karis. (1993). "Community Service Writing in an Advanced Composition Class." In *Praxis I: A Faculty Casebook on Community Service Learning,* edited by Jeffrey Howard. Ann Arbor, MI: University of Michigan, OCSL Press.

Describes the integration of community service learning into Practical English, an advanced writing course at the University of Michigan. Crawford compares two sections of Practical English — one in which students worked as volunteer writers at community organizations, another in which the group writing project did not involve community service — finding that students in the service-learning course rated their experience more positively and made comparable gains in their writing. Crawford identifies some of the administrative difficulties created by the campus-community link, suggesting practical measures to address them.

Ede, Lisa. (1984). "Audience: An Introduction to Research." *College Composition and Communication* 35:40-54.

A bibliographic essay surveying research on audience in a series of related disciplines, including Cognitive Psychology, Composition, Speech Communication, Rhetoric, and Philosophy. Ede describes the review as "introductory and exploratory, rather than exhaustive or definitive." Includes sections on audience analysis, empirical research, and humanistic theory. A vast number of sources, with helpful pointers to areas of interest, gathered into a compact essay. In this same CCC issue are two other articles on audience: Ede and Lunsford's seminal "Audience Addressed/Audience Invoked: The Role of Audience in Composition Theory and Pedagogy" and Barry Kroll's "Writing for Readers: Three Perspectives on Audience."

Franco, Robert W. (1996). "Integrating Service Into a Multicultural Writing Curriculum." In *Promoting Community Renewal Through Civic Literacy and Service Learning,* edited by M.H. Parsons and C.D. Lisman. San Francisco: Jossey-Bass.

Describes an ambitious service-learning program at Kapi'olani Community College. One strand of the program, based in a sequence of English courses, has community college students working as literacy tutors to at-risk youth, producing a newsletter for a network of community agencies, and writing oral histories of elders. The article sketches features of Hawaii's history and culture that faculty considered in order to design service-learning curricula sensitive to the needs and values of their community.

Greco, Norma. (1992). "Critical Literacy and Community Service: Reading and Writing the World." *English Journal* 81:83-85.
This short piece, written by a high school English teacher from Pittsburgh, describes how she facilitated a course in which seniors undertook community volunteer work in inner-city schools and day-care centers and wrote about it in their journals. Greco notes in several of the students a greater grasp of diversity and social inequities in their communities and society at large, and ultimately the emergence of a "socially aware voice" in many of the journals.

Heath, Shirley Brice. (1993). "Inner City Life Through Drama: Imagining the Language Classroom. *TESOL Quarterly* 27:177-192.
Drawing on a five-year ethnographic study on the life of young people in inner-city youth organizations, Heath focuses on a group of adolescents who, while many are nonnative speakers of English and/or struggling in school, demonstrate mastery of complex linguistic problems through their hands-on, collaborative, and contextualized production and performance of drama in a neighborhood youth group. She notes "a host of abilities undiscovered in the ordinary run of classroom requests for *displays of knowledge* rather than full *performances of knowing*."

——, and Leslie Mangiola. (1991). *Children of Promise: Literate Activity in Linguistically and Culturally Diverse Classrooms*. Washington, DC: National Education Association and American Educational Research Association.
This brief monograph profiles two cross-age tutoring projects in which students were asked to read to younger children, keep notes recording the children's progress, and write various documents to reflect on and advance their work (including, for example, letters to the children and a handbook for parents). The tutors grew increasingly self-assured and sophisticated in their analysis of the children's learning. They were encouraged to be self-conscious about their own use of language, as well; Heath and Mangiola stress the pedagogical advantage of presenting language as both the instrument and the object of study. Although the authors describe tutoring programs located in elementary schools, they make recommendations for implementing cross-age literacy tutoring that could easily be adapted to high schools and colleges.

Kendall, Jane, and Associates. (1990). *Combining Service and Learning: A Resource Book for Community and Public Service*. 3 vols. Raleigh, NC: National Society for Internships and Experiential Education. (ph. 919/787-3263; now, National Society for Experiential Education)

Volumes I and II each contain more than 50 short essays, articles, and program profiles; Volume III is an annotated bibliography. Sections to Volume I include: "Essential Principles in Combining Service and Learning"; "Rationales and Theories for Combining Service and Learning"; "Public Policy Issues and Guides"; "Institutional Policy Issues and Guides"; and "History and Future of the Service-Learning Movement." Volume II: "Practical Issues and Ideas for Programs and Courses That Combine Service and Learning" and "Profiles of Programs and Courses That Combine Service and Learning (College, K-12, Community-Based and Government)." Most articles relate directly to higher education and are authored by university faculty and administrators, but few explicitly intersect with issues in Composition.

Knoblauch, C.H., and Lil Brannon. (1993). *Critical Teaching and the Idea of Literacy*. Portsmouth, NH: Boynton/Cook.

Through a combination of personal and teacher narratives and critical theory, the authors argue for a pedagogy aimed at "critical literacy," which "entails an understanding of the relationships between language and power together with a practical knowledge of how to use language for self-realization, social critique and cultural transformation." Drawing on the liberatory theory and pedagogy of Paulo Freire, Henry Giroux, and Ira Shor, they offer an accessible study of how to unpack the complex issues of power, politics, and literacy in the reading and writing classroom. Chapters include: "Representation: Naming the World in Schools"; "The Real Political Correctness"; "Images of Critical Teaching"; "Functional Literacy and the Rhetoric of Objectivism"; "Literacy and the Politics of Nostalgia"; "Expressivism"; "Critical Literacy"; and "Teacher Inquiry."

Kraft, Richard, and Marc Swadener, eds. (1994). *Building Community: Service Learning in the Academic Disciplines*. Denver: Colorado Campus Compact. (ph. 303/620-4941)

An overview of service-learning courses in the liberal arts and professional schools, including syllabi and faculty reflections, from Colorado colleges and universities. Of special note are the chapters "Incorporating Service Learning Into Writing and Literature Classes" (Eleanor Swanson) and "Literature and Service Learning: Note Strange Bedfellows" (Cathy Comstrock). The collection also includes a "Review of Research and Evaluation on Service Learning in Public and Higher Education" and an extensive bibliography.

Mansfield, Margaret. (1993). "Real World Writing and the English Curriculum." *College Composition and Communication* 44:69-83.
Analyzes a graduate course called Writing for the Public, in which students developed a questionnaire to advance the work of a college senate committee. Mansfield shows that the inclusion of this assignment enriched her course because it complicated students' understanding of audience, gave them experience with collaboration, and challenged their view that only extended expository texts count as "real" writing. She stresses the importance of academic reflection and analysis in helping students recognize the rhetorical complexity of their task and extend their insights to other kinds of writing, academic and professional.

Matalene, Carolyn B., ed. (1989). *Worlds of Writing: Teaching and Learning in Discourse Communities of Work*. New York: Random House.
A collection of 23 essays investigating the uses of writing in a range of discourse worlds, including journalism, finance, computers, and law. Of special interest are the first six essays investigating the relationship between academic and nonacademic writing; these include Kristin Woolever's "Coming to Terms With Different Standards of Excellence for Written Communication," Stephen Doheny-Farina's "Case Study of One Adult Writing in Academic and Nonacademic Discourse Communities," Mary Ann Eiler on "Process and Genre," William E. Rivers's "From the Garret to the Fishbowl: Thoughts on the Transition From Literary to Technical Writing," Janette S. Lewis on "Adaptation; Business Writing as Catalyst in a Liberal Arts Curriculum," and "Rhetoric and the Discourse of Technology" by Theresa Enos. Taken as a whole, the volume suggests that the forms and functions of writing in the society as a whole are widely variable and substantially different from what students practice in school. Matalene observes that, of the common themes emerging from all the articles, "perhaps the most important . . . is the call for writing instruction genuinely grounded in rhetorical theory."

Minter, Deborah Williams, Anne Ruggles Gere, and Deborah Keller-Cohen. (1995). "Learning Literacies." *College English* 57:669-686.
Describes a service-learning seminar paired with an after-school tutoring program for children. Starts by noting the shift in English studies from the study of a few culturally sanctioned texts to the

wider consideration of "social products and agents," which in this case are the texts and contexts of undergraduates enrolled in the service-learning seminar focusing on literacy. The authors trace the development of the participants' primarily traditional and static conceptions of literacy as they evolve, through tutoring experiences, readings, and discussion, toward understanding "literacy as sets of practices that change with circumstances and their use." Includes the syllabus and readings for the seminar.

Odell, Lee, ed. (1993). *Theory and Practice in the Teaching of Writing: Rethinking the Discipline.* Carbondale: Southern Illinois University Press.

An anthology of 10 essays on contemporary composition research, theory, and pedagogy. Especially pertinent to service-learning are Shirley Brice Heath's "Rethinking the Sense of the Past: The Essay as Legacy of the Epigram," which investigates the origins of the essay and suggests that "learners are preparing for adulthood in a world of work and public service that differs radically from that of the centuries in which our expectations of the essay originated"; and Sally Hampton's "The Education of At-Risk Students," which argues against traditional remedial education for at-risk students and for a curriculum that emphasizes "real life," purposeful, contextualized writing projects.

——, and Dixie Goswami, eds. (1985). *Writing in Nonacademic Settings.* New York: The Guilford Press.

Recognizing the gulf between composition studies and the world of nonacademic writing, Odell and Goswami bring together studies of workplace writing, theoretical work on the relationship between text and context, and discussion of research methodologies (survey research and ethnography) to inform further investigation. The volume includes Lester Faigley's influential essay "Nonacademic Writing: The Social Perspective," in which he defines the social perspective in writing scholarship, contrasting it with the "textual" and the "individual" (or cognitivist) perspectives; introduces the concept of discourse community; and recommends an ethnographic approach to writing research.

Peck, Wayne, Linda Flower, and Lorraine Higgins. (1995). "Community Literacy." *College Composition and Communication* 46:199-222.

The authors describe the history of the Community Literacy Center in Pittsburgh, the educational practices of the center, and its commitment to literate social action. They explicate the principles of "community literacy," which is dedicated to (1) social change and action;

(2) intercultural conversation, collaboration/"bridging conversations"; (3) strategic approaches to learning, problem solving, argument, planning, collaboration, and reflection; and (4) shared inquiry, which actively explores "the logic of how you and I are using our literate practices to make meaning," and which in this case is facilitated by a university-community partnership. Examples include working with adolescents and a local high school in negotiating a fair suspension policy, and bringing community members and landlords to the table to craft more appropriate housing agreements and documents. In the words of the authors, "One can say that community literacy occurs wherever there are bridging discourses invented and enacted by writers trying to solve a community problem . . . community literacy as an emerging discourse recognizing that its forms are experimental, provisional, problematic, and, in our experience, generative."

Rubin, Sharon. (1990). "Service Learning: Education for Democracy." *Liberal Education* 76:12-17.

Concerned with both intellectual and ethical development, Rubin elaborates on how service-learning fits into the aims of higher education in helping students to be "full participants in democratic processes." Concerned with democratic values, active learning, and curricular and institutional reform, she calls for renewed dialogue about the possibilities for integrating service and learning, and in-class and out-of-class experiences. She also poses several practical questions that require attention when colleges and universities undertake more ambitious service-learning efforts.

Scholes, Robert. (1985). *Textual Power: Literary Theory and the Teaching of English*. New Haven: Yale University Press.

Argues for "shifting our concerns as English teachers from a curriculum oriented to a literary canon toward a curriculum in textual studies." Although Scholes concerns himself primarily with how we teach students to interpret and criticize literary texts, one particularly engaging chapter ("Is There a Fish in This Class?") brings structuralist and poststructuralist theory to bear on composition, articulating a vision consistent with writing across the curriculum and Community Service Writing programs: "As teachers of writing we have a special responsibility to help our students gain awareness of discourse structures and the ways in which they both enable and constrain our vision. And the only way to do this is to read and write in a range of discursive modes."

Watters, Ann, and Marjorie Ford. (1995). *Writing for Change: A Community Reader*. New York: McGraw-Hill.

A thematic reader intended for use in first-year or advanced composition courses. Readings include essays, stories, poems, and speeches about social issues including the family, education, poverty and homelessness, health, and the environment. Each section ends with examples of student writing drawn from Watters and Ford's experience in Stanford University's Community Service Writing Program; these include research papers and several documents written for community agencies. A companion volume, *A Guide for Change: Resources for Implementing Community Service Writing* (McGraw-Hill, 1995), provides more examples of students' projects as well as curricular and administrative materials to help teachers develop community-based assignments and establish productive relationships with community organizations.

Appendix

Program Descriptions

Arizona State University

Students do internship activities (tutoring and mentoring) in addition to classroom activities, receiving six credit hours for both. English 102 begins with readings and discussions about tutoring and reading acquisition. In English 215, students write four essays that link their research to their service-learning. In English 217, Service Learning: Personal and Exploratory Writing, students draft and revise four essays on their own experiences as well as poverty, school funding, and self-esteem. Students identify issues in their tutoring activities and research, and write about these issues.

Contact: Gay W. Brack, Director, Service Learning Project, Arizona State University, PO Box 873801, Tempe, AZ 85287-3801, ph 602/965-3097, IEGWB@ASUVM.INRE.ASU.EDU

Augsburg College

The college motto is: "Education for Service." Approximately 10 percent of academic courses include service-learning components. Journalism (English 227) is open to students who have completed a composition course prerequisite (English 111). Journalism fulfills college graduation requirements in "writing." Students select a 10-hour service assignment in literacy, inner-city schools, homeless shelters, food banks, transitional housing, AIDS programs, and women's and children's shelters. Students work at the site and then define an "urban issue beat." Students then write three assignments on that beat — simple news, a meeting or speech, and a feature interview.

Contact: Cass Dalglish, Assistant Professor of English, Augsburg College, 2211 Riverside Avenue, Minneapolis, MN 55454, ph 612/330-1009, dalglish@augsburg.edu

Chandler-Gilbert Community College

Service-learning in English 101 and 102 combines community service with academic instruction. Both courses focus on the theme of community. In 101, students read about community issues and serve at an agency of their choice for three to four hours. The readings, service experience, and reflection then become the focus of the students' essays. In 102, the students' service-learning experience is extended. Students keep a journal while serving 20 hours in an agency as part of their research on a social problem in their community related to their career aspirations.

Contacts: Pamela Davenport, Language and Humanities Division Chair, davenport@cgc.maricopa.edu; Marybeth Mason, English Faculty, mason@cgc.maricopa.edu; and Maria Hesse, Business Faculty, hesse@cgc.maricopa.edu, Chandler-Gilbert Community College, 2626 E. Pecos Road, Chandler, AZ 85225, ph 602/732-7000, fax 602/732-7090

Colby College

Students have the option of taking a composition section with a service-learning component. Next year, all placements will be in local elementary schools. Students work 16 hours, keep a journal, and are encouraged to do a research project that relates to education, social justice, gender, race, and class.

Contact: Peter B. Harris, pbharris@COLBY.EDU

DePaul University

English 409, Urban Literacy, is offered to both graduate and undergraduate students to explore the multiple definitions of literacy, with a special emphasis on adult literacy in an urban environment. Including both theory and practice, the course combines class discussion and assigned readings with a service component. Students work at five independent adult literacy sites in the Chicago area. The theoretical part of the course consists of the study of definitions of literacy, the politics of literacy, and the history of literacy and draws upon the work of major literacy theorists from the fields of Psychology, Cognitive Science, Education, History, Composition and Rhetoric, and Linguistics.

Contact: Darsie Bowden, English Department, DePaul University, 802 W. Belden, Chicago, IL 60614, ph 312/325-7000 x1769, dbowden@wppost.depaul.edu

Foothill College

Several sections of English 110, Basic Writing Skills, include a community service writing focus and optional service-learning projects. Although students are trained in a variety of reflection activities and are asked to reference their service experiences in their essays, much of the writing in Foothill's CSW program is analytical and text-based and community service experiences are seen as another development resource.

Contact: Rosemary L. Arca, Language Arts Division, Foothill College, 12345 El Monte Road, Los Altos Hills, CA 94022, ph 415/949-0543, arca@admin.fhda.edu

Gateway Community College

English 101 students first write about their own writing process and hear about universal safety precautions from nursing students. Then students have a choice of writing an essay about service-learning, which they must research, or writing about their tutoring experience at one of three school sites. Tutors must be on-site for four hours and either teach the writing process or help with an English assignment from the teacher.

Contact: Dean Stover, Gateway Community College, 108 N. 40th Street, Phoenix, AZ 85034-1795, ph 602/392-5275, Stover@GWC.maricopa.edu

George Mason University

As part of the Linked Courses Program, English 101 (Composition) and Sociology 101 are linked along with an experiential link: service consisting of nine 2-hour sessions assisting teachers and schools. Students write field notes of observations and reflections; questions coming out of these notes are then used by the sociology professor to help students relate their class work to wider issues of social justice. The notes also foster critical-thinking skills, and students write a researched essay based on issues raised in the field notes.

Contact: Ruth Overman Fischer, English Department, George Mason University, MSN 3E4, 4400 University Drive, Fairfax, VA 22030-4444, rfischer@gmu.edu

Hibbing Community College

A part-time director has established community partnerships with diverse agencies; representatives from agencies, faculty, students, and an administrator form an advisory board that monitors communication. Faculty provide guidebooks on service-learning goals and requirements. Service-learning is required in Technical Writing, a first-year composition course. At service sites, students become a part of the working community and reflect on the dynamics of that experience. Their research reports offer suggestions for change at these sites.

Contact: Lois A. Schmidt, 1515 E. 25th Street, Hibbing Community College, Hibbing, MN 55746, L.Schmidt@HI.CC.MN.US

Indiana University

English L240 ,Writing for a Better Society, includes volunteer work at a community service agency and a writing assignment for in-house use or public distribution by the agency. Students also focus on a social issue or problem and write a research paper.

Contact: Joan Pong Linton, Department of English, Indiana University, Bloomington, IN 47405, ph 812/855-2285, jlinton@indiana.edu

Johnson County Community College

Service-learning is integrated into the composition program as an option by individual instructors. Their approaches vary within the guidelines of program goals for a transferable writing course. Students work for schools, care facilities, social service agencies, environmental groups, women's shelters, homeless shelters, and soup kitchens.

Contacts: Marcia Shideler, Service Learning Coordinator, mshideler@jcccnet.johnco.cc.ks.us; and Joan Gilson, Composition Instructor, jgilson@jcccnet.johnco.cc.ks.us, Johnson County Community College, 12345 College Boulevard, Overland Park, KS 66210-1299

Kapi'olani Community College

Some instructors offer service-learning options in basic writing, introductory exposition, and advanced composition. Goals include enhancement of oral and written literacy and the celebration of culture, communication, and community. Because KCC offers a competency-based educational program, instructors also select specific course competencies to be developed through each service-learning project. Some experiences, such as tutoring and conversation in reading, writing, and English as a second language, are available through established contacts with schools and agencies in targeted neighborhoods. Other special projects for the community include newsletters, oral histories, story collecting and storytelling, and read-aloud programs.

Contact: Irena M. Levy, Department of Language Arts, Kapi'olani Community College, 4303 Diamond Head Road, Honolulu, HI 96816, ph 808/734-9435, irena@hawaii.edu

Lafayette College

Some courses of the required First Year Seminar include service-learning, such as Dealing With Differences: Views From the Margins; Challenging Differences: Discovering the Possibilities of Community; and The College Student in America. Students volunteer one to two hours per week in a local agency or program and reflect on the experiences in journals, essays, and class discussion.

Contact: Gary R. Miller, Chaplain, Lafayette College, Easton, PA 18042, ph 610/250-5320, millerg@lafayette.edu

Louisiana State University

The English department uses several service-learning models. In first-semester composition, students serve as mentors and tutors in public schools and agencies that promote literacy. Student writing examines various academic and nonacademic discourse communities. Second-semester students use persuasive writing to address immediate and systemic social concerns through work in a range of agencies.

Contact: Rhonda Atkinson, LSU PLUS (Louisiana State University Program for Learning ThrU Service), Louisiana State University, Coates Hall, Suite B-31, Baton Rouge, LA 70803, ph 504/388-5762, http://www.lac.lsu.edu/lsuplus.htm (Submitted by Jan Ophelia Shoemaker)

Marquette University
Service-learning is coordinated through a campus-wide service-learning program, which provides placements, coordinates details, and conducts cultural sensitivity training. In Marquette's two-semester, required, first-year writing course and in upper-division classes connected with the writing major, individual writing instructors choose whether or not to include a service-learning component; student participation is almost always optional. Some students write about their service experience; some upper-division students may also write for a particular agency.

Contacts: John Boly, Director of First-Year English, ph 414/288-7179, BOLYJ@vms.csd.mu.edu; and Virginia Chappell, ph 414/288-6859, CHAPPELLV@vms.csd.mu.edu, Department of English, 335 Coughlin Hall, Marquette University, Box 1881, Milwaukee, WI 53201-1881

Michigan State University
The Service Learning Writing Project (SLWP) is a multidisciplinary program of service-learning, writing instruction, and public culture studies. It is a joint effort of the College of Arts and Letters, the Department of American Thought and Language, the Service Learning Center, and the Writing Center.

Contacts: David Cooper, cooperd@pilot.msu.edu; and Laura Julier, julier@pilot.msu.edu, Department of American Thought and Language, 229 Ernst Bessey Hall, Michigan State University, East Lansing, MI 48824-1033

Portland State University
In English Composition (Writing 323), each student spends four weeks in a community project/agency developing writing that meets course and agency goals. Community Service Writing, an upper-division course, places students in projects of their choice. In Composition Research, students become a part of a community-based literacy project and write a reflective essay. In Immigrant Experience in American Literature and Film, students integrate classroom understandings about the representation of immigrant experience with a community experience.

Contact: Jacqueline Arante, Senior Instructor in Composition and Community Service Writing, Portland State University, PO Box 75, Portland, OR 97207

San Francisco State University
English 416 — Writing for the Community — has a thematic focus in which the class, through reading, discussion, service, and journal and essay writing, examines and reflects on community. Students serve in teams of two or three as volunteer writers for community agencies. Also, students in basic reading and writing courses participate in The Village Words Project, an after-school program where youngsters from disadvantaged backgrounds learn about language and literacy and perform and publish their work in their communities.

Contact: Michael Martin, Department of English, San Francisco State University, 1600 Holloway Avenue, San Francisco, CA 94132, ph 415/338-3089, mmartin@sfsu.edu

Stanford University
Community Service Writing is a project of Stanford University's Program in Writing and Critical Thinking. Students involved in the project are assigned, as part of their coursework for a first-year writing class, to write for a community service agency. Students write a wide variety of documents, such as news releases, grant proposals, brochures, editorials or letters to legislators, and researched reports.

Contact: Leslie H. Townsend, Program in Writing and Critical Thinking, Mail Code 2087, Stanford University, Stanford, CA 94305, ph 415/723-2631, townsend@leland.stanford.edu

University of Colorado-Boulder
Writing in Arts and Sciences, Farrand Academic Program. The ARSC1150 service-learning practicum pairs Farrand students with young readers from the Boulder County Family Reading Program. Training for students includes theories of illiteracy and literacy acquisition, introduction to children's books, and reading exercises. After training, students meet for one and a half hours a week with their "reading buddy" and spend another one to two hours a week preparing for these sessions. On the last day of class, students present a portfolio of work completed with their buddy, including reading lists, "books" written and illustrated by the young readers, and book reviews. Class sessions help connect student experiences as tutors with their own writing skills.

Contact: Kayann Short, Farrand Academic Program, CB180, University of Colorado, Boulder, CO 80310, ph 303/492-1267, fax 303/402-1207, shortk@spot.colorado.edu

University of Massachusetts, Amherst
Special sections of College Writing with a community service emphasis are offered through Residential Academic Programs. Recently, Community

Service Writing, an experimental seminar, was offered to upper-division students and included substantial reading and writing on the social and ethical dimensions of service, in addition to a major agency project. Student projects include press releases, brochures, manuals, research for internal use and for grants, and articles for newsletters. Agencies include Big Brothers/Big Sisters, The Food Bank, a public-interest research group, and Student Disability Services.

Contacts: Peter Elbow, Director; Tom Deans, Teaching Associate, tdeans@english.umass.edu; and Zan Meyer-Goncalves, Teaching Associate, zmg@english.umass.edu, University Writing Program, 305 Bartlett Hall, University of Massachusetts, Amherst, MA 01003, ph 413/545-0610

University of Minnesota, General College

General College's mission is to prepare for transfer students not admitted to other, degree-granting colleges within the university. GC's community service program, therefore, helps students capitalize on community-based knowledge and integrate it into academe. The program has used three models: one where students produce writing used by nonprofit agencies, one where students perform internships in conjunction with their courses, and one where students are participant-observers in organizations and analyze the effectiveness of some of the site's workers.

Contact: Linda Adler-Kassner, General College, University of Minnesota, Minneapolis, MN 55455, ph 612/625-6383, kassn001@maroon.tc.umn.edu

University of Washington

Two programs link service-learning with writing, both of them built on the Interdisciplinary Writing Program's model of linking writing courses to specific academic contexts: Community Literacy Program and Seattle Tutoring Center Writing Link Program. The goals include having students understand what constitutes a valid, well-structured argument in this particular context. Typical assignments ask students to do ethnographic research at their tutoring sites or write a case study.

Contact: Elizabeth Simmons-O'Neill, ph 206/685-3804, esoneill@u.washington.edu; and Catherine Beyer, ph 206/543-4892, cbeyer@u.washington.edu, Interdisciplinary Writing Program, Department of English, University of Washington, Box 354-330, Seattle, WA 98195

Villanova University

Social Justice Writing focuses on the visual and written rhetoric of materials published by nonprofit agencies and other organizations working for social justice in Philadelphia and suburban communities. Students write and design leaflets, brochures, newsletters, press releases, fund-raising letters, and grant proposals. In the Literacy Practicum, students examine theories of literacy, undergo literacy training, and tutor worker-students in union literacy programs.

Contact: Karyn Hollis, Director of the Writing Program, English Department, Villanova University, 800 Lancaster Avenue, Villanova, PA 19085, ph 610/519-7872, Hollis@ucis.vill.edu

West Texas A&M University

Workshops are offered with the intent of providing an opportunity for positive personal change through writing. The program is available to various populations, from runaway youth to senior citizens. Students at WTAMU accompany the instructor and participate in leading the workshops. Future plans include a university course on the philosophy, theory, and practice of service-learning.

Contact: Sandra Gail Teichmann, PO Box 955, West Texas A&M University, Canyon, TX 79016, ph 806/655-1288, muriel_bonness@msn.com

Appendix

Contributors to This Volume

Linda Adler-Kassner is a teaching specialist in composition and the writing program codirector at the University of Minnesota-General College, where she regularly teaches service-learning courses. Her interest in the relationship between student and academic literacies has led her to publish articles about service-learning as well as composition and literacy history. In the fall of 1997, she will join the faculty at the University of Michigan-Dearborn as assistant professor of composition and rhetoric.

Chris M. Anson is Morse-Alumni Distinguished Teaching Professor at the University of Minnesota, where he directed the Program in Composition during 1988-1996 and teaches graduate and undergraduate courses on language and literacy. He has published widely on composition, writing across the curriculum, and response to student writing.

Rosemary L. Arca is the fourth-generation teacher in her family. She teaches online reading and writing classes in the shadow of her great-grandmother's teaching contract from 1892 and she is currently an instructor of developmental reading and writing classes and the Community Service Learning Across the Curriculum coordinator at Foothill College.

Nora Bacon is a doctoral candidate at the University of California-Berkeley. She taught in Stanford's Community Service Writing program from 1989 to 1992 and helped launch a similar program at San Francisco State University. In the fall of 1997 she will join the faculty at the University of Nebraska at Omaha as assistant professor of English.

Gay W. Brack is the director of the Arizona State University Service-Learning Project. Students in her project have contributed more than 100,000 hours of supplemental education to the community's most in-need children.

Lillian Bridwell-Bowles is a professor of English language and literature and director of the Center for Interdisciplinary Studies of Writing at the University of Minnesota. She also codirects the Minnesota Writing Project, a collaborative of writers and teachers committed to improving the teaching of writing at all levels, and is a past chair of the Conference on College Composition and Communication (CCCC), the international scholarly and professional organization for teachers of writing. Her recent research focuses on characteristics of writing in various fields, rhetoric, and the teaching of writing.

David D. Cooper, an associate professor in the department of American Thought and Language and the American Studies Program at Michigan State University, founded its Service-Learning Writing Project in 1992.

Robert Crooks teaches composition and also literary, film, and communication theory at Bentley College. An associate professor of English, he has incorporated service-learning projects into a number of different courses and has presented a paper on "Service-Learning, Composition, and Cultural Studies" at CCCC.

Tom Deans is completing a dissertation at the University of Massachusetts at Amherst on the relation of community-based writing initiatives to composition studies. He teaches writing, literature, and service-learning courses, and his essays have appeared in *College Teaching* and *Composition Chronicle*.

Wade Dorman and **Susann Fox Dorman** are instructors in English at Louisiana State University. Currently on leave, they are making classroom connections from the Real World side of the gap, designing a corporate training program for The Fox Group.

Linda Flower is professor of rhetoric at Carnegie Mellon University and director of the Center for University Outreach. She is the author of *Problem-Solving Strategies for Writing in College and Community* and *The Construction of Negotiated Meaning: A Social Cognitive Theory of Writing.*

Leanna R. Hall is assistant professor of English at Grand Canyon University. She is a former coordinator of the Service-Learning Project at Arizona State University. Her dissertation, "Transforming the 'Empty Assignment Syndrome': A Study of Rhetorical Context for Service-Learning Composition Students," was an ethnographic study of service-learning.

Paul Heilker is the director of English Department Writing Programs at Virginia Tech. He is the author of *The Essay: Theory and Pedagogy for an Active Form* (NCTE, 1996) and coeditor of *Keywords in Composition Studies* (Heinemann, 1996).

Bruce Herzberg is professor of English at Bentley College, where he directs the Expository Writing Program. He is coauthor, with Patricia Bizzell, of *Negotiating Difference* and *The Rhetorical Tradition,* and has also written a number of articles on composition and rhetoric.

Laura Julier is an associate professor in the department of American Thought and Language at Michigan State University, where she teaches writing and women's studies, and is also a founding faculty of the MSU Service-Learning Writing Project. In 1995, she was honored with the Michigan Campus Compact/Kellogg Foundation Community Service Learning Award as Outstanding Faculty.

Working currently as associate executive director of the National Council of Teachers of English, **Patricia Lambert Stock** is professor of English at Michigan State University. Her most recent book, *The Dialogic Curriculum,* presents the theory of curriculum that underlies the Write for Your Life Project.

Janet Swenson is a visiting assistant professor in the Writing Center at Michigan State University, where she directs the Red Cedar Writing Project and the Write for Your Life Project.

Ann Watters is a lecturer in the English department at Stanford University, where she has directed the Program in Writing and Critical Thinking and currently serves as associate director. A member of the Invisible College of educators involved in service-learning, she cofounded Stanford's Community Service Writing Project. She has coauthored and edited five books, including *Writing for Change* and *Guide for Change,* two textbooks for college composition courses that integrate service-learning.

Edward Zlotkowski is professor of English at Bentley College. Founding director of the Bentley Service-Learning Project, he has published and spoken on a wide variety of service-learning topics. Currently, he is also a senior associate at the American Association for Higher Education.

About AAHE's Series on Service-Learning in the Disciplines

The Series goes beyond simple "how to" to provide a rigorous intellectual forum. *Theoretical essays* illuminate issues of general importance to educators interested in using a service-learning pedagogy. *Pedagogical essays* discuss the design, implementation, conceptual content, outcomes, advantages, and disadvantages of specific service-learning programs, courses, and projects. All essays are authored by teacher-scholars in the discipline.

Representative of a wide range of individual interests and approaches, the Series provides substantive discussions supported by research, course models in a rich conceptual context, annotated bibliographies, and program descriptions.

Visit AAHE's website (www.aahe.org) for the list of disciplines covered in the Series, pricing, and ordering information.